The
Same Great Struggle

THE HISTORY OF THE VICKERY FAMILY
OF
UNITY MAINE
1634–1997

Ada Josephine Berry (1881–1903)
The daughter of Reuel and Hattie Myrick Plummer Berry and niece
of Ralph Berry, Sam Berry, and Mary Berry Cook, in the family
parlor, Unity, Maine, c. 1891. Photographs that documented the
growth and accomplishments of family members were requisite for
decorating middle-class homes at the turn of the twentieth century.

The Same Great Struggle

THE HISTORY OF THE VICKERY FAMILY
OF
UNITY, MAINE
1634–1997

ANDREA CONSTANTINE HAWKES

TILBURY HOUSE, PUBLISHERS   GARDINER, MAINE

Tilbury House, Publishers
2 Mechanic Street
Gardiner, ME 04345
800-582-1899 • www.tilburyhouse.com

First Edition May 2003

10 9 8 7 6 5 4 3 2 1

Library of Congress Cataloging-in-Publication Data

Hawkes, Andrea Constantine, 1953-
 The same great struggle : the history of the Vickery family of Unity,
Maine, 1634-1997 / Andrea Constantine Hawkes.— 1st ed.
 p. cm.
Includes bibliographical references and index.
 ISBN 0-88448-251-0 (alk. paper) — ISBN 0-88448-252-9 (pbk. : alk.
paper)
 1. Vickery family. 2. Pioneers—Maine—Unity—Biography. 3.
Pioneers—Montana—Biography. 4. Frontier and pioneer
life—Maine—Unity—Biography. 5. Frontier and pioneer
life—Montana—Biography. 6. Unity (Me.)—Biography. 7.
Montana—Biography. I. Title.
CT274.V53 H39 2003
929'.2'0973—dc21

2002153611

Cover and text designed on Crummett Mountain by Edith Allard, Somerville, Maine.
Editorial services by Jennifer Bunting and Barbara Diamond.
Layout by Nina DeGraff, Basil Hill Graphics, Somerville, Maine.
Scans by Integrated Composition Systems, Spokane, Washington.
Jacket and covers printed by the John P. Pow Company, South Boston.
Printing and binding by Maple Vail, Kirkwood, New York.

Contents

FOREWORD

As ANDREA C. HAWKES has so well conveyed in *The Same Great Struggle*, family history was a central force in the life of James B. Vickery III. His passion for collecting genealogical information and his 1954 publication *A History of the Town of Unity, Maine* are but the outward manifestations of a complex drive to document the generations of Vickerys and related families who came before him.

The death of his older brother Eric in 1991 prompted Jim to prepare a will. Given his multiplicity of interests and his valuable collections, this was no ordinary task. The question of what should go where was the topic of several of our Sunday afternoon telephone conversations. Fortunately, Jim was assisted by a very talented and understanding attorney, Stuart M. Cohen of Bangor, and his wishes were carefully translated into a legal document which has achieved his intentions.

When Jim Vickery died on June 13, 1997, it became my responsibility as his personal representative to work with Stuart Cohen to carry out the several provisions of his will. The most challenging one was a directive to publish "a book of the genealogy of the Vickery Family of Unity, Maine." For this I turned to Dr. Martha J. McNamara, professor of history at the University of Maine at Orono, to locate a qualified individual to prepare a Vickery family history. Martha recommended Andrea C. Hawkes, and from my first meeting with her, I knew that she was the right person for the job.

Andrea has demonstrated an impressive array of professional skills during the research, writing, and publishing of *The Same Great Struggle*. This volume reflects her thorough analysis and organization of Jim's extensive genealogical notes, supplemented by her own investigations into the Vickery family and their relations. Her narrative has transformed the dry facts of births, marriages, and deaths into a compelling and compassionate human story, so local and at the same time so universal. Finally, with the help of Jennifer Bunting at Tilbury House, Publishers and designer Edith Allard, Andrea has fashioned her manuscript into a handsome volume, complete with the many family photographs which Jim gathered and cherished.

In the publication of *The Same Great Struggle* I am deeply gratified that Jim's lifelong goal of a Vickery family history has been accomplished in such a meaningful way. I only wish that he would be here to leaf through the chapters with us, but his spirit is on every page.

Earle G. Shettleworth, Jr.

ACKNOWLEDGMENTS

FIRST AND FOREMOST, I want to thank Earle G. Shettleworth, Jr., for his support, patience, insights, and faith in me. Earle's sense of excellence and commitment to preserving and sharing Maine's history is an inspiration and model to me; it has been a privilege and an honor to work with him.

I want to thank Carol Oberweiser and Eileen Hyem in Montana, Mary A. Dell in California, Nora Robertson in Arizona, and David F. Vickery in Idaho, the grandchildren of Eli Ayer and Carrie Brandenburg Vickery who shared their cherished memories and photographs with me, and Jim Vickery's cousins in Maine, John A. Vickery, Sr., and John A. Vickery, Jr., for their help and interest.

If I was able to do justice to the history of the Vickery family it was because I have trained at the University of Maine with some of the finest historians working today. I want to thank Dr. Martha J. McNamara for knowing that I was the right one to write this history. I am indebted especially to Dr. Marli F. Weiner (ever my mentor and ideal) and Dr. Richard Judd at the University who took time from their own important scholarship to read the manuscript and make incisive comments that challenged me to make this a better book. I am also grateful to Dr. Mazie Hough, Dr. Pamela Dean, and Dr. Pauleena MacDougall for their hours of invaluable discussions. And to Dr. Alan Taylor at the University of California at Davis—his kind words and suggestions meant more to me than he could know.

I want to thank people at several institutions for their invaluable help securing materials: Tracy Elizabeth Robinson at the Smithsonian Institution Archives; Dave Burgevin at the Smithsonian Institution; Betsy Paradis in Special Collections, Raymond H. Fogler Library at the University of Maine; Bill Cook at the Bangor Public Library; Christopher Hartman at the New England Historic Genealogical Society; Jim Small in Public Affairs at L. L. Bean; Richard R. Shaw and Charles A. Campo at the Bangor Daily News; Elaine Ardia in the Edmond S. Muskie Archives and Special Collections Library at Bates College, Terry Baillargeon in the Office of Development at Bates College, Nancy LePage in the registrar's office at Bates College, and Joan Roming at the Unity Historical Society.

A special acknowledgment to Brian Robinson in the Quaternary Institute at the University of Maine for rescuing crucial Vickery family papers "in the nick of time"; to Ethel Farrington Smith for graciously allowing me to reproduce the map she drew of the Vickery community in seventeenth-century Hull, Massachusetts; to the Honorable Frank M. Coffin for his help in making Jim Vickery's college years come alive; to David Mishkin at Just Black & White in Portland, Maine, for his expect care of precious images; to Stuart Cohen for fulfilling Jim Vickery's wishes; and to Jennifer Wixson for sharing her knowledge of Waldo County and its people then and now.

I owe much to my dear friends; to Cynthia O'Neil and Nancy Torresen for their discerning reading of the manuscript; to Judy Kirk, Cheryl Wixson, Lori Edwards, Nancy Graham, Jan and Dan Olmstead, and Lynn and Tom Woods, who never tired of hearing about the Vickery family; to Dr. Celeste DeRoche whose steadfast encouragement and enthusiasm throughout this project helped make it happen; and to Berry Manter who read my mind in her creation of the wonderful maps for this book and the Vickery family crest of back-to-back dolphins that graces the genealogical chart and chapter headings.

I want to thank those at Tilbury House, Publishers who have made the production of this book a most pleasant experience; Jennifer Bunting for her immediate zeal, fine advice, and unwavering spirit; Barbara Diamond for her good copy editing; and Edith Allard who skillfully captured the sense of the book in her design, and Nina DeGraff whose skill facilitated the layout.

I dedicate this book to James "Jim" Berry Vickery III who gave me this opportunity, and to my husband Donald and my daughter Nicole who made it possible for me to realize it.

—ACH

INTRODUCTION

*THIS IS A PORTENTOUS PERIOD of history that this old world is going
through, and students some day will find the record of thrilling reading
and I hope in large degree inspiring as well, but the drama [of World War
II] is so tremendous that it is hard for us here and now to comprehend its
full significance or even to live through it with the patience, confidence,
and steadfastness that I feel we should. I do hope that all will go well with
you and your part in it and that in years to come those to carry on your
name and blood will find pride in your record as you and I do in that of
old David Vickery of Monmouth and Valley Forge. After all this is simply
a logical and continual part of the same great struggle.*
—S. Stillman Berry III to James B. Vickery III, 25 June 1942[1]

*T*HIS BOOK TELLS THE STORY of ten generations of one branch of
the Vickery family who settled and created communities in Massachusetts, Maine, Montana, and Wyoming. In this history each of these
ten generations is placed within the context of the time and place that
influenced the choices it had and the decisions it made.

The Vickery family began in the 1640s with the marriage of
George Vickery and Rebecca Phippen of Massachusetts Bay Colony.
George and Rebecca's children and their grandchildren in the second
and third generations of the Vickerys created a complex family network
in Massachusetts that stretched from Cape Cod to Boston. Just before
the American Revolution Hannah Parker Vickery, who was a widow,
and her six children came to the District of Maine. They extended this
family network from Cape Elizabeth, east to Calais, and north to Unity.
One of Hannah's sons, David Vickery II, and his wife Sarah Stone Vickery later settled Unity, Maine, where five generations of this Vickery
family thrived for the next two hundred years. In the 1870s and 1880s
Eli Ayer Vickery and his cousins Ralph and Evie Kelley Berry of the
ninth generation in Unity expanded the family network across the
United States to the borderlands of Montana and Wyoming. The direct
lineal line of this branch of the Vickerys that began in 1634 ended
when the last member of the tenth generation, James B. Vickery III,
died in 1997.

The obvious question, of course, is why should we care about the history of the Vickery family? Whether we are a member of this family and its communities or not, reading stories like the Vickery family's history can help us see that our histories are connected—we are truly all engaged in, as S. Stillman Berry III told his cousin James Berry Vickery III during W.W. II, "a logical and continual part of the same great struggle." We depend on our connections to other people, our families, our communities, and the land or region where we live, and this has been true throughout history. The Vickery family history underscores how these connections define our identities. According to historian William Cronon, in order to come to a more complete understanding of who we are, our history should be studied in "terms of *connection*" and the "interactions among different regional economies, cultures, and environments.[2] This narrative reveals some of those consequential connections between Vickery family members and dozens of individuals, families, and communities that shaped the history of New England, the West, and in turn the United States.

Specifically, the history of the Vickery family shows how the concept of family and community has endured over more than three hundred years of American history even as its meaning has been transformed. Focusing on just one family history like the Vickerys gives a more personal meaning to the changes in the economy, religion, demography, politics, and gender roles that caused this transformation. It also allows us to question the romantic notion of the harmonious "traditional family." Social, cultural, and economic changes, the tension between individual aspirations and the family's common good, idiosyncrasies; and illness often caused conflict within families. "Without those [family] conflicts," states historian Linda Gordon, "we'd have no Shakespeare!"[3] Correspondingly, the Vickery family had their share of intergenerational and gender conflicts, repression of individualism, idiosyncrasies, illness, and despair, and without these we would have no Vickery family history.

This book has a history of its own. Writing the history of the Vickery family was a lifelong aspiration of James "Jim" Berry Vickery III (1917–97), a "teacher, historian, and antiquarian" of Unity, Maine.[4] Early in his life Jim sensed the significance of being "one of the Unity [Maine] Vickerys."[5] It certainly was meaningful, as one relative put it, that "nearly all of the families in Unity were related to them."[6] Being a Vickery, being from Unity, and being from Maine forged Jim's identity. While still in his teens he began his genealogical search to find the roots of this layered identity. Who were the Unity Vickerys? From where did they come? How were they related to the other Unity families and what did it mean to be connected to most of these families? What part did the Vickery family play, as Jim's friend historian Elizabeth Ring might ask, in the making of Maine and the nation?[7] Jim spent his life collecting and preserving the genealogical data and local history material that might help him answer these questions, intending in due time to publish a history of the Vickery family based on these documents.[8]

Genealogy—an endeavor based on making connections—was mainly a hobby for "gentlemen of leisure" in the nineteenth century and, though some research from this time is still valued, it was little more than ancestor worship.[9] In the early twentieth century genealogy became popular with many native-born New Englanders when immigration, race issues, and profound changes in society and the economy threatened their identity. They did genealogical research to find their inherited lineage in order to reinforce their authority and superiority. They strove to find family connections to the MAYFLOWER or service in the Revolutionary War to give themselves "a kind of nobility of native origins."[10] Genealogy appealed to people for nostalgic reasons, too, and "curiosity or the pleasure of the hunt" engaged others.[11] By the time that Jim Vickery started to trace his family tree in the 1930s, genealogy had become a scholarly profession based on "objective" methods of research and exacting standards of documentation.[12] As a professional, Jim used these methods and adhered to the standards. This did not lessen his pride, however, in discovering his own family's connections to the MAYFLOWER, or in documenting his great-great-great-grandfather David Vickery II's role in the American Revolution.[13]

Jim Vickery began to gather the pieces of his family history in the early 1930s by sending out query letters to people throughout the United States and Europe. It was well that he did so, as many of those who responded to Jim were elderly. Most were clearly excited by the prospect of his book on their shared family history and sent him touching letters filled with names, dates, and memories. Cousin Elizabeth Crockett, however, was not sure she could be much help. "I might have found out all about our folks years ago I suppose, but I never was interested in them as they never seemed real to me," she wrote. "No one ever talked about them to me and some of them I suppose I never even heard of."[14] Like Cousin Elizabeth, another connection said she could be little help, and stated the obstacle that many genealogists encounter:

> I CANNOT GIVE ANY particular information, as no record was kept by my grandparents, until their marriage. Then the record was kept in their family Bible, of their children's births, marriages and deaths…. It's too bad families kept no records, except orally, in days of old.[15]

Wary of how the information might be used, one relative highlighted the issue of privacy not often addressed by genealogists:

> MOTHER HAS AN AVERSION which she feels her sisters would share, to having a personal matter of record, as date of birth, published in a book, and as you are compiling a history, and not genealogy, it does not seem necessary. However if you wish the year of death, that is another matter, and following is the items…. I wish you all success in your book.[16]

While these women were concerned about divulging a "date of birth," it was not the most personal information a genealogist might uncover.

Several relatives like Gertrude Vickery Fisher, S. Stillman Berry III (who was related to Jim "in two different ways"), Theoda Mears Morse, and James E. Kelley were genealogists themselves, and they readily shared their own years of research.[17] Their letters not only show how scholarly and serious these people were, but also how much fun and meaning genealogy—with all its research "problems"—brought to their lives. Seventy-year-old Cousin Gertrude Vickery Fisher encouraged sixteen-year-old Jim's new interest:

> I AM MOST PLEASED that you are interested in genealogy and I hope it will lead to a live study of history, genealogy is to me as absorbing as a cross-word or jig-saw puzzle and far more worth while. I was 17 when my Father had letters from Vickery's in

Indiana and in New York asking for family history, he gave them to me and I went to the Worcester Antiquarian society and began my search. I wrote to my Aunt Ann Stone, she and My Father gleaned enough family traditions to give me working clues.... I will send you genealogical lines as soon as I can go through my papers for I am delighted that you wish them.[18]

Seventy-six-year-old Cousin James E. Kelley, a Boston lawyer, gave young Jim some sound advice:

DO NOT LET YOUR AGE stop you from taking up genealogy and history as hobbies. They will be a great help to you in getting pure joy and satisfaction out of life. Job Chap. 8 v 8 says: "For inquire I pray you, of the former age, and prepare thyself for the search of their fathers." And Sewall [Rufus King Sewall] in his introduction to his "Ancient Dominions of Maine" says, in substance, that a love of the study of history is no mean indication of intellectual attainments. The only thing for you to watch out on is your duty to your family and your farm. You must not neglect those duties. If one has abundant means he may indulge his hobby, otherwise he must use only his spare time.[19]

Jim heeded his cousin's advice. He never neglected his duty to his family, his community, or his country. Graduating from Bates in 1940, he served in World War II, earned a Master of Arts degree in history from the University of Maine in 1950, and "paid his dues" by teaching in Maine secondary schools for almost forty years.[20] He wrote *A History of the Town of Unity, Maine* (1954), articles, and exhibition catalogues, and edited *An Illustrated History of Bangor, Maine* (1969), *A Pictorial History of Brewer, Maine* (1976), and the three volumes of *The Journals of John B. Godfrey* (1979, 1984, and 1985). He was the president of the Bangor Historical Society and served the Penobscot Heritage Museum and Maine Historical Society in many capacities. "In his rumpled tweed jacket and Hush Puppies, he shuffled through decades of antique shows, book stalls, and collectors' booths" where he collected thousands of books, pamphlets, newspapers, manuscripts, photographs, prints, and maps pertaining to Maine history and literature, conserving many rare materials, artifacts, and first editions.[21] When he had his collection appraised in 1972, even he was surprised at its magnitude and exclaimed, "I fear I have created a monster."[22] He donated this extraordinary collection to the University of Maine in 1978. According to Earle G. Shettleworth, Jr., director of the Maine Historic Preservation Commission, Jim's collection "is a legacy that could never be duplicated today."[23]

All the while, Jim used his "spare time" to further his research, accumulating more Vickery-related names, dates, places, and provocative bits of family lore.[24] He filled in pedigree charts, took copious notes on yellow legal pads, and typed up pages of his findings, placing this work in piles until the right time—after the endless research was finished—to write the book. But the right time never came. "Goodness knows," he once professed,

> WHEN I AM GOING to be able to complete my Vickery Genealogy for publication, although I have certainly made serious progress in the last two years. I am teaching in Dexter High, my second year. We are having a splendid fall and the leaves have remained on the trees and such a burst of gaudy color everywhere; still very warm and Indian summer lingers to my delight.[25]

As Jim frankly admitted, "it's more fun researching than writing.... But to be a historian you have to do the hard work, which is to plop yourself down in a chair for hours and write. It is a fault of mine."[26] Rather than seeing this as a fault, rare book dealer Francis O'Brien put Jim's work into perspective. "There are different kinds of historians," stated O'Brien, "those who write a lot and those who discover information and provide the tools that pave the way for other historians to write.... Jim has searched out the minutiae that fills all the wonderful little spaces."[27] Without a doubt, Jim's commitment to advancing the scholarly value of genealogy and local history, and his careful collecting and preservation of our cultural heritage has enriched and will continue to better our understanding of American history, bringing us closer to understanding our own lives and times.

Jim Vickery understood himself well, and realizing at the end of his life that he was not able to write his family history, he made provisions in his will to have the book written at last. I was born, raised, and lived most of my life in Bangor, Maine, and as many people do, I remember Jim as a fixture of the Bangor Public Library.[28] Already exploring ideas about identity, place, and family history in my own scholarship, and eager to keep *my* connection to Maine, I accepted the challenge of writing the Vickery family history. My task was to bring order to Jim's research (even Jim said that his filing "system" left "something to be desired") and to place his genealogy in historical context.[29] Genealogy distills life to its most basic elements of birth, death, marriage, and family and provides the essential groundwork of history. To create a narrative, however, I aspired to give force to all these elements, make meaning of family lore, and unveil the human drama embedded in this "cold" genealogical data. For example, on 17 January 1883 Samuel "Sam" Stillman Berry II and Florence Ellen Bartlett were married in Maine, on 20 May 1885 Sam died in Montana, and on 19 October 1885 Florence gave birth to their daughter Sybil Samuel Berry in Maine. While these are just Vickery family names, places, and dates, if we think about them as more than data on pedigree charts, they represent the mixture of joy and despair that is the meaning of life across time and place.

Names are the most problematic issue in doing genealogy. The spelling of surnames through time and place has changed and before a time of standardization, people during any one time and place spelled a name differently. Gertrude Vickery Fisher described to her cousin Jim how the Vickery name originated in France and came to England in a number of variations:

VICARS, VICARY, Vickere, Vickrey, Vickery from Normany. William de la Vackerie was granted estate of his Uncle Richard by King John. Richard de la Vachery came to England from Normandy 1272.[30]

While troublesome, surnames can give valuable clues to genealogists about the work or calling of their ancestors. The Vickery name is listed in one source as all part of "The Vicars Line" and is linked to the occupation of one who is part of the administration of an English parish:

VICARY, VICERY, Vicarey, Vicars, Vicors, Vicaris, Vicaridge, Vickerage, Vickeridge are forms of one name and, with many others of the same origin but of various spellings, mean of the vicarage, or office of the vicar, or at the vicars. They are official or sometimes local names, and are found very early in England.[31]

Forenames can be particularly frustrating for genealogists. People named children for themselves and their ancestors, generation after generation and through different branches of their families in concurrent generations. Though this might have helped families to sustain a sense of family continuity (a particularly poignant custom when a child died and the name was given to the next child born), it can complicate research.[32] When families did introduce a new name or abandoned a time-honored one, as historian David Hackett Fisher suggests, it "probably reflected major transformations in the trend of family relationships" that do not correspond to urbanization, industrialization, and modernization periods that historians have used to explain change in the United States.[33] Changes in Vickery forenames seem to support Hackett Fisher's thesis. In the Puritan patriarchal era the names George, Jonathan, Rebecca, and Mary are prominent. The rise of the intimate and sentimental family after the American Revolution introduced David, Eli, Hannah, and Sarah. As "companionate" families (based on mutual affection and respect) evolved in the late nineteenth century, these names were replaced by James, John, Lydia, and Olive. In the early 1930s Cousin Gertrude Vickery Fisher explained the pattern of choosing forenames for men in the early generations of the Vickery family:

[DAVID VICKERY II] had come to Maine from Massachusetts but claimed his forbears had come from England, he said his Grand father's name was Jonathan; that there "had always been Davids and Jonathans way back" This was true back to the immigrant ancestor George. George Vickery came from a family of seafaring from the Island of Jersey or from Bideford in Devonshire England…. The names most used in the Vickery families in St. Helios, Jersey and in Bideford were George, Thomas, William, and James. When George Vickery of Hull married the daughter of David Phippen of Hingham, the next town to Hull the line of Jonathans and Davids began.[34]

Thus, the same names repeated again and again in the Vickery family makes some mistakes inevitable. I expect that new and conclusive evidence about Vickery family dates and names will surface after this book is published, and it is welcomed.

For expediency, I narrowed the scope of the history, since the ever-growing branches of the Vickery family tree reach throughout Maine, across the country, and around the world. I "listened" to Jim's evidence to help me do this. Because of his strong sense of place, I decided right away that I would concentrate on the branch of Vickerys who founded and lived in Unity. The overwhelming amount of attention Jim paid to the ten generations of his direct ancestral line from their arrival in New England in 1634 convinced me that this was the story Jim most wanted to tell. But Jim's great fascination with the West and the group of Unity Vickerys and their Berry relatives who settled Montana and Wyoming borderland communities in the late-nineteenth century compelled me to include some of their story as well.

I also decided to use family lore and traditional stories as valid evidence, fully aware of their weaknesses as primary sources. In his classic 1970 *The Saga of Coe Ridge: A Study in Oral History,* William Lynwood Montell convincingly puts to rest the debate about the use of traditional stories or folklore as valid evidence. "No historian who is aware of the ways of the people on a local level, especially in rural areas where ties with the land are strong," contends Montell, "will question the importance played by oral traditions in the lives of the people.... It can serve as a historical record in those areas where written accounts have not been preserved."[35] While laden with nostalgia and the possibility of inaccuracies, a historian cannot ignore the sound information about social history and family life at the turn of the twentieth century in the American West that can be garnered from recollections like the following, however sentimental:

THE SCHOOL HOUSE became the center of all social life; election days, Christmas programs, basket socials, dances.... When we got ready to drive over to the schoolhouse for one of these events Father would fill the wagon box with hay and all the children sat in the hay with Father and Mother up on the one spring seat of the wagon. When we arrived, the dear old team would be unhitched and tied at the end gate so they could munch hay while waiting for the return trip. Father was always kind and thoughtful of the horses.[36]

Oral histories and family and traditional stories, or folklore, are no less reliable than conventional archival documents; any evidence a historian uses can be adulterated and should not be accepted uncritically.

I used personal letters (which some historians consider "folk documents") as evidence in this study, too. Jim Vickery not only saved seemingly all of his own correspondence, he also acted as the conservator of precious letters sent home to Maine in the 1870s and 1880s from his Berry ancestors who emigrated to Montana. Written by his cousins Mary Berry Cook and Evelyn Kelley Berry, this correspondence is presented in Part Three and is rich in the little known experiences and attitudes of women on sheep ranches. They present an intimate account of the wool-growing industry and sheep culture in Montana, and the relationship between white settlers and the Native Americans on whose land the industry depended. These letters also suggest that women sustained the connections between Maine and Montana as people, culture, and money flowed continuously back and forth between the two states in an exchange that extended and connected families and communities over 2,000 miles. I quoted at length from these letters so that the voices of these women can be heard on their own terms. The correspondence in Jim's cousin S. Stillman Berry III's papers at the Smithsonian Institution Archives complements and informs these western letters.

"Through photographs," states social critic Susan Sontag, "each family constructs a portrait-chronicle of itself—a portable kit of images that bears witness to its connectedness" and often, "a family's photograph album … is all that remains of it."[37] As he was for his family's genealogical history, Jim Vickery was also the guardian of his family's photograph albums and these images kept him further connected to his disappearing family. Thus, there are numerous images to illustrate the history of the seventh, eighth, ninth, and tenth generations of the Vickery family, such as daguerreotypes and tintypes from the mid-nineteenth century, cartes de visite, and studio portraits from the late-nineteenth century and twentieth century, as well as candid photographs that the Vickery family took of themselves throughout the twentieth century. Jim was a collector and connoisseur of historical iconography in general as well, and he was especially intrigued with daguerreotypes. "What makes me get rather ecstatic over these as early forms of photography is difficult to write," he once commented. "Nevertheless they have a charm of their own whether it is the forbidding visage of an old deacon or the artless innocence of a child. They convey an artistry of another period and provide considerable historical clues."[38] Indeed, I based some of my analysis of the life and times of the latter generations of Vickery family on clues from their photographs.[39]

Here is a good place to note some of my editorial conventions. I did not correct the grammar or spelling in letters from which I quoted nor did I use the expression *sic* to call attention to variant words. To clarify an extrapolated passage I used information within brackets. To simplify the "tangle of names" I spelled out ordinal numbers to designate each generation (the first generation, the second generation, etc.) and I used Roman numerals after a simultaneous forename used in consecutive generations, such as David I, David II, David III.[40] There were a number of ancillary family stories in Jim Vickery's papers that might have impeded the immediate narrative, but were too interesting and telling not to include, so I placed them in the endnotes. I made several decisions early in the process that may not please those who desire a standard genealogical history. I used only what genealogical material Jim had amassed. I did no more genealogical research, but cross-referenced conflicting evidence and made judgments on what seemed probable. I recorded here only the parents, their children, and their children's spouses in each generation. All the other material Jim Vickery collected is in his papers and accessible to other genealogists and scholars.

This book was written for the Vickery family, the beginning history student, and the general reader. I hope that members of the Vickery family will be proud of the pioneering and entrepreneurial spirit, faith in family, and community-mindedness of this branch of their family, and perhaps they might be challenged to enhance this history with the story of other branches of the Vickery family tree. I hope that this story engages other readers and perhaps inspires them to know their own family history. Most of all, I hope Jim Vickery would approve.

Andrea Constantine Hawkes
Arlington, Massachusetts
September 2002

THE VICKERY FAMILY

The First Generation

GEORGE VICKERY I and **REBECCA PHIPPEN**
(c.1615–1679)   (c.1628–after 1679)

1. **JONATHAN I**   2. George II   3. Isaac   4. Israel   5. ?John   6. Benjamin   7. ?Joseph
(c.1648–1702)   (c.1651–   (c.1654–   (c.1660–   (c.1662–   (c.1664–1718) (c.1666–1739)
M.   1721)   1726)   1710)   1703-17)
ELIZABETH HUDSON

The Second Generation

REVEREND JONATHAN VICKERY I and **ELIZABETH HUDSON**
(c.1648–1702)   (1659–1706)

1. Elizabeth   2. **JONATHAN II**   3. David   4. Joanna   5. Mary   6. Rebecca   7. Sarah   8. ?Hudson (?)
(c.1679–1714?) **(1683/4–1741)**   (c.1685–   (1686–   (c.1689–   (?–living   (?–died
M.   1714?)   1720)   1702-12)   in 1714)   before 1714)
MARY ELDREDGE

The Third Generation

DEACON JONATHAN VICKERY II and **MARY ELDREDGE**
(1683–1741)   (1682–1745)

1. **DAVID I**   2. Jonathan III   3. Matthias   4. Mary   5. Isaac   6. Nathaniel   7. Ebenezer   8. Paul   9. Joanna
(1704–1744) (1709–1744)   (1711–?)   (1713–   (1716–?)   (1718–?)   (1721–?)   (1724–?)   (1726–
M.   after 1731)   after 1745)
HANNAH PARKER

The Fourth Generation

DAVID VICKERY I and **HANNAH PARKER**
(1707–1744)   (1710–c.1752)

1. Hannah   2. **DAVID II**   3. Elizabeth   4. Mary   5. Matthias   6. Matthias
(1732–c.1782) **(1734/35–1823)** (1737–?)   (1739–1822) (1741–   (1743–1812)
M.   before 1743
Lydia Atwood

The Fifth Generation

DAVID VICKERY II and **1. LYDIA ATWOOD** and **2. SARAH STONE**
(1735–1823)   (?–c.1768)   (1746–1830)

With Lydia Atwood: 1. Deborah   2. Lydia
(c.1766–?)   (c.1768–1852)

With Sarah Stone: 1. Hannah   2. Jonathan   3. Sarah   **4. DAVID III**   5. Susanna   6. Joel
(1771–1833) (1774–1847) (1777–1852) **(1780–1847)**   (1784–?)   (1798–1869)
M.
LYDIA COBB BARTLETT

The Sixth Generation

DAVID VICKERY III and **LYDIA COBB BARTLETT**
(1780–1847)   (1787–1865)

1. **ELI**   2. Damaris   3. Sarah   4. Joseph   5. Ann   6. Benjamin Bartlett
(1807–1877) (1809–1879) (1811–1888) (1813–1876) (1815–1901)   (1817–?)
M.   7. Nelson   8. David   9. John   10. Charles Augustus   11. Albert
CLARISSA BERRY (1819–1895) (1821–1879) (1823–1870) (1827–1891)   (1831–1858)

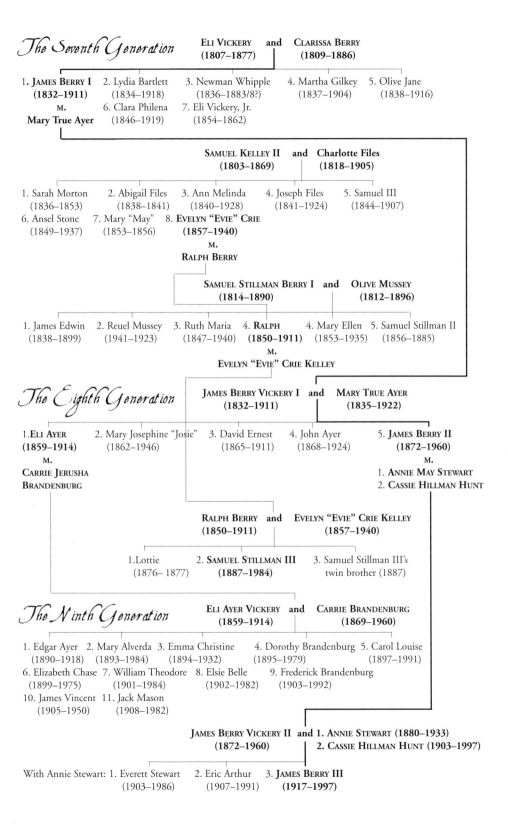

The Seventh Generation
ELI VICKERY and CLARISSA BERRY
(1807–1877)   (1809–1886)

1. JAMES BERRY I   2. Lydia Bartlett   3. Newman Whipple   4. Martha Gilkey   5. Olive Jane
(1832–1911)   (1834–1918)   (1836–1883/8?)   (1837–1904)   (1838–1916)
M.   6. Clara Philena   7. Eli Vickery, Jr.
Mary True Ayer   (1846–1919)   (1854–1862)

SAMUEL KELLEY II and Charlotte Files
(1803–1869)   (1818–1905)

1. Sarah Morton   2. Abigail Files   3. Ann Melinda   4. Joseph Files   5. Samuel III
(1836–1853)   (1838–1841)   (1840–1928)   (1841–1924)   (1844–1907)
6. Ansel Stone   7. Mary "May"   8. EVELYN "EVIE" CRIE
(1849–1937)   (1853–1856)   (1857–1940)
                                     M.
                                     RALPH BERRY

SAMUEL STILLMAN BERRY I and OLIVE MUSSEY
(1814–1890)   (1812–1896)

1. James Edwin   2. Reuel Mussey   3. Ruth Maria   4. RALPH   4. Mary Ellen   5. Samuel Stillman II
(1838–1899)   (1941–1923)   (1847–1940)   (1850–1911)   (1853–1935)   (1856–1885)
                                                   M.
                                   EVELYN "EVIE" CRIE KELLEY

The Eighth Generation
JAMES BERRY VICKERY I and MARY TRUE AYER
(1832–1911)   (1835–1922)

1. ELI AYER   2. Mary Josephine "Josie"   3. David Ernest   4. John Ayer   5. JAMES BERRY II
(1859–1914)   (1862–1946)   (1865–1911)   (1868–1924)   (1872–1960)
M.   M.
CARRIE JERUSHA   1. ANNIE MAY STEWART
BRANDENBURG   2. CASSIE HILLMAN HUNT

RALPH BERRY and EVELYN "EVIE" CRIE KELLEY
(1850–1911)   (1857–1940)

1. Lottie   2. SAMUEL STILLMAN III   3. Samuel Stillman III's
(1876–1877)   (1887–1984)   twin brother (1887)

The Ninth Generation
ELI AYER VICKERY and CARRIE BRANDENBURG
(1859–1914)   (1869–1960)

1. Edgar Ayer   2. Mary Alverda   3. Emma Christine   4. Dorothy Brandenburg   5. Carol Louise
(1890–1918)   (1893–1984)   (1894–1932)   (1895–1979)   (1897–1991)
6. Elizabeth Chase   7. William Theodore   8. Elsie Belle   9. Frederick Brandenburg
(1899–1975)   (1901–1984)   (1902–1982)   (1903–1992)
10. James Vincent   11. Jack Mason
(1905–1950)   (1908–1982)

JAMES BERRY VICKERY II and 1. ANNIE STEWART (1880–1933)
(1872–1960)   2. CASSIE HILLMAN HUNT (1903–1997)

With Annie Stewart: 1. Everett Stewart   2. Eric Arthur   3. JAMES BERRY III
(1903–1986)   (1907–1991)   (1917–1997)

O N E

The Massachusetts Families

1634–1746

GEORGE VICKERY I (c.1615–1679)
and
REBECCA PHIPPEN (c.1628–after 1679)
Married c.1647
England
Hingham and Hull, Massachusetts

CHILDREN:

1. *Jonathan I (c.1648–1702) m. Elizabeth Hudson*
2. George II (c.1651–1721) m. Lucy Hodson
3. Isaac (c.1654–1726) m. (1) Elizabeth Cromwell Price, (2) Lydia Jones
4. Israel (c.1660–1710) m. Judith Hersey
5. ?John (c.1662–between 1703 and 1717) m. Sarah Croakum
6. Benjamin (c.1664–1718) m. (1) Dorcas Paine, (2) Mary Coom
7. ?Joseph (c.1666–1739) m. Abigail?

Other children some notes mention, but do not seem probable: Anna, Rebecca, Mary, Roger, Gamaliel.

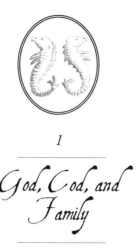

1

God, Cod, and Family

THE FIRST GENERATION

I CAN NOT GIVE YOU *many particulars, I am afraid, for my father and mother were very careless over these things and I was so much abroad that it was too late to collect the history of the family when I settled down for the reason that their memories were not accurate and they had destroyed any archives.... The family was an old Devonshire family and some of them are buried in Bideford church yard and I have always heard my father say that we originally did come from the Channel Islands.... The family crest is two dolphins back to back and I am enclosing a wax impression of my ring.*
—Colonel C. E. Vickery to James B. Vickery III, 27 August 1937[1]

HISTORIANS CALL IT the "Great Migration." Between 1630 and 1642 thousands of average English men, women, and children—some estimate 20,000—migrated to New England. Known as Puritans, these migrants felt compelled to leave their homeland, their friends, extended family, and all things familiar, because they believed the English government and Anglican Church were morally corrupt. They embarked on a precarious 3,000-mile journey across the Atlantic Ocean that would cost them about a thousand dollars per family in modern terms and take two to four months to complete.[2] They planned to create a "new" England in what they considered wilderness. They hoped to reform their impure church and build a more secure society where their hard work, frugality, and orderliness would bring them prosperity and a better life. With God's grace (and a charter from the king) they would bring together a new church and state to create model communities where individuals worked together for the good of all.[3] Among those who came during the Puritan "Great Migration" and helped build one of these communities were George and Rebecca Phippen Vickery—the founders of the Vickery family that five generations later settled Unity, Maine.

Rebecca Phippen came to New England from Weymouth, in Dorsetshire, England, about 1635 with her parents David and Sarah Phippen, her sister Sarah, and her four brothers Joseph, Benjamin, Gamaliel, and George.[4] Most of the migrants who came to New England came in families like the Phippens. These families were usually made up of married couples with an average of three or more children. Since many women were still of childbearing age, they continued to add to their families after arriving in New England, with more of their children reaching adulthood in the healthier environment than would if they had stayed in England. Because families like these came to the northern colonies, unlike the overwhelming population of young, single men who migrated to the southern colonies, New England society became stable in a remarkably short time.[5]

Rebecca Phippen's fifty-year-old father, David, received a grant of five acres in Hingham, Massachusetts, in September 1635 and it was there the family settled first. The Phippens probably received their land grant from the incorporated town of Hingham, that in turn had received a land grant from the Massachusetts Bay General Court. This town-grant settlement policy, versus land given to individuals by headrights as was the policy in the southern colonies, made certain that those who came to New England would settle together in communities.[6] Like the other Puritan settlers who were mostly farmers, or yeomen, the Phippen family probably farmed their land. The short season of farming in New England, however, required that settlers work in a variety of occupations. Rebecca's brothers were also involved in carpentry, blockmaking (making blocks from stone or timber for building materials), and seafaring. While keeping their land in Hingham, her mother and father moved to Boston about 1641 where they were granted another house-lot in September 1641. David Phippen was also given "liberty of wharfing near the Milne Creek," and later appointed a constable in Boston. As her older brothers lived in Boston at this time as well, thirteen-year-old Rebecca Phippen most likely moved there with her family.[7]

George Vickery I, who came to New England in the late 1630s, was not the typical Puritan settler. He was a young fisherman and he came, if not on his own, then with other unmarried fishermen from his region of Devonshire in England. Family lore claims that George Vickery I was descended from a seafaring family from the Island of Jersey and later, from Bideford, England.[8] Since at least the early sixteenth century Europeans had fished for cod along the North American coast. Every spring thousands of Englishmen left West Country ports like Bideford, fished the grounds off northern New England and maritime Canada throughout the summer, and returned in the fall with enormous quantities of dried fish to sell to the European markets. George Vickery I may well have fished the area before he came to settle permanently. At any rate, he would have been aware of the promising livelihood Massachusetts Bay's cod-rich waters offered him.[9]

George Vickery I might even have been recruited to bring his fishing skills to the new colony. Soon after the first settlements were organized, Puritan leaders realized that they needed to do more than farming if they were going to develop a commodity they could trade in Europe for the goods they needed that they could not yet produce, like paper, ironware, and gunpowder. Cod was an important commodity in the European market and one New England had in abundance. But the Puritans were mostly farmers and craftsmen and did not have the skill or the desire for commercial fishing. Puritan leaders decided that they needed to recruit unmarried fishermen to do this work, but they feared allowing them to join their family-based colony. They believed that an ordered and disciplined family lifestyle was fundamental for a stable society, and they disapproved of those who lived alone and outside the control of a family and the community. Fishermen were individualistic, itinerant, and had a reputation for violent and "sinful" living. So, the General Court of the Massachusetts Bay Colony established fishing plantations. They hoped to encourage fishermen to settle down, marry, raise families, and lead more respectable and "pure" lives. In these plantations fishermen received house lots and a small amount of land for planting—lest too much entice them to become farmers.[10]

After arriving in New England, George Vickery I spent his first years fishing out of Salem, Marblehead, and Boston. He and Rebecca Phippen probably met in Boston, which was still a village, and they were married in the late 1640s. By 1650 they had started a family and were living in Hull, a fishing plantation established in 1641.[11] Before colonization, Hull—sometimes called Nantascot or Nantasket—was a traditional summer fishing camp for Native Americans. Later, the Plymouth colonies used it as a trading post with the natives. It is a narrow peninsula curling out seven miles into Boston Harbor and surrounded by a number of small islands. Less then a mile wide and with the sea surrounding three-quarters of the land, Hull has a real sense of being an island. From the top of one of its oval hills, one could see far out to sea, and off its northeast shores, the important Boston market. It was ideal land for a fishing plantation.

George and Rebecca Phippen Vickery's Massachusetts Community.
"Nantascot-Hull 1642–1657" excerpted from Ethel Farrington Smith,
"Seventeenth-Century Hull, Massachusetts and Her people,"
NEW ENGLAND HISTORIC GENEALOGICAL REGISTER, *116.*

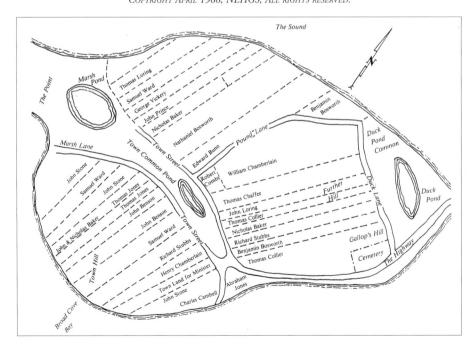

Most of the first settlers came from Hingham. Indeed, a part of Hingham's land was annexed to develop Hull, much to Hingham's dismay. The name Phippen appears in the earliest Hull records indicating that some of Rebecca Vickery's family might have settled out on the peninsula as well. George I and Rebecca received a house lot on the northeast side of the peninsula facing Boston. On their forested lot that extended from the town common to the beach, they could build the preferred home at this time, a "saltbox" with two rooms on either side of the center chimney on the first floor and lofts for sleeping and storage above. With the abundance of trees, they might side it with wooden planks and put wooden shingles on the roof—a great improvement over the thatched roofs to which they had been accustomed in England.[12] They also had access to a meadow for their cattle and rights on the nearby islands for drying fish. It was a promising community for George I and Rebecca Phippen Vickery and their children.[13] However, like Gloucester, Marblehead, and Provincetown, Hull was different than the majority of farming communities in the colony because its economic, political, and social rhythms depended on the inconstant sea.

Fishing for cod in the deep waters in the Gulf of Maine or the shallow waters off the Massachusetts coast was hard and dangerous work. A son and a grandson of George I and Rebecca Phippen Vickery were drowned, and a grandson and two great-grandsons were lost at sea.[14] Unpredictable and foul weather conditions; idle times when the fish did not bite; exhausting, hectic times when they did bite; the necessity of depending on merchant patrons for credit to buy salt, provisions, and equipment each season, and to provide shipping to markets; fluctuating market prices; ever-threatening legal entanglements; and the risky industry of curing the fish without damaging it made life in fishing communities tense.[15]

George Vickery I was in court at least twice concerning his fishing business. In November 1651 he and his brother-in-law Thomas Ewe (husband of Rebecca's sister Sarah Phippen) were in Suffolk County Court, Boston, for sailing out of Annisquam Harbor in Gloucester "upon the Sabbath day morning"—the day designated strictly for worship, irrespective of migrating cod.[16] In 1677 William Green took George I to Suffolk County Court again "for refusing to give an account of 1,500 cod fish put into his hands," but the jury found George blameless.[17] Such court cases were heard more frequently by the end of the seventeenth century as budding individualism and self-interest conflicted with Puritan ideals of cooperation and community.[18]

Despite the inherent hardships of fishing, an inventory of George I and Rebecca Phippen Vickery's estate in 1679 was valued at £220. It was a modest sum, yet considerably more than the average fishing family was worth at this time in nearby Essex County.[19] They owned a home, several lots of land, cows, sheep, pigs, and oxen. They were in the minority of fishing families to own part of a light open boat called a shallop that they used mainly in shallow waters and propelled by oars or sails.[20]

George I did the fishing and, by Puritan beliefs, he was the unquestioned patriarchal head of the household, but the success of the Vickery family depended equally on Rebecca, whose duties were very different. Rebecca Phippen Vickery was an ordinary colonial woman, known in the vernacular of the times as a "Goodwife."[21] The inventory of the Vickery estate hints at a few of Rebecca's household duties, in addition to giving birth to at least seven children (the colonial average), caring for them, and acting as helpmate to George I. She built and kept the fires going and cooked and baked the food (liquids and cereals, bread and cakes, and meat, poultry, and fish) using the "tramels, and irons, and spit." She milked and made cheese from their cows, and tended their oxen and swine. She spun the fleece from their sheep into "yarn" on the "wheeles." Rebecca's work, like her husband's, was hard, and facing death with each pregnancy, it was dangerous. Her daughter-in-law Dorcas Paine Vickery, whose great-grandfather arrived on the Mayflower, died at the birth of her seventh child.[22]

The famed minister in Massachusetts Bay Colony, Cotton Mather, stated that families were "the nurseries of all societies."[23] The "range of functions" performed by these nurseries were all encompassing, according to historian John Demos. The household was the center of all work to produce food, shelter, and clothing that sustained the family, and the "vocational institute" that trained the next generation for work. It was the school where most people learned to read the Bible. The family home was "a house of correction" where discipline and punishment were enforced, and a "welfare institution" that cared for orphans, the ill, the aged, and the poor. "The gradual surrender" of these private family responsibilities to public control since George and Rebecca Phippen Vickery's lifetime is the central theme of the history of the family in America.[24]

Respect for authority was the foundation of an ordered and disciplined family that Puritans thought was fundamental for a stable society. They believed that there was a natural hierarchical chain of authority that began with God, flowed through the church, and rested on the patriarch, or father in each household.[25] As the patriarch of the Vickery family, George Vickery I was responsible for the control and discipline of his children and his wife. He was a freeman in 1665, which meant he was a member of the church; only male church members, or freemen could vote for rulers or be elected to office. So George I represented his family in all church and government decisions. He also controlled the means of income and all property. His sons depended on him to inherit a share of the Vickery property.[26] When they married (and George I and Rebecca played a big part in deciding who they married) he decided when and how to distribute his property, although both he and Rebecca signed the deeds for land they sold or gave to their sons.[27]

In April 1679 George I and Rebecca deeded "a small piece of the homelot in Hull" to their third son, Isaac.[28] Isaac already had a dwelling on the lot, as he was married and headed a family of his own. Puritan communities continued to be made up of small nuclear families where a married couple and their children lived under one roof. It was rare for a married son and his family to live in the same household as his mother and father.[29] Isaac's land lay next to his brother George II's house lot, which was probably given to him as well by George I and Rebecca. Lucky it was for Isaac that his father acknowledged the deed to his house lot promptly because on 12 July 1679 George Vickery I died "suddenly" and he did not leave a will.[30]

According to colonial law, without a will designating George Vickery I's wishes, Rebecca Phippen Vickery would have inherited only a third of the Vickery household goods and could only use or receive income from a third of their house lots and land. Rebecca was supported in her widowhood to some degree, especially since she still had underage children to care for, but she did not necessarily have control over what she must have considered was hers.[31] Tradition and the evidence suggest that the Vickery family's eldest son Jonathan I inherited the original house and lot in Hull. Yet Rebecca and Jonathan I were both appointed to administer the Vickery estate, which was not unusual. While the principles of patriarchy were maintained, the reality was Rebecca probably assisted George I in their economic affairs and could handle the details after his death better than anyone else could.

Records related to Rebecca Phippen Vickery seem to end with her husband George's death. But since her son Jonathan I did not sell his house in Hull until 1699, a good two years after he had moved to Cape Cod, one might speculate (and hope) that Rebecca lived the rest of her life in the home that she and George built.[32] Living to be eighty years old in seventeenth-century New England, as Rebecca might have, was not uncommon. The longevity of the first generation in the colonies, according to some ministers at the time, was proof of God's grace.[33]

George and Rebecca Phippen Vickery and the other first-generation pioneers who came during the "Great Migration" and stayed (for as many as one in six became discouraged and fearful and returned to England) settled two hundred towns in New England in their lifetime and increased the population to almost 100,000.[34] But it was the second generation—the first born in New England—who knit together through marriage the towns and communities into a network of family relationships.[35] The second generation of the Vickery family actively participated in creating a complex extended family network in communities that stretched over an ever-widening area of New England.

REVEREND JONATHAN VICKERY I (c.1648–1702)
and
ELIZABETH HUDSON (1659–1706)
Married c.1678
Duxbury, Hull, Scituate, and Chatham, Massachusetts

CHILDREN:
1. Elizabeth (c.1679–1714?) m. Jonathan Collins
2. *Jonathan II (1683/4–1741) m. Mary Eldredge*
3. David (c.1685–Missing at sea, whereabouts unknown after 1714)
4. Joanna (1686–1720) m. Samuel Treat, Jr.
5. Mary (c.1689–between 1702 and 1712)
6. Rebecca (?–living in 1714) m. John Wing
7. Sarah (?–died before 1714) m. Thomas Higgins or ? Nickerson
8. ?Hudson (?)

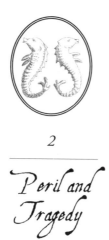

2

Peril and Tragedy

THE SECOND GENERATION

NO HISTORY OF *the Vickery family would be complete without an account of the exciting adventure of Elizabeth Vickery.... [She] was born probably at Hull, Massachusetts about 1685, the second child of the Rev. Jonathan and his wife, Elizabeth (Hudson) Vickery. She came to Chatham with her parents and might have died years later and be completely forgotten except for the unusual sea voyage and captivity on a bleak and desolate island when she was eighteen years old.*
—James Berry Vickery III[1]

WHEN THE PURITANS arrived to create a "new" England, they considered the land wilderness. In fact Native American communities had long inhabited and worked the land. The Massachusetts Bay Colony intruded on the communities of Wampanoags, Narragansetts, Nipmucks, Pequots, Monhegans, Pennacooks, Sokokis, Niantics, and Abenakis. Puritans met little resistance at first in appropriating the land that supported these communities because the Native American population had been devastated by smallpox, typhus, measles, and respiratory illnesses brought over by earlier European explorers.[2]

Since so much of this land looked uncultivated to them, Puritans felt justified in taking possession of it for some small compensation. It was their responsibility, according to the Bible, to civilize and improve the "wilderness" with permanent settlements. Puritan ideas about land differed dramatically from those of Native Americans.[3] They thought it strange that Native Americans moved each season in order to take advantage of the best sites for food, shelter, and clothing. Most shocking to Puritans, however, was seeing Native American women tilling and planting the fields. This was men's work in civilized English society.[4] As the English population in New England grew and the second generation pressed inland from the coast, conflicts between the two cultures, especially concerning the uses and ownership of land, were the basis for several brutal wars between Native Americans and the Puritan settlers in the seventeenth century.

King Philip's War, one of the most vicious conflicts, directly affected the Vickery family who were all still living in Hull. Whole communities of Puritans and Native Americans were destroyed in a horrific and barbaric guerrilla war from 1675 until 1676 that, in proportion to the population, inflicted greater casualties than any other war in American history.[5] George Vickery II fought as a private in the Narragansett campaign during King Philip's War and lived. In 1733 his son Israel Vickery claimed land in Bedford, New Hampshire, for his father's service.[6] But while Hull was never attacked, the Vickery family and their community suffered economically when George II and his brothers Jonathan I, Isaac, Israel, and the other men were kept from their livelihood of fishing in order to defend their village during the war.[7]

The four Vickery men and their neighbors signed a petition presented to the colonial government in Boston asking for help in March 1675. The petition speaks to the nature of the community's tenuous economic survival and the men's passion for their community, as well as Hull's differentiation in the colony as a fishing plantation.

THE WHOLE COUNTRY is Exposed to the wasting ffury off the most barbarous heathen, Which wee are sensible off, and therfore ffreely willinge to spend our care, our strength, yea, Wee hope our very lives, in, and for the defense off this place, and the Country, yet, beinge persons whose sole employment is ffishinge, and soe att sea, havinge noe lands, nor Cattle to mayntayne ourselves, or familyes, but what wee must have hitherto done by the blessinge of God on our Labours produced ffrom the sea; beinge therefore now Commanded by our Cheife officer, not to goe forth on our imploy, desired then to know, how Wee and ours shall bee maytayned, they havinge a year's provision aforehand, Wee none; they havinge cattle to give milke to theire familyes in the summer, Wee none; they havinge Cattle and swine to kill for meate, Wee none; soe that Wee are like to bee put to Extremity, both Wee and ours ... iff wee must be Constrayned to leave our imploy and not goe to sea, but bee kept here to garison the Town, that then your Honourr would please to gratifie this our Wee hope, but reasonable request, that Wee and ours may bee provided for, or liberty to follow our imploy.[8]

While the response to the petition is unknown, the Vickery family and their community most likely endured their hardships for about sixteen months. The death and mutilation of the Wampanoag chief King Philip, also known as Metacom, in August 1676 ended both the war and the efforts of Native Americans to drive out the English settlers in this part of New England. Again, because the Puritans saw God's power behind everything that happened, they saw their victory over Native Americans as more proof of God's grace.[9]

While memories of this devastating war remained with the English settlers for years (historian Jill Lepore argues that as a cultural war, King Philip's War has never ended), the people in Hull returned to their livelihood of fishing and to the continued growth of their families and community through marriage.[10] In 1678 Jonathan Vickery I, George I and Rebecca's oldest son, was declared a freeman, which by 1673 meant even without membership in the church, he could vote and be elected to office.[11] As an acknowledged member of the community in his own right, he and Elizabeth Hudson, the daughter of John and Ann Russell Hudson of Duxbury, married at this time, extending the Vickery network of family relationships down the south shore of the colony.[12]

In their fishing excursions people of Hull often came in contact with the communities along the south shore and on Cape Cod.[13] Duxbury and most of these communities were part of the original Plymouth Colony, whose settlers came to North America to separate from, not reform, the Anglican Church. Their expansion into the interior of New England; the death of the original leaders and their vision; and no doubt, the economic ties and uniting of the second generation with outsiders, such as Elizabeth Hudson's marriage to Jonathan Vickery I, weakened these communities. In 1691 the Massachusetts Bay Colony swallowed up the Plymouth Colony.

Elizabeth Hudson Vickery moved from her home in Duxbury and came to live in her husband Jonathan's home in Hull, as was the custom.[14] They began their family with the birth of a daughter who was named for Elizabeth, then a son named for Jonathan, followed by six more children. Jonathan I continued, like his father George I, to fish, and Elizabeth's work was little changed from her mother-in-law Rebecca's work. Their nuclear family was still the center for the production of the food they ate and the clothing they wore, the place their children learned to read, and the only place all were cared for in sickness and old age.[15] While family life and work seemed to stay the same for the second generation of Vickerys at the end of the seventeenth century, church leaders feared that the social order in Massachusetts Bay Colony was changing for the worse. They felt that this second generation had strayed from the original Puritan mission of their mothers and fathers.

To combat this perceived changing attitude, ministers all over the colony lambasted their congregations with scathing sermons known as jeremiads. They accused Jonathan I and Elizabeth's generation of immorality—especially being too concerned with making money, lacking piety, and failing their communities.[16] As an example, they might have pointed to George Vickery II and several others from the area who were "fined 20 shillings for not attending their service upon the jury according to summons."[17] Thus, the ministers declared, this second generation was responsible for God's wrath shown through disasters like King Philip's War. They entreated their congregations to look fervently inward for personal salvation and diligently outward for ways they might be of more service to God and their communities.[18]

Most Puritans in seventeenth-century New England felt that they served God and reached their highest spirituality by performing their callings well and remembering their place in the social hierarchy of authority.[19] Apparently for Jonathan Vickery I, however, this was not enough. Sometime between his father's death and the late 1690s, he became an acknowledged minister employed at Chatham (earlier called Monomoit) on Cape Cod. Many of the ministers at this time were educated at Harvard College, but there is no evidence that Jonathan was formally trained. One history of Chatham states that he "was not an educated man nor an ordained minister, but a lay preacher."[20] His character obviously commanded respect for his congregates called him "Reverend."

It is not known what drew Jonathan Vickery I into the ministry. Perhaps the jeremiads he heard affected him deeply and propelled him to a higher service. Or perhaps Jonathan offered his life in the service of God because his wife's life was spared after she was assaulted and robbed. While visiting Boston with his aunt, Elizabeth Phippen, Jonathan I's thirty-four-year-old wife Elizabeth was robbed and nearly strangled by "Samuel White Labourer of Boston" on the evening of 19 June 1693.[21] Elizabeth Hudson Vickery told the superior court about the crime in her deposition the next day:

> THAT LAST NIGHT being the 19th of June Currant about nine or tenn of the Clock, going to Mrs Harris's house in Boston near the draw Bridg as shee was in the narrow lane by sd Harris's house a man clothed in whitesh garments with a Jackett whose voyce she can remember came to her & with violence assaulted her saying I swear I will have a kiss or something & then took her by the throat & put his hand in her pockett & took from thiner a child's linnen bed [cloth] wherin was tyed up thirty shillings & upwards, an allamode scarfe & a pr of gloves worth about sixteen shillings & then ran away, but shee crying out severall men ran after him & catcht the man that goes by the name of Samuell White with is the verry man that robbt her to the best of my knowledge it being pretty dark & can only know him by his Jackett & voyce.[22]

Late-seventeenth-century Boston was fast becoming a major seaport and commercial center, as well as a staging ground for military operations against the French. Its population exploded, precipitating disorder and a rise in crime and violence.[23] The rule of law still prevailed, however, and on 31 October 1693 Samuel White was indicted for his offense against Elizabeth Hudson Vickery.[24] By the spring of 1697, for whatever reasons, Jonathan I and Elizabeth Hudson Vickery and their children were living on a thirty-acre farm in Chatham (far from Boston) and he was the spiritual leader of the First Congregational Church.[25] He was paid £20 a year, and by convention, the community supplied all his hay and wood needs.[26] Jonathan I's new profession would certainly bring honor and status to the Vickery family.

Shortly after the Vickery family moved to Cape Cod, their lives were sensationally affected by world politics. While Native Americans no longer posed a major hindrance to English land acquisition and settlement in this part of New England, the French did. From 1689 to 1713 Britain and France fought for domination in Europe and North America. In the first war, known here as King William's War (1689–97) the French and their Native American allies fought the English for control of Arcadia and the fort at Port Royal. The fighting destroyed settlements all along the Maine coast and made the Gulf of Maine and Massachusetts Bay a battleground. Privateers were a constant source of danger in these waters. Authorized by both the English and French governments to cruise the seas and seize the ships and commerce, or "prizes," of their enemies, these private armed vessels differed from pirate ships only in their official commissions called "letter-of-marque and reprisal."[27]

In the fall of 1697 Jonathan I and Elizabeth Hudson Vickery's eldest child, eighteen-year-old Elizabeth Vickery, boarded a fishing vessel in Truro, Cape Cod, bound for Boston. Before she reached her destination, a French privateer seized the fishing vessel and four Frenchmen headed their "prize" towards Arcadia. While they apparently removed the English fishermen, they either left Elizabeth alone because she was a woman or she might have been in hiding, as she later appeared on the vessel while en route. As if her capture was not nightmare enough, the vessel was then caught in a gale and Elizabeth and the four Frenchmen were shipwrecked on Sable Island.

A 50-mile-long sand bar, Sable Island lies about 100 miles southeast of Cape Canso, Nova Scotia. The island is about 20 miles long and one mile wide, and it has a smooth coastline and grasses, but no harbor or trees. It is known as "the graveyard of the Atlantic" because of its frequent fog and storms. The wreck of Elizabeth Vickery's vessel is one of over 200 known shipwrecks off Sable Island. In 1697 all aboard appeared to survive their unfortunate accident, and Elizabeth and her French captors built a hut from the damaged remains of the vessel and settled in to wait out the long winter.

The English were the first to arrive on the island in the late spring of 1698 and they took everyone prisoner. Since Elizabeth Vickery was English, she was transported home to Cape Cod. What Elizabeth went through those cold, isolated months stranded on an island, with little or no food, probably unable to speak or understand French, and living with four men in a hut can only be imagined. Though suspect, one nineteenth-century historian claimed:

> TO THE HONOR of these French sailors, be it remembered that during all these trying experiences, they never failed in their kindness or honorable protection to their helpless prisoner, and that she received only marked respect from their hands.[28]

A few years after her sensational "adventure," Elizabeth married a man from Cape Cod, and became, as this same nineteenth-century historian declared, "the mother of many generations."[29]

Elizabeth Vickery's disappearance surely distressed her family. After learning that she was captured, they might have tried to follow the privateers themselves, or petitioned the government to help them find Elizabeth. They probably thought her another victim of the sea to which their community had become accustomed. They no doubt rejoiced and thanked God upon her return. One might wonder if the French had been the first to arrive on Sable Island in the spring, whether Elizabeth would have come home? Many captive women decided to make new lives with their captors and by their own decision, never returned.

Elizabeth's capture highlights the dangers that average men and women in the colonies faced every day. Confronting these dangers called for the strength that many colonists derived from their intense religious faith. While there is no evidence that Elizabeth wrote about her capture, a number of women who were captured by Native Americans allied with the French against the English settlers wrote first-person accounts about their experiences. The words of Mary Rowlandson, who wrote the most well known of the seventeenth-century captivity narratives, might have been spoken by Elizabeth Vickery after her ordeal: "Yet I see when God calls a person to any thing, and through never so many difficulties, yet he is fully able to carry them through, and make them see and say they have been gainers thereby."[30]

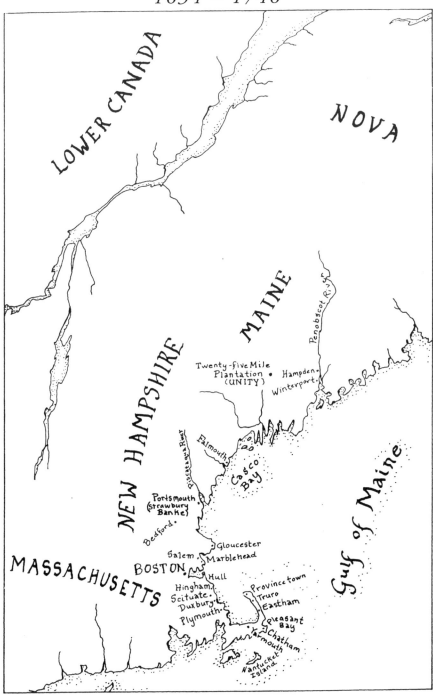

Map by Berry manter

The Massachusetts Families

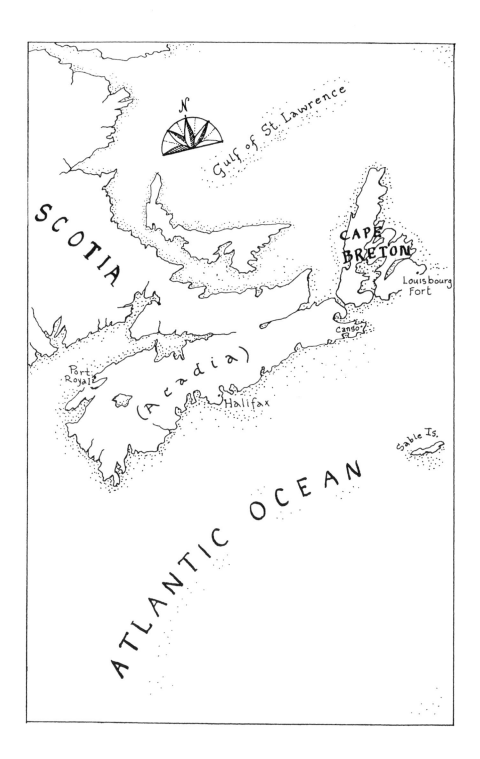

In 1702 tragedy struck the Vickery family again. On April 30th Jonathan Vickery I was in a boat on Pleasant Bay with several of Chatham's leading citizens, perhaps fishing for small whales called blackfish, or "drift fish," that swam into the Cape's shallow waters and then were easily driven ashore. Jonathan I had earlier signed a compact with Native Americans concerning the ownership of these fish.[31] Fishing, work Jonathan I knew well, would be necessary for supplementing his modest income as a minister. While fishing on this particular day, the boat overturned and all the men drowned. This disaster "cast the village into a state of gloom for many months."[32] Reverend Vickery was a crucial member of his family and community. He was described as a "gifted preacher" and "a man of unusual mind and spirit."[33] He had been elected to represent them in Boston when they petitioned the court for their official designation as a township. He helped spur the building of the community's first meetinghouse that had only just been completed at the time of his death. Reverend Vickery's leadership would be missed.[34]

Jonathan I's sudden death must have crushed his wife, Elizabeth Hudson Vickery. Left with six underage children, she suffered "a lingering illness" that sounds like depression, and died only a few years after her husband. Before she died, she lost all interest in her home, and it became so run down that the court turned the care of the house over to her oldest sons, Jonathan II and David. After Elizabeth Hudson Vickery's death in 1706 the estate was divided among the children, with Jonathan II as the eldest son receiving the greatest share.[35] But Jonathan II did not stay in Chatham for long after the death of his parents. Stretching the Vickery network of family relationships further out Cape Cod, he and his wife Mary Eldridge Vickery moved to Truro to become valued members of this community by 1707.

DEACON JONATHAN VICKERY II (1683–1741)
and
MARY ELDREDGE (1682–1745)
Married c.1705
Hull, Chatham, Truro, Massachusetts

CHILDREN:

1. *David I (1704–1744) m. Hannah Parker*
2. Jonathan III (1709–1744) m. Susanna Thomas
3. Matthias (1711–?)
4. Mary (1713–after 1731) m. Thomas Paine, Jr.
5. Isaac (1716–?)
6. Nathaniel (1718–?)
7. Ebenezer (1721–?)
8. Paul (1724–?) m. Elizabeth Thomas
9. Joanna (1726–after 1745) m. Ephriam Lombard

3

An Interwoven Community

THE THIRD GENERATION

By 1710 JONATHAN VICKERY [II] *was fully established at Truro.*
Jonathan Vickery [II] became thus a proprietor of the town of Truro and
early settler. He is listed among those who owned cattle. And soon he became
a influential and prominent personage in the small fishing town.
—James Berry Vickery III[1]

JONATHAN VICKERY II and Mary Eldredge, who were both from Chatham, married about 1705. Mary's father, Lieutenant Nicholas Eldredge, led Chatham's military and was its representative at the general court of Massachusetts Bay in the 1690s. He was one of the men in the boat with Reverend Vickery who drowned in April 1702. Mary's mother, Elizabeth Eldredge, like Jonathan II's mother, was left alone to care for a number of underage children.[2] So Jonathan Vickery II and Mary Eldredge were brought together in grief several years before they were brought together in marriage. They moved to Truro shortly before their first child David I was born, but they did not sell the Vickery homestead in Chatham until after Jonathan II's brother David Vickery disappeared at sea in 1714.[3] The Vickery family was by this time, as a historian of Truro states, "quite a large family," and though they lived in Truro, Jonathan II and Mary Eldredge Vickery remained "considerably interwoven" by marriage with the communities of Chatham and Hull.[4]

25

Jonathan Vickery II was both a farmer and a fisherman in Truro. Although Henry David Thoreau wrote in 1857 that Cape Cod's name derived from "that great store of cod-fish which Captain Bartholomew Gosnold caught there in 1602," farming was the basis of the Cape's economy in the seventeenth and early eighteenth centuries.[5] Its tall trees, fertile soil, and lush salt marshes had made it attractive at once to the Pilgrims who came from England's farming areas. All around Eastham, which bordered Chatham and Truro, colonists grew great crops of corn. This crop was so important to the economy of the community in 1695 that to protect it from the birds, a law was passed mandating that every unmarried man in the township had to "kill 6 blackbirds, or 3 crows" (following an unspecified schedule) as long as he remained single.[6] Thus, two problems were eradicated with one law; unattached men, so it seems, were as much a threat to communities as the birds.

As more and more settlers moved out to Cape Cod, deforestation and soil depletion made farming unproductive and towns turned exclusively to fishing for their economic base. As early as 1733 many marginal farming families from outer Cape Cod began a concerted migration to the Penobscot River valley in the District of Maine.[7] No doubt some of the extended Vickery family network migrated to central Maine in the early eighteenth century, but Jonathan II and Mary Eldredge Vickery stayed in Truro. They successfully practiced a mixed economy of fishing and farming, involved themselves in church and community affairs, and lived and raised their nine children much as their parents and grandparents had before them.

Community commitment and the worship and service of God were as important to Jonathan Vickery II as they were to his father. He was chosen moderator of the Truro town meeting and was active in starting schools in the town. He was a town selectman and was on the Committee of Proprietors that was responsible for selling the town's land. The Vickery family bought a pew in the new Church of Christ that Jonathan II helped to build and on 13 November 1728, Jonathan II was elected to be one of its deacons.[8] In this position Deacon Vickery advised and assisted the minister, served the communion, kept the treasury of the church and took care of its charities, as well as attended to its secular affairs.

Mary Eldredge Vickery was baptized in the Truro church in 1713. Individual church membership was one of the few ways that Mary could gain some independence outside her role as a "Goodwife." Religious faith continued to be a major source of strength for women as they faced potential death from childbirth every two or three years. Women in general also began to gain more authority in church affairs in Mary's generation (most often by influencing their husbands and sons) and they initiated the establishment of new church congregations, controlled the behavior of ministers, and acted as visionaries. Yet, even though there were now more women than men in most congregations of New England, they could not assume leadership roles in their church.[9]

Mary Eldredge Vickery and Deacon Vickery placed the Puritan, or Congregational church as it was now known at the center of their community. They baptized their children in the Truro church, which was made easier by the Halfway Covenant. This new church policy allowed the baptism of children whose parents had been baptized and "were living sober Christian lives," but who had not had the requisite conversion experience to become full members of the church.[10] Mary and the Deacon believed, as their parents had, that children were capable of religious experience and should take responsibility for their actions at an early age, as Puritan culture presumed children were "miniature adults."[11] The Vickery family, however, was not necessarily following the current trend.

The majority of Deacon Jonathan and Mary Eldredge Vickery's generation were not carrying on the same religious commitment as the first generation of settlers. By the beginning of the eighteenth century membership in the Puritan churches had declined, especially for men, who were increasingly concerned with economic achievements and less with spiritual fulfillment. To bring people back to religion—a more egalitarian religion—a new style of itinerant preacher, frequently without an elite theological education, traveled everywhere in the colonies in the 1730s and 1740s and held revival meetings. These emotionally charged revivals (in direct contrast to the reasoned and controlled Puritan worship services) were often held in open fields and drew crowds of thousands of individuals who tearfully converted, though not always to Puritan congregationalism. Called the "Great Awakening," this was the most important religious event in the eighteenth century.[12]

The Great Awakening and the new religious denominations that developed from it finally split the Puritan idea of a society that fundamentally linked church and state. Since the time that Deacon Vickery's grandfather George I arrived in the colony, this link defined community. Indeed, churches were supported by town taxes. But this idea had been slowly eroding from the beginning. One example of this erosion was the concept of church membership and suffrage. In 1650 George Vickery I was required to be a member of the Puritan church to vote for political officers. Though there were still religious requirements, Reverend Vickery could vote in 1678 because he owned land, not just because he was a member of the church. Deacon Vickery could vote because he owned land, but in 1735 he could chose to belong or not belong to the Congregational church or any one of the Methodist, Baptist, Anglican, or Quaker churches that "invaded" the Puritan stronghold in the 1700s.[13]

Without the common bond of one religion, town governments became secular in order to function without ill will and community took on a new meaning. The Puritan model of community where individuals worked together for the good of all was replaced with the model of community where individuals worked for the good of themselves and learned to cooperate in town matters in order to accomplish that. "Enlightenment" was the spirit of the times and it advanced the ideas of individual choice and individual gratification that would come to be the cornerstone of the American free-enterprise system.[14] Yet the church continued to be the center of community for the Vickery family and many others in New England. Regardless of the prevailing trend of individualism, acquisitiveness, and the secularization of society, or perhaps because of it, people still turned to religion to give thanks for God's grace and to help them cope with the harshness of life.[15]

Deacon Vickery died in Truro on 19 November 1741 at the age of fifty-eight. He was spared the loss three years later of his two oldest children, David I and Jonathan III, who, like his brother, were lost at sea. Mary Eldredge Vickery was still alive in 1744 to feel the pain and to witness another maritime tragedy that again ruptured her family. She died shortly thereafter on 13 November 1745 at the age of sixty-three. Deacon Jonathan II and Mary must have felt that God blessed their lives in spite of their losses. He "said unto them, Be fruitful, and multiply, and replenish the earth, and subdue it," and they did.[16] Two hundred and fifty years later their gravestones are still standing in the old North Cemetery in Truro, Massachusetts. They are tangible symbols of the fortitude, religious faith, and commitment to community that marked the lives of "Deacon Jonathan Vickery" and "Mary Vickery, widow of Jonathan Vickery [II]."

DAVID VICKERY I (1707–1744)
and
HANNAH PARKER (1710–c.1752)
Married 1731
Yarmouth, Truro, and Boston, Massachusetts

CHILDREN:

1. Hannah (1732–c.1782) m. (1) Barnabas Paine, Jr., (2) Isaac Whitney
2. *David II (1734/35–1823) m. (1)Lydia Atwood, (2) Sarah Stone*
3. Elizabeth (1737–?) m. Nathan Starbird
4. Mary (1739–1822) m. (1) Edmond Weston, (2) John Mitchell
5. Matthias (1741–before 1743)
6. Matthias (1743–1812) m. (1) Ruth Horton, (2) Elizabeth Wagg

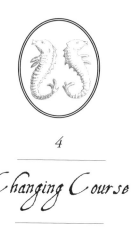

4

Changing Course

THE FOURTH GENERATION

*IN YOUR LETTER you wondered why there was not a settlement of an estate
for Capt. David Vickery. Well, my opinion is this: I am SURE that he was
lost at sea—everything points to that, and probably in the same ship that his
brother Jonathan was on…. I take it that David had not lived in Boston for
any length of time, and therefore probably had not accumulated any estate,
and if there was any settlement of his estate it would be in Barnstable
County, and … Barnstable county records have been burned several times.*
—Theoda Mears Morse to James Berry Vickery III, 18 June 1951[1]

THE COURSE OF THE VICKERY FAMILY history was definitively
changed when Captain David Vickery I, the son of Deacon and
Mary Eldredge Vickery was lost at sea in 1744. It started the family on
a path that would turn future generations away from the sea and towards
a livelihood dependent solely on agriculture. The Vickery family would
again be cast in the role of settlers of the "wilderness" in the District of
Maine, and they would populate it with an extended family network
that reached from Cape Elizabeth east to Calais and north to Unity. In
the 1730s, however, this history was inconceivable.

The fishing industry on Cape Cod in the first part of the eighteenth century, like farming, was changing radically. With the development of larger vessels like two-masted schooners and more precise

navigational instruments, fishermen could sail further offshore. New methods of curing fish by salting them right on the vessels allowed crews to stay out longer. The larger catches meant steadily declining prices for cod. Fishermen who still fished inshore on modest shallops could not compete. The merchants who once supplied them with credit now invested in the more profitable schooners. Many fishermen on the Cape and neighboring Nantucket Island aggressively turned to whaling for its lucrative oils and products, and soon the shore fishery died out.[2]

David Vickery I and his brother Jonathan III might have joined the crew of one of the whaling or offshore-fishing vessels at this time, but it would not be as promising a career for them as commanding a trading vessel. While a captain was paid about £8 a month (only about twice as much as an ordinary seaman), he had the opportunity to make even more money by purchasing shares in his trading voyage.[3] Both David I and Jonathan III became captains of vessels that shipped out of Boston. Captain David Vickery I was, by his own account in 1742, "Employed as a Master of a Vessell" involved in the "Virginia Trade."[4]

New England had by this time become dependent on grains and flour imported from the middle colonies and the upper South, so the coastal, or Virginia trade was important. In Boston Captain David Vickery I's vessel might take on a cargo of beer, lumber products, fish oil, and salt and sail down the coast to Virginia where the goods were exchanged for tobacco, peas, and pork. Perhaps Captain Vickery carried this cargo to the West Indies to swap for molasses, sugar, rum, and slaves. He could either head back to New England or take the West Indies cargo to the Chesapeake, use it to purchase a full cargo of tobacco, take this to London, and sell it for the manufactured articles that people back in Boston craved.[5]

Slavery was integral to most of the Atlantic trading patterns in the eighteenth century. Most obvious were the trade routes that included stops in West Africa to buy slaves. Not so obvious was the fact that vessels like Captain Vickery's often carried the dried cod that was used to nourish slaves. Slaves labored to produce the sugar, molasses, rum, and tobacco that were exported by the West Indies and southern colonies, imported north, and enjoyed by all New Englanders. New England's complicitious support of slavery made the fortunes of its merchants and provided income for its fishermen and mariners.[6]

Captain Vickery's trading ventures kept him away from home and his wife Hannah for long periods of time. He and Hannah Parker were married in Truro on 23 September 1731; the same day, and perhaps as part of the same ceremony in which his younger sister Mary Vickery and Thomas Paine were married. Hannah Parker was from Yarmouth on Cape Cod, one of ten children born to Benjamin Parker (sometimes referred to as "Reverend") and Rebecca Lombard Parker who could trace their lineage to the MAYFLOWER.[7] At this point the early interconnectedness of the Vickery family network becomes particularly noticeable. The following is a good example of the complexity of New England's genealogy: Thomas Paine's mother was a Cobb, as was Hannah Parker Vickery's grandmother; David I's great-great-uncle Benjamin Vickery, his sister Mary, and his daughter Hannah all married members of the Paine family; David I's brothers Jonathan III and Paul both married women from the Thomas family; and both David I's sister Joanna and Hannah Parker Vickery's sister Sarah married into the Lombard/Lumbert family, which of course was the maiden name of Hannah's mother. Community on Cape Cod was hard to separate from family.

Captain David I and Hannah Parker Vickery added a child to their family about every two or three years from 1732 until their last child, Matthias, was born in 1743. Hannah had much to keep her busy while David I was out at sea. Having joined the Truro church with David I in 1734, she had the spiritual community as a support system in his absences and, of course, her extended network of family was everywhere around her. More than likely, regardless of her support systems and days full of work and children, Hannah Parker Vickery fought, as did every mariner's wife, "a ceaseless, changeless war with fear" until Captain Vickery returned.[8]

In 1742 Captain David I and Hannah Parker Vickery decided to move to Boston. Since the 1640s the Vickery family had been connected to Boston through their network of relatives and the fish markets. David I's brother Captain Jonathan Vickery III had already moved to Boston, where he and Susanna Thomas had married in 1734, and where they had started a family. Since Boston was where David I usually shipped out, it seemed sensible to move there. Imports and exports were on the rise in 1742, as was the construction of new houses, churches, and pub-

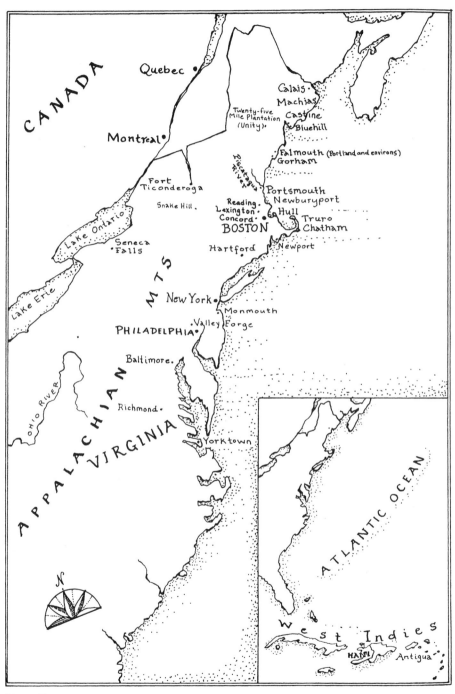

MAP BY BERRY MANTER

lic buildings.[9] Seaports were the places where all the newspapers were published, and David I could get the important maritime news immediately. He certainly could stay with Hannah and the children longer in Boston and see them sooner if the trip to Truro was eliminated. Perhaps he and Hannah desired a more cultivated lifestyle that cosmopolitan Boston could give them. But before David I and Hannah could move to Boston, David I had to ask permission from the selectmen of Boston.

It was the law that before families moved to a new community, they had to inform the officials of that community of their intentions and ask for permission to be admitted as members of the community. If the officials "voted in the negative," individuals or families were "warned out" of town.[10] The law was enacted to keep communities stable and discourage newcomers from moving into town with only marginal resources, suffering an economic downturn, and then ending up on public relief as a "town charge."

The Vickery family was just the sort of people Boston selectmen would want to admit into their town. According to the selectmen's minutes, Captain David Vickery I informed them that

HE HAD BROUGHT TO the Value of Five Hundred Pounds Old Tenor with him in Household Goods Chiefly, and that he is Employed as a Master of a Vessell out of this Town in the Virginia Trade and hired a House about Sixteen Days ago in mr. Stanifords Buildings at New Boston.[11]

After a week, Captain Vickery learned that his family's request had been "Voted in the affirmative, Provided he gave Bond with Sufficient Suretys to Indemnify the Town as the Law directs."[12] Apparently the stability of those who worked at sea was still questionable.

Officials cannot be faulted for their discrimination and caution, as Boston was in a state of chaos in the early 1740s. England and the colonies had just finished one war with Spain over trading rights in the Caribbean and Central America, the War of Jenkins' Ear (1739–42), and were preparing to declare war on France again. The focus of this conflict in New England, known as King George's War (1744–48), was the capture of the French fort at Louisbourg on Cape Breton Island. This naval station gave shelter to French privateers that attacked English ships, and it controlled the fishing waters around the Grand Bank area that had become the destination of New England fishermen in their new schooners. In preparation for the attack on Louisbourg, Boston became the embroiled gathering place for supplies, warships, and men from all over New England. The attack was successful and the English captured the important fort, but over 500 colonists were killed in the effort, and in the inexplicable dealings of world politics, Britain gave Louisbourg back to the French within a few months.[13]

While the Vickery family might have found opportunity in Boston in the 1740s, it was not so for many others. Aside from the general urban problems of sanitation, public health, and crime which seaports now faced, Boston also became, as historian Gary Nash put it, "the New England center of mass indebtedness, widowhood, and poverty." The war years brought inflation that caused the price of bread to increase six-fold between 1742 and 1749. Violent riots erupted because the British navy tried to impress, or "recruit" men right off the streets for service on their ships. Out of Boston's total population of 17,000 in 1742, 30 percent of adult women were widowed. The "successful" Louisbourg expedition, as Nash points out, made hundreds of Boston families "father-less, husbandless, and dependent on charity for food and fuel."[14]

Hannah Parker Vickery, widowed with five children after her husband was lost at sea, became a Boston statistic in 1744. Captain David Vickery I had been shipping to Antigua since at least 1738. There was great money to be made by seizing prizes at sea; he might have commanded a privateer. Tropical hurricanes, coastal shoals, enemy privateers, disease, and accidents always made seafaring hazardous, but King George's War made the trade to the West Indies even more risky and mortality rates extraordinary. French privateers out of Louisbourg seized thirty-six colonial vessels that were mostly from Massachusetts in the first weeks of the war.[15] Word came on 31 December 1744 that "Captain Vickery in a brigantine belonging to Boston" had been taken in the West Indies.[16] He never returned. Captain Jonathan Vickery III also died at this time, and family lore speculates that he might also have been on the same vessel as his brother David I.[17]

Even with some small estate her husband might have left her, Hannah Parker Vickery, now a widow, had few choices to secure her family's future at this time. Most women in the mid eighteenth century depended on men for their livelihood, and there is no evidence that Hannah ever started a business of her own as wives of Nantucket whalers sometimes did. As the wife of a mariner she could not continue her husband's business as some Boston artisans' wives did. Cities did offer women more opportunities to work in shops or taverns, but with her youngest child just over a year old and her eldest only twelve, this was difficult. If she stayed in Boston the chance that she might become a "Town Charge" was ever present. Hannah and her children might have gone to her parents' home on Cape Cod, but her father was dead, and there is no evidence that her mother could support her, or even if her mother was still alive. Broken households were common in early America as children were farmed out as apprentices or domestics in order to survive after the death of a parent. To keep her family together Hannah made the decision that most colonial women and many men had to make after the death of their spouses—she remarried. The man that Hannah Parker Vickery decided to marry lived in the District of Maine. It was Hannah who changed the course of Vickery family history when she moved to Falmouth and she and widower Joseph Weston married in May 1746—melding her family with his.[18]

T W O

*The Maine
Families*

1746–1860

DAVID VICKERY II (1735–1823)
and
LYDIA ATWOOD (?–c.1768)
Married 1760
and
SARAH STONE (1746–1830)
Married 1769
Truro and Boston, Massachusetts
Falamouth, Cape Elizabeth, Gorham, Standish, and Unity,
District of Maine

CHILDREN:

With LYDIA ATWOOD:

1. Deborah (c.1766–?) m. James Hunt
2. Lydia (c.1768–1852) m. (1) John Mitchell, (2) William Boynton

With SARAH STONE:

1. Hannah (1771–1833) m. Isaac Mitchell
2. Jonathan (1774–1847) m. Ruhamah Gould
3. Sarah (1777–1852) m. Samuel Kelley
4. *David III (1780–1847) m. Lydia Cobb Bartlett*
5. Susanna (1784–?) m. John Hanscom
6. Joel (1798–1869) m. Priscilla Bean

5

Revolution!

THE FIFTH GENERATION

THE HISTORY OF *the Unity [Maine] branch of the Vickery family begins with David Vickery II, the first of this name to settle in that town.*
—James Berry Vickery III[1]

ORIGINALLY INHABITED BY the Algonquin community of Native Americans called Wabanaki, or Abnaki until they were devastated by European settlers, the District of Maine was a contested area of land throughout the seventeenth century. It was bestowed, chartered, and granted to a number of European proprietors until it was officially appropriated by the Massachusetts Bay Colony in 1691. Thus, by the time that the Vickery family arrived, Maine was a colony of Massachusetts Bay Colony, which in turn was part of England's growing global empire of colonies.[2]

Massachusetts used Maine as a buffer to protect "civilized" Boston from attacks by the "savage" French and Native Americans, while Maine and its natural resources of fish, fur, and timber made Boston land speculators and merchants wealthy. It remained a contested area throughout the Revolutionary War and then into the nineteenth century as wealthy land speculators and settlers bitterly struggled over the rights to land ownership. Far from being the isolated demarcation between "civilization" and "savagery" wedged between the French colonies of Canada and Arcadia, Maine was an "international crossroads," according to historian Alan Taylor, where the diverse cultures and economies of North American and European peoples came crashing together in the mid eighteenth century.[3]

David Vickery II was about twelve years old when he and his older sister Hannah, his two younger sisters, Elizabeth and Mary, and his youngest brother Matthias, moved with their mother Hannah Parker Vickery to Falmouth, Casco Bay, in the District of Maine, upon her marriage to Joseph Weston in 1746.[4] Falmouth, which encompassed the modern towns of Portland, South Portland, Cape Elizabeth, Westbrook, and Falmouth, was the largest seaport in Maine just before the Revolutionary War, rivaling Portsmouth, New Hampshire, as a harbor for shipping the massive white pine trees needed for ship masts.[5] It was also a significant port in the trading routes with Boston, Virginia, and the West Indies and one that was probably frequented by Captain David Vickery I, so he may very well have known Joseph Weston.[6] The bustling waterfront and cosmopolitan air of Falmouth was similar to Boston, albeit on a lesser scale, and would have been a familiar environment for the transplanted Vickery family.

Joseph Weston had moved to Falmouth from Reading, Massachusetts, about 1729. Before that time, France and its Native American allies had destroyed the fledgling settlement of Falmouth in 1690, leaving the community, as historian Charles E. Clark described it, "a charred, nearly deserted army post." When peace was declared in 1713, an act was passed that gave land and citizenship to English men who promised to settle in Falmouth and pay the town £10.[7] Once families from Massachusetts like Joseph Weston, his first wife Sarah, and their four children felt safe enough, they hastened to settle Falmouth and other southern coastal towns of Maine. Joseph and Sarah Weston had at least three more children after they arrived in Maine before Sarah's death and the marriage of Joseph and Hannah Parker Vickery in 1746.

Hannah Parker Vickery was still of childbearing age when she and Joseph married, but there is no indication that they had children together. Evidence, or rather lack of evidence suggests Hannah Parker Vickery Weston died within a decade of arriving in Maine and by 1760 most of the Weston family were living in Gorham. Land in Gorham, known as Narragansett #7 in reference to the defeat of the Narragansett community of Native Americans, was granted to veterans of King Philip's

War and their heirs. It was advantageously linked to Falmouth by the Presumpscot River and was one of several towns on Maine's eastern frontier that was settled in the 1730s to act as a line of defense for Falmouth, Portsmouth, and Boston from northern attacks by Native Americans and the French.[8] The Weston family's move to Gorham had important consequences for drawing the Vickery family into Maine's interior and eventually to Unity.

According to family legend and expectations of the times, David Vickery II "followed the sea from his earliest days" as had the previous four generations of his family.[9] Living in Falmouth offered him the opportunity to fish of course, but there were plenty of other jobs available, too. He could build, load, and sail schooners and sloops, or navigate a gundelow (a low, flat, barge-like vessel) to port with loads of firewood and lumber from the many sawmills that lined the banks of the Presumpscot River.[10] However, when he was twenty-one the fourth and final war between England and France over control of frontier lands in North America put a halt to young David Vickery II's maritime career.

This final war which lasted from 1754 to 1763 was called the "French and Indian War" by the English colonists. At the same time, England, France, and the other European powers were fighting on that continent where it was called the "Seven Years' War." Since it was also fought for control of colonies in Asia and Africa it is more appropriately called the "First World War" by some historians. Although the many northeastern Native American communities in North America wanted to remain neutral in the war, they chose sides from the beginning because the French and the English compelled them to ally themselves with one side or the other. In spite of this, Native Americans still had the freedom to choose sides for their own purposes and they often changed sides when it was to their advantage.[11]

The war broke out in North America when the French expanded into the upper Ohio River valley area that the English claimed was part of their Pennsylvania and Virginia colonies. With the help of their Native American allies the French captured, killed, or drove out English traders and then fortified their western posts, preventing English colonists from settling any land near the Appalachian Mountains. With the help of their Native American allies the English waged a number of retaliations (including one led by young George Washington) but were repeatedly defeated. War then erupted in other tense "international crossroads" of the colonies where Native American, French, and English cultures came together.[12]

Not the least of these tense areas was the District of Maine. Twenty-two-year-old David Vickery II joined Colonel Ezekeil Cushing's militia company from Cape Elizabeth as a private for service "to the eastward" in 1757.[13] His service "to the eastward" at this time might mean service in colonial fortifications along the coast to Penobscot Bay and along the Kennebec River, or in one of the captured French forts in Acadia and Nova Scotia. David II could even have been a part of the forces massed in Halifax in the summer of 1757 that prepared yet again to capture the French fort at Louisbourg.[14]

David II's brother Matthias Vickery, who was only fourteen years old, also served in Cushing's company. In fact, most Massachusetts colonial soldiers were as young as David II and Matthias. Their ages ranged mostly between fourteen and twenty-nine years old, versus the experienced British regular troops who averaged thirty years or older. There were other important differences between the colonial and regular soldiers as well. Their ideas about military service, warfare, and general values were incompatible. While there was yearly compulsory service in the colonial militia for all men between the ages of sixteen and sixty, the colonists were not professional soldiers, but citizen-soldiers. They were farmers, woodsmen, fishermen, and mariners who felt they were serving out of community obligation when they went to war. They mustered up with their friends, neighbors, and families—the members of their communities—and they felt, as historian Fred Anderson put it, "knit together as one in the common pursuit of God's will." They were not concerned with military order and it shocked them to see the brutal way that aristocratic English officers treated English regular career soldiers.[15]

In the early years of the war the French overwhelmed the English regular and colonial troops. It was not until the English government realized that a global empire was at stake that they finally made major financial and military commitments to winning, and thus turned the war around. They captured the French strongholds of Quebec in 1759 and Montreal in 1760, and with the treaty of 1763 they eliminated France as a colonial rival in North America.

Ironically, defeating the French contributed to the loss of England's original colonies in North America twenty years later. For the first time in their lives many of the colonial soldiers were exposed to English-born soldiers and their rigid class system. David Vickery II and most other fifth-generation colonists still felt "English," but interactions with these soldiers, as well as their own unique colonial environment and experiences gave the colonists a real sense of their distinct and separate "American" identity, and they began to call themselves Americans. The egalitarian thinking of the "Great Awakening" in the early part of the eighteenth century contributed to the creation of this "Americanism" as well. So, while the "Great Awakening" might have seemed to erode the old Puritan notion of community, it helped generate a new community idea based on nationalism. Much like their great-great-grandfathers and grandmothers, these Americans thought the English class system and government were morally corrupt. It was during the French and Indian War that the idea that they wanted a more equitable government began to take root.[16] After the war Americans felt constrained under the increasing authority and new economic policies of the king and Parliament and fomented the Revolution. David Vickery II's military service and experience in the French and Indian War, like other colonial veterans, would be important for the success of this revolution.

In 1760, however, it was peace, not notions of revolution that brought hope for a better life to most colonial settlers like David Vickery II who were already in the District of Maine, as well as the hundreds who now swarmed in from Massachusetts and New Hampshire. David II, who would call himself a "seaman" until after the Revolution, returned to his maritime career after the war and put down roots in the Falmouth region. After posting their intentions in September 1759, David Vickery and Lydia Atwood were married at Cape Elizabeth in the spring of 1760. Lydia's parents, Joseph and Lydia Atwood, had come to Falmouth from Truro, so the marriage of David II and Lydia helped to bind the widening Cape Cod community together as the migration of its settlers to Maine accelerated. David and Lydia's marriage would be a good economic match as well, for according to family lore, Lydia Atwood's father operated a fishing fleet—a propitious enterprise now that French competition in the Gulf of Maine and along the Canadian coast was eliminated. It was about this time that David Vickery II requested and was granted land in the region of Mt. Desert for his service in the French and Indian War. Though he apparently never "took up" this grant, his brother Matthias did and started the Blue Hill branch of the Vickery family. Life looked promising for David and Lydia Atwood Vickery in the early 1760s.

It should have been a prosperous time in the northern colonies as a whole, but it was not, as a postwar depression developed that affected everyone from wealthy Boston merchants to small farmers, fishermen, and woodsmen in Maine. To make matters worse, throughout the 1760s the English government enacted a series of new taxes, or acts. They also decided to clamp down on smuggling by actively enforcing the Navigation Acts that had been in place since the 1660s. The intention was to make the colonies defray the costs of governing the new lands won from France. Since most of these tax acts revolved around controlling and profiting from the colonial trade and navigation system, colonists who lived in areas like the District of Maine, whose economy depended on trade, felt particularly threatened. They did not want interference in a trade and smuggling system that had served them well for generations.

The Sugar Act of 1764 restricted timber exports in Maine and attempted to control trade with the French West Indies and to curb smuggling, which was an important hidden economy along the northeast coast. The Stamp Act in 1765 was a tax on paper—all newspapers, almanacs, pamphlets, legal documents, ship's papers, licenses, and even packs of playing cards in the colonies. The Townshend Acts in 1767 added more duties on imports to the colonies. Each new tax act resulted in escalating protests, boycotts, and violence from the colonists. In David and Lydia Atwood Vickery's town of Falmouth there were riots, boycotts, and attacks on customs agents throughout these tense years. The "nonimportation" protests, in which colonists refused to buy imported goods from England, surely affected the livelihood of the Vickery family in Falmouth. No doubt, they would be well aware of, if not influenced by the growing center of revolutionary radicalism in Gorham, where their extended Weston family network lived.[17]

For the Vickery family these times of political and economic turmoil were overshadowed by personal tragedy when Lydia Atwood Vickery died suddenly in 1768. Lydia had given birth to a daughter Deborah in 1766. Two years later she gave birth to her second daughter, who was named Lydia. The date of baby Lydia's birth in 1768 and mother Lydia's death that same year suggests that she died from complications of that birth. It would have been very difficult for David to raise a motherless infant, and he would have needed to find a wetnurse to feed his new-born daughter. Left with two young children to care for, David II could waste no time in finding a new wife. In the fall of 1769 he and Sarah Stone were married in the Second Parish Church of Falmouth.

Twenty-three-year-old Sarah Stone of Scarborough would have known David Vickery II all of her life. She was the granddaughter of David's stepfather Joseph Weston, and she was born in Falmouth a few months after David's mother Hannah and Joseph Weston married. David's sister Mary Vickery and Joseph Weston's son Edmond had married in 1757, making Mary Vickery Weston an aunt of Sarah Stone. Sarah Stone's mother was Sarah Weston Stone, Joseph's oldest child. Sarah Stone's father Archelaus Stone, whose family were seventeenth-century Maine settlers, served in the French and Indian War alongside David Vickery II in Ezekeil Cushing's Company. The complex interrelated Vickery family and community network in Maine began from this marriage of David Vickery II and Sarah Stone. Much like they had in seventeenth- and eighteenth-century Cape Cod, this Vickery family would become related by birth and marriage to an extraordinary number of families in central Maine during the nineteenth century.

While David II and Sarah Stone Vickery began their family together in the early 1770s with the birth of a daughter Hannah in 1771 and then a son Jonathan in 1774, the tensions between American colonists and England accelerated. In 1770 a clash between English soldiers and colonists in Boston known as the Boston Massacre resulted in the death of five colonists. An attempt in 1773 by the English government to monopolize the tea trade in the colonies culminated in the infamous Boston Tea Party. As retribution, England initiated the "Intolerable Acts" prohibiting loading and unloading ships in Boston Harbor in 1774 and then passed laws in March 1775 restraining New England maritime trade and barring New England fishermen from the North Atlantic. These economic and political tensions, inflamed by festering ideas of colonial independence, exploded into the Revolutionary War when colonial militia men met English soldiers in armed battle in Lexington, Massachusetts, in April 1775.[18]

The Revolution in the District of Maine officially started in June 1775 when protests against English maritime trade policies propelled colonists in Machias (the leader of whom was David Vickery's brother-in-law John Mitchell) to capture three English naval vessels.[19] Earlier that spring, colonists in Falmouth had aggravated the English navy by capturing one of its commanders in another trade protest. In return, the English navy attacked Falmouth and burned two-thirds of the Vickery family's hometown to the ground in October 1775. Apparently this was enough for David Vickery to enlist in the Continental Army on 1 December 1775.

David Vickery II was forty years old when he enlisted in Falmouth as a private in the Eighteenth Continental Regiment. He was 5 feet 7 inches tall, with a dark complexion, dark hair, and gray eyes, according to the official "Descriptive List of Enlisted Men."[20] Private Vickery would spend most of the next seven years of his life fighting in the Revolutionary War, with occasional interruptions. His older age, his economic status as a taxpayer in Falmouth, his occupation as a seaman, and his continued, faithful service throughout the entire war as a private made him an anomaly. Most Continental soldiers from New England were half his age, did not own taxable property, were unskilled, and did not serve in the war for more than one year. In fact, often older settled men like David Vickery II paid younger, poorer men to fulfill their military obligations during the war.[21] David Vickery II's years of committed service seem praiseworthy because in the latter years of the war, it was difficult to find patriots in Maine who were willing or financially able to leave their families to join the military for extended periods of time.

Private Vickery began his service in Colonel Edmund Phinney's Eighteenth Continental Regiment by marching 300 miles from Falmouth to Cambridge, Massachusetts, then west to Fort Ticonderoga, New York. A small colonial force led by Ethan Allen had captured the fort from the British in 1775 and the Eighteenth Regiment was sent there in 1776 to help hold it. It was that summer that Private Vickery probably heard the Declaration of Independence for the first time. It was surely the most powerful articulation of why men like him had left their wives, children, and livelihoods to fight for "life, liberty, and the pursuit of happiness" so far from home. In December Private Vickery was discharged from duty and when he returned to Maine, he and his

James Berry Vickery III commissioned this idealized bookplate of his great-great-great grandfather Revolutionary War veteran David Vickery II: "I am enclosing my new book plate. It represents David Vickery and I looked up the description of the type of uniform which his regiment wore. However, I expect he never wore such as elaborate uniform as this."

family moved away from the risky coastal area inland to Gorham where Sarah Stone Vickery's uncle Joseph Weston II now lived. Sarah's brother Archelaus, her six sisters, and her widowed mother would also move to Gorham by the end of the war.[22] Private Vickery was home barely a month when he enlisted for three more years as a private in the First Massachusetts Regiment. In January 1777 he marched south under the command of Colonel Joseph Vose.

Sarah Stone Vickery, like other American women, also served in the Revolutionary War, although her service was not officially recognized. Inconsistent and meager military pay paid to their husbands, wartime scarcity, inflation, the extra work of producing substitutes for boycotted English goods, and the constant fear of capture and rape by enemy troops made life a constant battle for women serving on the home front.[23] When her husband first marched off to Ticonderoga, Sarah was left with her young stepdaughters and two small children. She gave birth to two more children during the war, a daughter Sarah and a son David III. There is some suggestion that she also gave birth to another son during the war years who was "drowned when a child."[24] With her husband away it became her sole responsibility to feed, shelter, and clothe her growing family.

If Sarah had been the wife of a farmer or a merchant, she might have taken over the tasks of running the farm or the business. However, like Sarah's mother-in-law Hannah Parker Vickery thirty years earlier, wives of seamen had no such recourse and women and children on the eastern coast suffered desperate poverty during the war. In order to survive, many women followed the troops from camp to camp with their families, cooking, washing, and working as nurses. According to family lore, Sarah Stone Vickery taught school during the Revolution, perhaps to support the family. Sarah and her children were not destitute and were safely ensconced in the Gorham community of Weston and Stone relatives. This might help to account for David Vickery II's consistent and unusual reenlistment for seven years of service in the war. Patriotism notwithstanding, these repeated reenlistments invite speculation on the nature and quality of David II and Sarah's marriage and his relationship with his family.

Private Vickery began his second tour of duty in Valley Forge, only 20 miles away from the British-occupied capital of Philadelphia. With 11,000 other men commanded by General George Washington, he endured the legendary brutal winter of 1777 through 1778, though there would be more such winters as the war dragged on. Camped in log huts, American troops received little food or clothing. Many went barefoot while they suffered starvation, smallpox, and dysentery. They were often so cold that they sat up through the nights huddled around fires. While there were desertions and some mutiny, most soldiers like Private Vickery suffered bravely. Surviving this ordeal turned Private Vickery and his fellow citizen-soldiers into more of a professional army—one that in June 1778 chased the English across New Jersey and surprised them with a new strength at the Battle of Monmouth Courthouse.[25]

After fighting in Rhode Island for the rest of his second enlistment, Private Vickery was discharged in January 1780 at Fishkill, New York, and he made his way back to Maine once again. "According to family tales of the fireside," Private Vickery was wounded in the hip during the Battle of Monmouth and "he is said to have walked with a limp during the rest of his life and in his old age he walked with two canes."[26] David II stayed home that year. While he surely needed time to recover from the hip wound, Maine's economy was in ruins and concern for his family might also have kept him home for a longer time.

David Vickery II enlisted once again in January 1781 as a private in Colonel John Greaton's Third Massachusetts. Although the English surrendered after the Battle of Yorktown in 1781, it would take more than a year and a half to end the Revolutionary War. England had also been at war with France, Spain, and the Netherlands, as well as the new United States, and the war did not officially end until the Treaty of Paris was signed by all in 1783. Since a standing army threatened the Ameri-

James Berry Vickery III (left), S. Stillman Berry III (center), and Eric Arthur Vickery (right) with one of Revolutionary War veteran David Vickery II's extant canes, Pittsfield, Maine, November 1951.

can ideal of the virtuous citizen-soldier, the Continental army was disbanded throughout that year and men trudged home to their families and communities.

Private Vickery was discharged after spending time convalescing from a shoulder wound he received somehow in July 1783 while stationed at Snake Hill, New York, a small village just south of Saratoga Springs. Wounded, and no doubt weary of war, he came home to his wife Sarah and their six children in Gorham, but he returned to a tense region in which the Revolution was not over. Many impoverished veterans believed that for their sacrifices in the war they were owed a parcel of frontier land and the chance to improve it. Many men in essence had joined the Revolution to fight for the liberty to own and farm land, free and clear, on which they could support their families. However, legal title to land in central Maine now belonged to wealthy American speculators known as the "Great Proprietors." After the Revolution, these proprietors gained control of the original English land grants in the District of Maine through political maneuvering that was sanctioned by the Massachusetts legislature and they had no intention of donating their land for the common good. Nonetheless, after 1783 hundreds of hopeful veterans and their families came in droves to settle land in central Maine, with or without a clear title of ownership. The conflicting ideas of some of these settlers—who called themselves "Liberty Men"—and the "Great Proprietors" about land ownership kept the revolutionary fervor alive in the District of Maine for another forty years.[27]

While the Vickery family would become embroiled in this land conflict, the most pressing problem for them right after the war was deciding what course to follow in their lives. David II and Sarah Stone Vickery's seventh child was born soon after he came home, and an eighth was born in 1789. The Continental bills David II received for his service during the war had depreciated to the point of worthlessness, and with a large family to support it was imperative that he find gainful work. Sarah's school-teaching days were over, as she and other married women went back to their traditional roles in the home when the men returned. Since the maritime trade in the District of Maine was all but destroyed by the war, and the nature of his wounds might have prevented him from continuing as a seaman, it is not surprising that David II and Sarah would attempt a new livelihood as farmers. Farming on their own land would offer David II and Sarah the independence and liberty that the revolutionary ideal for which they had fought promised. More important, David II and Sarah's sons could stay with them on a farm and work to improve land they stood to inherit. In a time long before Social Security, keeping their sons living close to them would be David II and Sarah's security in old age. This would be fifty-four-year-old David II and forty-three-year-old Sarah Stone Vickery's last chance to create a homestead and security for themselves and their family.

Deciding not to buy land in Gorham, and being warned out of town in 1790 because of it, the Vickery family moved up the road to Standish, seemingly looking for the best land to begin farming. Remaining in Standish but a few years, they headed north in 1794 to their final destination—Twenty-Five-Mile Pond Plantation, known as such because it was twenty-five miles from Fort Halifax at Winslow. David II Vickery's sister Mary Vickery Weston Mitchell with her second husband John Mitchell and children had already moved to the plantation from Machias, and in the early 1790s David II's daughters, Lydia and Hannah had both recorded their intentions to marry two of the Mitchell sons who were also their cousins, John and Isaac. Thus, the Mitchell family's established presence and success, as well as their growing familial connections would have been influential factors for drawing the Vickery family to this new farming community, which in turn began a chain migration of others from the Gorham region.

Most of the men who came with their families to farm in central Maine were Revolutionary War veterans like David Vickery II and John Mitchell. The names they chose for their new settlements such as Washington, Freedom, New Canaan, Union, Hope, and Liberty reflected their politics as well as their hopes for their futures on the land.[28] Going forward into the nineteenth century the Vickery family's new community of Twenty-Five-Mile Pond Plantation, united in its patriotism, chose to call itself "Unity." It was a particularly apt name, because by the end of the century most people in Unity would be united either through marriage or by birth.

DAVID VICKERY III (1780–1847)
and
LYDIA COBB BARTLETT (1787–1865)
Married 1805
Plymouth, Massachusetts
Gorham, Standish, Unity, District of Maine

CHILDREN:

1. *Eli (1807–1877) m. Clarissa Berry*
2. Damaris (1809–1879) never married
3. Sarah (1811–1888) m. Stephen Thayer Rackliff
4. Joseph (1813–1876) m. Martha/Bertha? Jackson
5. Ann (1815–1901) m. (1) William Stone, (2) Josiah Fogg
6. Benjamin Bartlett (1817–?) m. (1)Adaline Stone, (2)Martha Church
7. Nelson (1819–1895) m. Isabelle Cornforth
8. David (1821–1879) m. (1) Luania Craig, (2)Sarah Barker, (3) Lucy Barker
9. John (1823–1870) m. Abigail Murch
10. Charles Augustus (1827–1891) m. Mary E. Heald
11. Albert (1831–1858) m. Louisa Craig

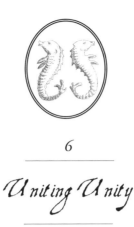

6

Uniting Unity

THE SIXTH GENERATION

He [DAVID VICKERY III OF UNITY] was styled "Black David" to distinguish him from his cousin, David Vickery [of Blue Hill] who was called "Red" David. The former David is described as very dark and was "hairy as the tribe of Esau."
—James Berry Vickery III[1]

To REACH THE BANKS OF their new community in 1794 David II and Sarah Stone Vickery and their children Deborah, Jonathan, Sarah, David III, Susanna, and Joel might have sailed up the Kennebec River past Augusta to Fort Halifax in Winslow. Then they would have cruised up the Sebasticook River into Twenty-Five-Mile Stream at Burnham and floated through an outlet into the waters of Twenty-Five-Mile Pond, much as the Stephen and Hannah Chase family had in 1783. Or like the Joseph and Lydia Bartlett family, the Vickery family might have taken a packet up the Penobscot River to Hampden and rode on horseback, "following a [blazed] trail of spotted trees through the woods," hauling all their worldly possessions behind them to Twenty-Five-Mile Pond Plantation. Now married, daughters Lydia Vickery Mitchell and Hannah Vickery Mitchell were most likely living in the new settlement and were there to greet their family when they arrived.[2]

The first order of business for the Vickerys was to build a shelter on land they claimed, but to which they probably had no clear title. The land all around them was heavily wooded. In fact trees were so plentiful that some families kept their babies in cradles hewn out of pine logs.[3] Like most of the other settlers, the Vickerys probably built a cabin of spruce logs. The cabin would be just one room between sixteen and forty feet long, twenty feet wide, and seven feet high in which all eight of them would live. There would be a door, perhaps a window or two covered with oil paper, a large stone fireplace at one end, a floor of either packed dirt or wooden planks, and a half loft for sleeping and storage. It must have seemed a primitive structure to David II and Sarah Stone Vickery who surely remembered the elegant homes in Falmouth, but they and the other early settlers of Unity had hopes of building respectable framed houses as they prospered.

Next, the Vickery family would have cleared five or six acres of trees on their land so that they could plant corn and a few vegetables. If they burned the deadwood and brush like so many of their neighbors, it formed a fertile layer of ashes on the soil, and they could plant corn and winter rye right away without plowing. This method of "slash and burn" farming in the new settlements of central Maine was productive, helped keep the legions of black flies and mosquitoes at bay, but it filled the air with smoke that sometimes turned the skies as black as night. Choking smoke, pests, wolves, and bears that killed their animals and destroyed their crops, scarcity of cash, mounting debts, starvation, accidents, isolation, and Maine's short growing season and brutal winters brought hardship, poverty, and tragedy to many of the postwar settlers.

Despite their privations the Vickery family believed that if they could endure they might realize their hopes of economic independence based on family farming—so they endured. They lived on cornmeal their first year of settlement. They raised wheat in the third year, and perhaps were able to build a small barn. By the fourth year they harvested English hay, wheat, rye, and corn, and with luck, by the seventh year these "old settlers" might finally build a frame house. David II and Sarah Vickery's children, "America's first generation," rewarded the perseverance of their parents by marrying and carrying on the independent family farm ideal.[4]

Most of the Vickery children married people in Unity or surrounding communities, and all but one stayed in central Maine to raise families. Deborah Vickery and James Hunt, the son of a Gorham war veteran and early Unity settler, married, moved to Charleston, Maine, and had five children. John and Lydia Vickery Mitchell stayed in Unity and had at least four children before John died and Lydia remarried. Isaac and Hannah Vickery Mitchell built one of Unity's first large two-story houses in which they raised their eleven children. Jonathan Vickery and Ruhamah Gould of Orrington married, had fourteen children, and started the Glenburn branch of Vickerys. Sarah Vickery and Samuel Kelley, the son of a Boothbay war veteran and early settler, married and raised twelve children in Unity. Joel Vickery and Pricilla Bean of Unity married and had two daughters and a son who died as an infant.

Susanna Vickery was the first in the family to leave Unity to go westward. She and John Hanscom, who had come to Unity from Gorham, married in 1810 and after the birth of several children moved to Ohio. The migration to Ohio of discouraged Maine farm families started as early as 1810. After the summer of 1816, when it was so cold that it snowed, puddles froze solid, crops failed, and birds dropped dead, the migration accelerated. Seeming like an epidemic, this migration was called "Ohio Fever." From 1810 to 1820 an estimated ten to fifteen thousand persons caught "Ohio Fever" and moved out of Maine.[5] While some families returned, the John and Susanna Vickery Hanscom family settled in Summit County, Ohio, and prospered. Four of the Hanscom sons were successful grocers in Akron until after the Civil War.

In the fall of 1805 twenty-five-year-old David Vickery III and eighteen-year-old Lydia Cobb Bartlett married. Lydia had come from Plymouth, Massachusetts, to Unity as a child with her father and mother, Joseph and Lydia Cobb Bartlett. Her father Joseph had served with David's father during the Revolution in the First Massachusetts Regiment. Her two brothers, Lemuel and Benjamin Bartlett had come to Twenty-Five-Mile Pond plantation years before and by this time were considered esteemed "town fathers." Thus, Lydia had prominent standing in the community as the sister of "Squires" Lemuel and Benjamin, and in her own right as a schoolteacher in the early settlement. She also had a worthy MAYFLOWER lineage on her father's side as the great-great-great-granddaughter of Edward Doty and as the great-great-great-great-granddaughter of Richard Warren. The marriage of David III and Lydia was a good social and economic alliance between the Vickery family and the powerful Bartlett family.

David Vickery III and Lydia Bartlett's wedding would not have been like today's celebrations. It occurred with little fuss within the daily activities of family farm life. After David and Lydia's intentions were announced in a public place, Lydia concentrated not on her wedding, but on preparing to move to David's farm and setting up her own household. Crockery and tinware had to be collected, blankets woven, and quilts constructed. On the wedding day a few family members gathered in the Bartlett home and David and Lydia were joined in marriage by a justice of the peace—probably Lydia's brother Benjamin—and her homemaking preparations continued. It might be a month before she was ready to set up housekeeping with David, and he would continue to visit, more like a suitor than a husband until the day he brought her home to his farm. Like most young couples at this time David and Lydia's marriage was probably not arranged, and in the beginning at least they surely felt some affection for each other.[6]

Called "Black David," David Vickery III was described as being dark complexioned, with dark black hair, and of medium height, much like his father. While the name "Black David" distinguished him from his cousin "Red David," son of Matthias Vickery of Blue Hill, it also described his personality. According to Unity lore David III was "a man quiet and moody, not talkative, close, and reserved," and he had a "very jealous temperament." At some point he began to tie Lydia's feet "to the bed post when he went to bed at night—just in case." It also appears to have been common knowledge that "frequent family quarrels" erupted on the Vickery farm that had to be settled by Lydia's brother Lemuel Bartlett "who would be called in to straighten matters out." This all suggests that David Vickery III might have suffered from a mental illness for which there was no real medical understanding or effective treatment at the time.[7] There is no evidence that liquor was a factor in David's behavior, but it would not be surprising. Liquor consumption had increased markedly after the Revolution, and drunkenness was common in the United States at this time. Rum drinking especially was widespread on the Maine frontier, and while this might have helped settlers endure hardships, it could just as often compound economic uncertainty and rupture family relations. Lydia, who was "optimistic, cheerful," and had a "good sense of humor," persevered in this stormy marriage. For twenty-five years she was either pregnant or nursing, giv-

Lydia Bartlett Vickery (1787–1865), c. 1850.
Wife of "Black David," she was "optimistic,
cheerful," and had a "good sense of humor."

ing birth to eleven children. A married woman like Lydia Bartlett Vickery had little recourse from domestic violence—"all that she had in life lay with the man she had married."[8]

Both religious and civil institutions in the early nineteenth century gave husbands complete power over their wives. According to the divine law of the Bible a woman's duty "should be to her husband, and he should rule over her."[9] Common law declared that the very being or legal existence of women was suspended during marriage. This meant that when a woman married she was civilly dead, and her identity was merged into that of her husband who had access to her body and owned any property she brought to the marriage or wages she earned.[10] Another common-law tradition called the "rule of thumb" condoned wife beating as long as a husband used a rod no thicker than his thumb. The early Puritan church and government of David III and Lydia's ancestors intervened in family disturbances to keep their society stable and orderly. As a result Massachusetts had passed the first laws in the colonies against wife abuse as early as 1672. After the Revolution the affairs of an individual family were considered private, and state governments were more hesitant to interfere or impose a standard morality. It was also more difficult to enforce such laws on Maine's frontier. So it was left to caring neighbors or relatives to protect and help an abused woman within a community. During the "frequent family quarrels" on the Vickery farm, it was lucky for Lydia Bartlett Vickery that her brother Lemuel Bartlett did not hesitate to come "to straighten matters out."[11]

The American Revolution established, in theory at least, that all white male citizens were equal, but it did not reward the loyal service and sacrifices of white women patriots. They remained politically, legally, economically, and socially subordinate to men after the Revolution, and most women did not overtly challenge this. Maine historian Elizabeth Ring has eloquently captured the acquiescence and rhythm of life for Lydia Bartlett Vickery and her contemporaries in the "Early Republic."

> LIKE MOST WOMEN of their day, these women accepted life as they found it. A fractious or exacting husband, the oft repeated pain of childbirth, the training of children, the making of soap, the churning of butter, the running of candles, the weaving of cloth, the carrying of water, the heft of the wood at the fireplace, the baking, washing, and mending of clothes—thus a woman went the rounds of the clock.[12]

Some women hoped, however, that the American Revolution might advance some protections for women's political, legal, economic, and social subordination. Abigail Adams implored her husband John Adams to address these issues when he helped to draft new laws for the country after independence was declared from England in 1776:

> DO NOT PUT SUCH unlimited power into the hand of Husbands. Remember all Men would be tyrants if they could.... That your Sex are Naturally Tyrannical is a Truth so thoroughly established as to admit of no dispute, but such of you as wish to be happy willingly give up the harsh title of Master for the more ten-

der and enduring one of Friend. Why then, not put it out of the power of the vicious and the Lawless to use us with cruelty and indignity with impunity.[13]

Abigail Adams later lamented that the Founding Fathers did not consider women's plight. They proclaimed "peace and good will to Men" and "emancipated all nations," but they continued to "insist upon retaining an absolute power over Wives." Thus the status of Lydia Bartlett Vickery and the other first-generation American wives remained about the same as before the Revolution with one exception. Where it had earlier been the duty of fathers to foster morality and good citizenship in their sons, it now became women's added responsibility as "Republican Mothers" to raise virtuous sons for the New Republic, preferably on the hallowed land of the independent family farm.[14]

Nor did the American Revolution do much to revolutionize the injustices in other people's lives in the new United States. Thousands of black slaves fought as American patriots, but slavery was incorporated in the new Constitution nonetheless. Native Americans again fought on whichever side seemed advantageous during the Revolution, but all were on the losing side at war's end as land-hungry Americans bolted for the northern, southern, and western frontiers. In the District of Maine Native Americans had become dependent on trade items and were reduced to want when trading posts were closed after the war. To combat destitution and to preserve what was left of their self-sufficiency, Native Americans sold their traditional lands, creating opportunities for settlers to establish family farms. Selling their land only made Native Americans poorer after the Revolution and eventually forced their dependence on the new United States government for their survival.[15]

The opportunity to own their own land was what brought most Europeans like George Vickery and Rebecca Phippen's family to Massachusetts Bay Colony in the first place and land ownership became the main criteria for belonging to a community. "All historic nobility rests on possession and use of land," Ralph Waldo Emerson affirmed in his 1858 essay on farming.[16] By 1809 David III and Lydia Bartlett Vickery had taken over the Vickery family farm—having received the new "Invalid Pension" from the federal government for his Revolutionary War disabilities in 1807, David's father must have felt he could retire—

and David III confirmed the Vickery family's community membership (and their "nobility" or power) in Unity when he legally purchased the land on which his parents had probably first settled and farmed. The original Vickery family land was part of a grant made to James Bowdoin of Boston by the Kennebec Proprietors in 1770.[17] In the early nineteenth century it belonged to Bowdoin's heirs, and David Vickery III paid Lady Elizabeth Bowdoin Temple $20.00 for a five-acre lot in 1810. In 1813 he signed a mortgage for $367.15 to Sarah Bowdoin in order to purchase an adjoining one hundred and forty-four acres.[18]

It was not unusual that Jonathan Vickery as David II's eldest son did not take over the family farm. While it was customary for some families in New England to leave the farm to the eldest son, a right known as primogeniture, other families practiced a different strategy. Apparently it made more sense to them to pass the farm to the youngest son, a system called ultimogeniture, because when the father turned sixty-five or seventy and was ready to slow down or retire the youngest son would be ready to take over the farm and care for his aging parents.[19] This might explain Jonathan Vickery seeming to make his own way in Unity, and from this point forward the Vickery family seemed to continue to practice the ultimogeniture system of inheritance. Of course, intergenerational conflict and personal relationships between family members often usurped land-inheritance traditions as well. Historian Joyce Appleby also suggests that the Revolution and the resulting focus on individualism (not to mention new economic opportunities on frontier land) caused problems between many fathers and sons. Not willing to wait around to inherit the family farm, many sons now felt confident to strike out on their own.[20]

Legalizing land ownership and community membership was not as easy for some of the settlers in Unity as it appeared to be for the Vickery family. Many families had come to the area and settled on land without a deed, believing their service in the Revolution gave them moral right to the land. At the very least, they believed that the improvements they made to the land should count for something towards a reasonable purchase price. However, some of the wealthy proprietors—who were, in fact, land speculators—refused to sell to many settlers, because they thought they could sell at a higher price later. They often set the purchase price beyond the means of many settlers who

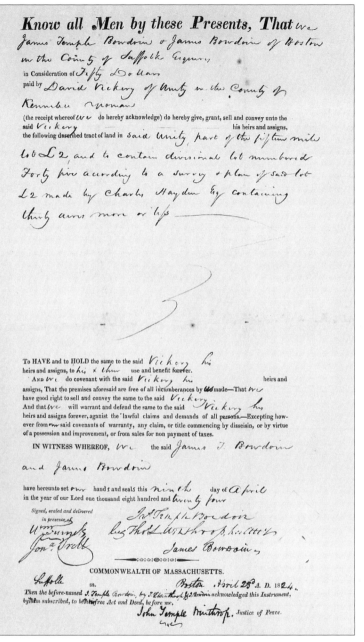

One of the several land transactions between the Vickery
family of Unity and the "Great Proprietors" of Boston, 1824.

COURTESY OF UNITY HISTORICAL SOCIETY.

were barely surviving on the land as it was. Because the proprietors legally owned the land, they could and did evict settlers with the support of the courts. Appeals to the government for help seemed futile to these frontier settlers; they had limited political influence, and it was too costly to send representatives to Boston. David Vickery III's brother, Jonathan Vickery, and other solid citizens who had earlier achieved Unity's incorporation (and would later become Vickery relatives) like the Jacksons, Rackliffs, Trueworthys, Kelleys, Berrys, and Mitchells sent a petition to the Massachusetts General Court in December 1807 that captures their desperation:

> YOUR PETITIONERS, inhabitants of Unity in the County of Kennebec, humbly sheweth that we are settled on land said to belong to certain proprietors, who are now endeavoring to eject us from our possessions, to the inevitable ruin of ourselves and our numerous families, though in making our settlements we have undergone hardships and difficulties which would baffle all description…. We are willing to pay a reasonable price for what the lands were worth in a state of nature…. And be allowed a reasonable time to pay…. We are a poor people, that we if we have but a short time to make payments, we shall be under the necessity of borrowing money and the rate of twenty-five percent interest which may operate to our utter ruin.[21]

In frustration and fear for the welfare of their families, as well as out of a commitment to Revolutionary War ideals, some of these men resorted to violence and intimidation in order to secure their land. They generally called themselves "Liberty Men," but others referred to them as "White Indians" because they disguised themselves as Native Americans while inciting riots and terrorizing the surveyors and land agents hired by the proprietors.[22] The racial implications of using the term "White Indians" suggest that some felt those who did not own their own land and had to resort to violence were, like Native Americans, "savages."

The Liberty Men also threatened some of the more secure settlers in the community who had successfully negotiated a deal with the proprietors. In one incident, they burned the house of Lydia Bartlett Vickery's brother, Benjamin Bartlett, who had received the deed to his land in Unity as early as 1802, and thus upheld the legal rights of the Great Proprietors. Perhaps because of their connection to the Bartlett family, the Liberty Men also attempted to burn the original Vickery homestead where David III, Lydia (who was probably pregnant), their baby son Eli, perhaps David III's young brother Joel, his sixty-two-year-old mother Sarah, and his father David II, now in his seventies, lived. Apparently while David III and Joel were away from home, Liberty Men descended on the Vickery farm in 1807. According to family legend, "the women of the household," believing that the sight of the "decrepit" and "ancient" Revolutionary War veteran David Vickery II might deter the "mob," placed him in the dooryard with his two canes and a "loaded rifle in his hands." Evidently this ploy worked, and the Liberty Men left "without any further action."[23]

Indeed the sight of the "ancient" veteran David Vickery II might have caused pangs of patriotic guilt for the Liberty Men in Central Maine. Revolutionary War veterans were honored members of a community and were looked upon as living symbols of the unity and republicanism that made America unique and great. Historians in the early nineteenth century who wanted to illustrate the patriotism and valor of veterans especially sentimentalized Valley Forge, where Private David Vickery had suffered through the famous winter. Politicians and community leaders referred often to these venerable veterans in their speeches and in newspaper articles. They hoped to awaken "the spirit of '76" in American citizens as new tensions between the United States and England escalated.[24] The Liberty Men's attempt to burn the farm of a Revolutionary War veteran shows just how desperate these men were.

In essence this bitter land struggle within several Maine communities like Unity and between Maine communities and the wealthier regions of Massachusetts was about the security and power that land ownership gave to some people and the uncertainty, anxiety, and resentment others felt when they were denied the opportunity to own land. The clashes resulting from this struggle surely must have threatened the unity of Unity, but what appears to have kept the settlement together was a common heritage, shared experiences of the Revolution, and their interconnections through marriage. In time disputes were reconciled and David III's brother Jonathan was finally able to purchase his one hundred

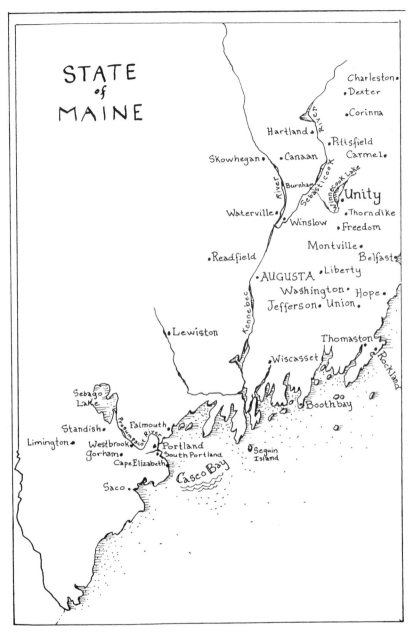

STATE
of
MAINE

Charleston•
•Dexter
•Corinna
Hartland•
Pittsfield
Carmel•
Skowhegan• •Canaan
Burnham
•Unity
Waterville• •Thorndike
Winslow •Freedom
Montville•
•Readfield Belfast•
•AUGUSTA •Liberty
Washington• Hope•
Jefferson• Union•
•Lewiston Thomaston
Wiscasset• Rockland
Sebago •Boothbay
Lake
Standish• •Falmouth
Limington• •Portland
Westbrook• •South Portland
Gorham• •
CapeElizabeth• •Sequin
Island
Saco• Casco Bay

THE MAINE FAMILIES

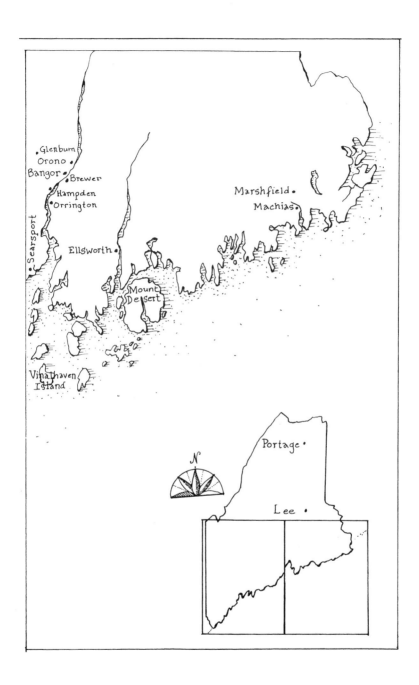

acres, but the sense of inequity lingered. The settlers never got over their resentment of being controlled by an elite authority in distant Boston. This conflict, compounded by the War of 1812, helped bring about the separation of the District of Maine from Massachusetts within the next ten years.[25]

This War of 1812 between England and the United States began because the United States government insisted on its neutrality after England and Napoleonic France went to war against each other at the turn of the nineteenth century. American shipping and commerce were prospering too much from European trade to encourage the United States to choose sides. Of course, the relationship between England and the United States had been strained ever since the end of the Revolution. Open hostilities began when England's navy blockaded American shipping to prevent American aid to France. When the English began to stop American ships to seize sailors whom they claimed were deserters, the United States retaliated. President Thomas Jefferson put an embargo on all trade with England and France, hoping that economic coercion would stop English aggression. It did not. It only harmed American trade, especially in New England where the trading ties to England were strongest.

The embargo devastated New England's economy, leading to the demise of such wealthy ports as Portsmouth, New Hampshire, and Newburyport, Massachusetts. It also caused the New England states to threaten secession from the United States—the first, but not the last time states would threaten secession when their economic survival was at odds with federal government policies. When other trade restrictions against England failed, war seemed the only alternative. Most of the celebrated battles with England in the War of 1812 were fought along the Canadian border in the Great Lakes region, though the English invaded Washington, D.C., and burned the White House in the summer of 1814. The famous Battle of New Orleans in which American soldiers under Andrew Jackson "kept the British running" was won after the treaty was signed between England and the United States in December 1814.[26]

As an international crossroad whose economy depended on shipping, Maine suffered from the embargo, compounding the desperate uncertainty wrought by the struggle between settlers and land speculators. Because the population was spread out and the district shared a border with the enemy, Maine suffered most from raids and invasion by the English during the war.[27] In the summer of 1814 the English conquered the entire coast of Maine east of Penobscot Bay and proceeded to pillage and terrorize Maine towns as far inland as Bangor. In September 1814 David Vickery III, his youngest brother Joel Vickery, and his brother-in-law Samuel Kelley marched to Wiscasset to meet the enemy threat as part of a militia company from Unity commanded by Benjamin Rackliff (his daughter Sarah's future father-in-law). Presumably when the men were away during this militia duty, "the war invaded the very hearthstones" of Unity. While on one of their "foraging expeditions" in the Unity area, English soldiers ended up at the farm of David III's sister, Sarah Vickery Kelley. According to family legend,

> SARAH KELLEY, undaunted by the looting enemy, stood unyielding. With a musket in her hands she defended her meager store of winter supplies. So impressive was her defense, so vehement was her attitude that the awed and frightened soldiers, admiring her resistance, left her unmolested.[28]

The war had begun to wind down by this time, and this might explain the nonbelligerent attitude of the English soldiers towards Sarah. Sarah's story joins that of other individual Maine women who fearlessly stood up to English soldiers who attempted to ransack their homes. The Unity militia only stayed in Wiscasset for about two weeks before they were discharged. It seemed that Sarah Vickery Kelley had seen more military action than they had.[29]

The War of 1812 had important consequences for the District of Maine. Mainers were angry because Massachusetts did not protect them from the English. This anger added to the resentment that Mainers still felt over the land conflicts with Boston land speculators. Shared resentment caused the interior farmers and the coastal merchants to put aside the economic differences that had impeded earlier attempts at separating from Massachusetts. They came together to demand statehood, and after years of political agitation and maneuvering (especially crucial were William King's political machinations in changing the federal coastal trading law to include all the east coast from Maine to Florida into one customs district), Maine finally became a state in 1820. That its entrance into the Union as a free state was contingent on Missouri's entrance as a slave state made Maine's statehood a bittersweet victory.[30]

After the War of 1812 Americans continued to focus on the patriotic sacrifices that Revolutionary War soldiers had made. They came to realize that the nation had a moral obligation to support all aged veterans who could not support themselves, and a law was passed in 1818 that gave veterans a pension for service during the war even if they had not been injured. In order to receive this new pension, a veteran had to prove that he had served in the war for more than nine months and that "from his reduced circumstances" he needed the "assistance of his country for support." In May of that year eighty-four-year-old David Vickery II applied for this veteran's pension. He would have to relinquish the disability pension he was receiving for the more substantial veteran's pension of $8.00 per month, but first he had to prove and then swear under oath that he was in reduced circumstances. His statement of proof is a poignant depiction of what it meant to be elderly in 1820:

THE FOLLOWING is a schedule of my whole estate and income necessary clothing and bedding excepted: I have no property in the world except my necessary clothing. I have no income. I am unable to labor and am nearly helpless from age and infirmity. I am at present without a family and live with one of my sons.[31]

David Vickery II obtained his pension. Probably like many of the veterans in the area, he was paid at first with supplies at Vose's store in Augusta. Later he received his pension in cash. In his last days the proud but ailing veteran "was wheeled around in a chair," and in the fall of 1823 he died. David Vickery II had survived the French and Indian War, and he and his wife Sarah both survived the Revolution, the creation of the community of Unity, and the establishment of the State of Maine, but stones marking their graves have not survived. Records about Sarah Stone Vickery's last days and death are slight. Census records hint that Sarah might have lived with one of her daughters until she died in 1830.[32] That David II felt "he was without a family," and his wife Sarah was not living with him and their son David III at the time he applied for his pension, adds to the speculation about family conflicts in the Vickery family. "Black David" III was now head of the Vickery household and he might not have treated his mother Sarah any better than he did his wife Lydia. "Seeking refuge with another married child," as historian Laurel Thatcher Ulrich has pointed out, is one way Sarah might have worked out problems that arose living in a house fraught with conflict.[33] It is rumored that David II and Sarah Stone Vickery were buried on the grounds of the family farm that they established in Unity, the town they helped found.

David III and Lydia Bartlett Vickery paid the mortgage in full on the Vickery farmland before David's parents died. By 1826 they had started to build a one-and-a-half-story frame house, and within the decade they were taxed for two barns, sixty acres of improved land, and one hundred ninety acres of woodlots and pasturelands.[34] They farmed over twenty-five acres of their tillable land and like their neighbors, they no doubt practiced a prudent "mixed husbandry." This meant growing a variety of crops like hay, wheat, barley, corn, oats, fruit, and vegetables that could be used both for the family's subsistence and for selling in the marketplace. If they had grown only one crop solely for their income, they might have risked starving or going into debt if that crop failed. The Vickery family owned a pair of horses for traveling, as well as several oxen that they could use to haul heavy loads like timber or slaughter for beef and leather. They also kept sheep, pigs, and seven to ten cows that gave them fleece, milk, and meat products for their own use or to sell for profit.[35]

David III and Lydia had worked hard to create a "thrifty" Maine farm which in turn, ensured their membership in the community. They could now afford possessions that bespoke their prosperity and a higher, more genteel standard of living in rural Maine. They purchased a Brackett tall clock for their home and a large leather-bound Bible on which they had their names embossed in gold. Their desire for a clock showed that they valued the new industrial sense of time outside the natural cycle of their farm life that started at dawn and ended at dusk. The "Great" Bible was a place to record family genealogy and suggests an appreciation of historical time as well. Both items could be passed on and treasured by the next generation. The Vickery family also owned a pew in Unity's new Congregational Church, and by 1835 they had $400 in bank stock and cash.[36]

David III and Lydia Bartlett Vickery bought this Brackett tall clock about 1823. It has a ship on its face that rocked back and forth, and it was still running in the 1970s.

David III held some minor yet respected town offices in Unity. As a fence-viewer he arbitrated boundary disputes between his neighbors. He was a school agent for a number of years, responsible for collecting the taxes (often in produce) that helped to support the school in his district, supplying firewood for the school, employing teachers, and determining school terms. He was involved in building and maintaining roads as a surveyor of highways, and he was on the committee to oversee fishing privileges in his community. As successful as David III and Lydia Bartlett Vickery were, however, it was their eldest child Eli Vickery and his wife Clarissa Berry Vickery who would assure that the Vickery family name would be held in high regard in Unity long into the twentieth century.[37]

ELI VICKERY (1807–1877)
and CLARISSA BERRY (1809–1886)
Married 1831
Unity, Maine

CHILDREN:
1. *James Berry I (1832–1911) m. Mary True Ayer*
2. Lydia Bartlett (1834–1918) m. (1) John Ferguson, (2) Joseph Higgins
3. Newman Whipple (1836–1883/8?) m. Sarah Sidlinger
4. Martha Gilkey (1837–1904) m. Edwin Whitney
5. Olive Jane (1838–1916) m. Otis Cornforth
6. Clara Philena (1846–1919) m. Eugene Boulter
7. Eli Vickery, Jr. (1854–1862)

SAMUEL KELLEY II (1803–1869)
and CHARLOTTE WESCOTT FILES (1818–1905)
Married 1835
Thorndike and Unity, Maine

CHILDREN:
1. Sarah Morton (1836–1853)
2. Abigail Files (1838–1841)
3. Ann Melinda (1840–1928) m. Charles Webster
4. Joseph Files (1841–1924) m. Adriana McGray
5. Samuel III (1844–1907) m. Sarah P. Harmon
6. Ansel Stone (1849–1937) m. (1) Celia R. Walker, (2) Violet Mixer, (3)?
7. Mary "May" (1853–1856)
8. Evelyn "Evie" Crie (1857–1940) m. Ralph Berry

SAMUEL STILLMAN BERRY I (1814–1890)
and OLIVE MUSSEY (1812–1896)
Married 1837
Thorndike and Unity, Maine

CHILDREN:
1. James Edwin (1838–1899) m. Mary Jane Adler
2. Reuel Mussey (1941–1923) m. Hattie May Myrick Plummer
3. Ruth Maria (1847–1940) never married
4. Ralph (1850–1911) m. Evelyn "Evie" Crie Kelley
5. Mary Ellen (1853–1935) m. Benjamin Bartlett Cook
6. Samuel Stillman II (1856–1885) m. Florence Ellen Bartlett

7

Faith in Farming

THE SEVENTH GENERATION

My Grandmother [Clarissa Berry Vickery] *and Grandfather*
[Eli] Vickery died before I was born so I do not know much about them.
I remember my Mother saying that when she was a girl, nearly all the
familys in Unity were related to them.
—Genevieve Boulter McAlary to James Berry Vickery III, 5 October 1936[1]

*T*HE LIVES OF ELI VICKERY and Clarissa Berry Vickery spanned
"The Farmer's Age" in the United States.[2] When they were born
in the early nineteenth century farmers made up 90 percent of the labor
force; at the end of their lives eighty years later, less than half the labor
force were farmers.[3] Yet, even as the family farm ideal diminished during Eli and Clarissa's lifetime, the legendary "yeoman" farmer was considered the most virtuous citizen in the United States. Thomas Jefferson
was the great promoter of this agrarian ideal, believing that the success
of the Republic rested on a nation of independent, property-holding
farmers. "Those who labour in the earth," Jefferson wrote at the end of
the Revolution, "are the chosen people of God, if ever he had a chosen
people, whose breasts he has made his peculiar deposit of genuine vir-
tue."[4] Jefferson's conviction defined the mythical way Americans would
feel about farmers and the simple virtues of rural life for the next two
hundred years and it was a major impetus in the settlement of American frontiers like Unity, Maine.[5]

Clarissa Berry was born in 1809 during the time of conflict between the settlers and the Great Proprietors in Unity, like her future husband Eli Vickery who was born in 1807. Both the paternal Berry side and the maternal Jackson side of Clarissa's family had been early settlers of the Piscataqua River region of New Hampshire. Her mother, Olive Jackson Berry, had come with her family to Unity from Limington, Maine, about 1800 and settled on Quaker Hill. Quaker Hill was where most of Unity's early settlers lived and was considered the center of town until 1830. Clarissa's father, James Berry, had come to Unity from Limington as well, and also established a farm on Quaker Hill a few years before he and Clarrisa's mother were married. James Berry, Clarrisa's grandfather Robert Jackson, and her uncle Peter Jackson had all signed the Unity settlers' petition to the Massachusetts General Court asking for help with the great land proprietors as they, too, like Eli's uncle Jonathan Vickery, were desperate to secure a legal deed to their land. The Jackson and Berry families did eventually come to terms with the proprietors and bought their farmland from the Bowdoin heirs like the Vickery family.

The farms on which Eli Vickery and Clarissa Berry grew up were family businesses as well as family homes. This was in sharp contrast to urban areas like Portland and Boston where the middle-class family home had become a separate entity from the place where a husband worked to support his family. As the nineteenth century progressed, the family home was promoted as a private refuge to which the husband could escape the public pressures of commerce and business. In theory a devoted and domestic wife, whose main concern was the development of the children, would cultivate this refuge. Childhood was now seen as a carefree time and new toys and books were produced specifically to engage children. Urban middle-class families began to practice birth control as well, so that more time and resources could be spent on an individual child. The post-Revolutionary War idea of "Republican Motherhood" which bid American mothers to raise virtuous sons for the New Republic was further refined. The model mother, or "True Woman" as she was called, was now the protector of all morality because it was assumed that a woman was more pious and pure than a man. She was the one who nurtured and gently instilled the proper middle-class values in the children—values that would ensure that daughters would marry well, be-

Olive Jackson Berry (1780–1863), c. 1855, mother of Clarissa Berry Vickery. "What a pretty old lady she was!"

coming "true" women in their own right, sons would be successful in business, and the nation as a whole would prosper. Historians have called this new sensibility about family and home the "Ideology of Domesticity," and it was spread throughout the United States by newspapers, magazines, and sermons.[6] Echoing the words of Cotton Mather two hundred years earlier the *Bangor* [Maine] *Register* stated this ideology clearly in 1830:

A FAMILY IS SOCIETY IN MINIATURE;—home is its location; woman its presiding spirit; and whatever destroys its primary feature must disturb the tranquility of its joys; introduce evil into its atmosphere of good; inflict the worst miseries, not only on her, but on all its members; and affect the whole community of which it forms a part.[7]

There was no separation between home life and business on the rural family farm, however. Farming was a business that was based on cooperation between family members, and everyone's efforts were needed to make their family farm business successful—especially children. While the "Ideology of Domesticity" pervaded rural America too, the economic reality was that children (as many as a family could produce) provided important labor on the family farm. Like New England families had been doing since the seventeenth century, some families hired out their children as laborers or domestic servants on neighboring farms.[8] Many rural families also took in outwork and children helped to stitch parts of shoes, braid palm-leaf hats, make buttons, or weave carpets. Farm parents believed that work built character, and they put their children to work at a young age.

By the time that Eli Vickery and Clarissa Berry were five or six they were helping with small chores on their parents' farms. When they were eleven or twelve, they were doing the same things that their parents of the same sex did, serving something like an "apprenticeship" for their future roles in life. Eli worked with his father and brothers to grow the crops, raise animals, and cut lumber. Clarissa helped her mother and sister maintain the household, grow vegetables and herbs, and preserve food. The women and girls also manufactured cloth and yarn, clothing, soap, and candles, raised poultry, and made cheese and butter to sell for cash or to barter for the items they did not grow or make. Sometimes women and girls helped the men and boys in the field during the haying season or to gather crops in crucial times. As the eldest children in their families, Eli and Clarissa might also be responsible for taking care of the younger children. There was no refuge from work on the family farm, nor from the tension and stress that surely arose within families because their work and home lives were so intimately intertwined.[9]

Though perhaps miles from other farms, Eli's and Clarissa's farms were not isolated family businesses. They were integrated into the larger farming community in Unity and surrounding villages by a sense of mutuality or cooperation. Networks of families and friends traded and bartered and shared labor, skills, farm tools, and products. They delivered each other's babies, gathered together for holidays and entertainment, loaned each other money, and helped each other in times of need. The other side of mutuality, however, was constant scrutiny and an obligation to conform to community standards. The paradox of an independent family farm was that it was never really self-sufficient; to achieve success beyond mere survival, farm families depended on other farm families. There were, of course, great diversities of wealth and power in Maine farm communities, and a good share of hard feelings, quarrels, and lawsuits—farm life was not utopia.

Much as it had been for the Vickery family ancestors on Cape Cod, community in Unity and in many other Maine villages was hard to separate from family. The connection between family, neighbors, and friends was a "defining characteristic of farm life" in the nineteenth century. Farm children usually married their neighbors (who often were cousins), increasingly knitting their communities together in intertwined "bonds of kinship."[10] Thus, the community's common good was personal and compelled members to work together to reach it. This was also true beyond the farmyard in civic obligations like maintaining roads and serving in militias.[11] Of course the intermarriages within Unity's middle-class community assured the continuation of shared values and kept the wealth concentrated in the same families.

Community support of district schools was another important example of mutuality in Unity. Eli Vickery and Clarissa Berry would have gone to a district school that was controlled by their community and supported in part by the taxes collected by Eli's father. They would have started school whenever their parents decided they were ready. Their schoolhouse was probably made of logs and located on a piece of land unsuitable for anything else. All ages would have been crammed in together for six hours; the younger children in the middle of the room and the older students around the perimeter. Eli and Clarissa would have used what schoolbooks their parents bought them or were passed down in their families. With this diversity of books and ages in their schoolhouse, they learned their lessons by memorization. Since Eli and Clarissa and the other children in their district came from farm families, school was probably only held in the winter months as they all were needed to work on their farms during other times of the year. The knowledge that Eli and Clarissa learned apprenticing on their family farms, of course, was as important for their futures as what they learned in the schoolhouse.[12]

When Clarissa Berry came of age in the late 1820s she took the opportunity to earn income outside her family's farm by teaching school in Unity, as would her sister Hannah Berry. Teaching, which had been the preserve of young men, was now becoming a respectable job for women. This corresponded with the prevailing "Ideology of Domesticity" based upon the assumption that women had a special ability and thus responsibility for child rearing. It was also economical, as Clarissa could be paid one-half or even one-third the amount paid a man who taught because a woman's labor outside the home was considered temporary and a diversion before her real career as a wife and mother began. Clarissa Berry was paid ten dollars for teaching school in the eighth district in 1829. She stopped teaching after she married Eli Vickery in 1831.

As a young single woman Clarissa might also have had the opportunity to leave her family's farm and work in the new cotton textile mills that emerged in New England towns in the 1820s. It had always been the special task of daughters on family farms to spin and weave the cloth used to make clothing. The textile mills were able to manufacture cloth more efficiently, making this traditional work of farm daughters less necessary. Freed from the tedious work of spinning and weaving, many young northern farm daughters of Clarissa's generation chose to leave their farms to work in the textile mills. While some took mill jobs because their wages were needed to support their family farms or they needed money for a dowry, many young women also went to work in the textile mills because they wanted social and economic independence—for a short time at least until they married. There is no evidence that Clarissa ever thought about leaving Unity to work in a textile mill. She surely would have been aware of this new choice for young women, as wagons rolled through Unity carrying farm daughters south to textile mills in Saco, Maine, or Lowell, Massachusetts.[13]

Young Eli Vickery was also given an opportunity for independence when he inherited ten acres of farmland on Quaker Hill from his Uncle Benjamin Bartlett's estate in 1819. Because he was only twelve years old, his father became the guardian of this land until Eli came of age. By this time it appeared to be a Vickery family custom for one of the younger sons to take over the family farm. Because Eli had inherited land at a young age, he was able to start building his own farm when he turned twenty-one. Eli's land was just a mile or so from the original Vickery family farm, but he chose to leave his father and mother's home at this time as well, and boarded with James and Elizabeth (Bartlett) Gilkey, his cousins and nearest neighbors on Quaker Hill. The Gilkey home was the former home of Eli's uncle and aunt, Benjamin and Esther (Chase) Bartlett, and the oldest wood-frame house in Unity. In the spring of 1830 Eli hired James Gilkey and other neighbors to help him build his barn. By early 1831 Eli had begun to enlarge his acreage in order to make his farm successful by buying the other parcels of land from Benjamin Bartlett's estate inherited by his mother, brothers, sisters, and cousins. He would continue to buy more land to add to his farm for the rest of his life.[14] At this point in establishing his independent family farm, the next important step for Eli was to take a wife.

"Began to Bord at miss Berrys," wrote Eli Vickery in his account book on 8 December 1830.[15] Technically, of course, Eli was now boarding at the home of Olive Jackson Berry, her daughters Clarissa and Hannah, and sons Samuel Stillman and Alfred whose farm abutted the eastern boundary of his property on Quaker Hill. Clarissa's father James Berry had died that summer and her brothers were still young, so perhaps Eli moved in with the Berrys to help them with their farm. Many farm families took in boarders as a source of income and no doubt after the death of Clarrisa's father, Eli's rent money in goods or in labor would have been needed. Eli's brief entry about boarding "at Miss Berry's" conveys that to him the most important person in the Berry household was twenty-one-year-old Clarissa, and it hints at a developing relationship between them before he came to live in the Berry home. Eli and Clarissa had grown up together in Unity. Throughout their lives they would have seen each other in school, in the Congregational church, in gatherings to watch Unity's militia train several times a year, at community barn raisings, at corn-husking parties in the fall, and no doubt, during

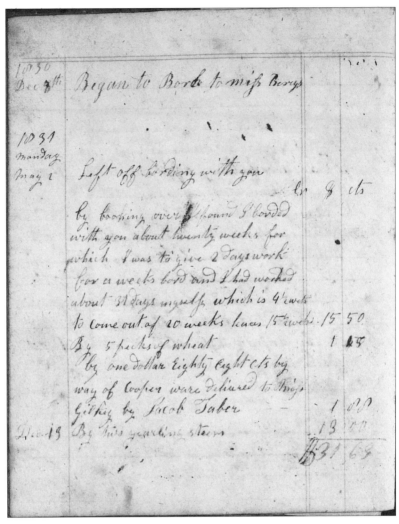

"Began to Bord to miss Berrys," wrote Eli Vickery
in his account book on 8 December 1830.

visits with their families to Vose's general store in Augusta or to market in Waterville. Within a year of moving to the Berry farm Eli and Clarissa were married, after the crops had been harvested of course, in late November 1831.[16]

Eli and Clarissa moved out of her family's home after their wedding, as no doubt Clarissa's brother Samuel S. Berry, now eighteen, must

1830			Dr
Nov	To myself and oxen 2 days brothy	2	94
Dec	To sledrunners		75
	To helping butcher Cow		25
Dec 22 1831	To helping hall wood with oxen ½ day		50
Jan 6	To 1 dy's Cutting logs - - -		50
7th	To helping get out Corn -		50
10th	To myself and Oxen halling wood	1	00
11th	To myself and Oxen ½ day halling wood		50
12th	To myself and Oxen halling logs	1	00
13th	To helping repair sled		50
14	To helping hall logs self and Oxen	1	00
15	To helping hall logs self and Oxen	1	00
17th	To helping hall logs self and Oxen	1	00
18th	To helping hall logs ??		50
20th	To helping haul logs self and Oxen	1	00
21	To helping haul logs self and Oxen	1	00
25th	To myself all day Oxen ½ day		75
26th	To myself and Oxen halling logs	1	00
31st	To cutting wood to the door		50
		15	4?

have felt he could run the farm himself.[17] Samuel later bought all the shares of the farm from his brother and sisters and became a successful farmer, a leading citizen in Unity, and a strong force in the anti-slavery and temperance movements.[18] While they built their own house on Quaker Hill, Eli and Clarissa rented two rooms in the Gilkey home. Their first child James Berry Vickery, who was named for Clarissa's father, was born on 26 July 1832 in these rented rooms.

The date of their first child's birth suggests that Clarissa could have been pregnant before she and Eli were married. This would not have been unusual in the 1830s as 20 percent of northern, white, Protestant, middle-class couples gave birth to their first child less than eight and a half months after their marriage.[19] Sexual relations were part of serious courtship for many rural couples at this time and if a woman became pregnant, her family and community were tolerant if there was a wedding. Bundling, an eighteenth-century custom that was practiced in rural New England well into the nineteenth century, allowed courting couples to spend the night in a bed together with their clothes on or with a "bundling board" between them as a step into marriage. While couples had many opportunities to find privacy in rural areas, if a young woman bundled with a suitor in her own home with the approval of her family, she might have more control of holding a man accountable for his actions. After almost a year of living and working with them, the Berrys must have felt like Eli was a part of their family, so it would not have been disturbing if Eli and Clarissa were intimate before marriage.[20]

By the time Eli and Clarissa's second child Lydia Bartlett Vickery, named for Eli's mother, was born in 1834, the Vickery family was living in their new home, though it would not be completely finished until spring 1835. They set their new center-chimney Cape Cod house on a knoll which would come to be known as "Vickery Hill," with the gable end facing Quaker Hill Road to the east. Their stylish Greek Revival front door opened south into the dooryard.[21] While ten acres had been cleared for the house and barn, they left a row of maple trees to extend along the road beside the farm. They built their barn in the older English style with its major door placed in the middle of the side wall and not in the gable end like newer New England barns of the time. They faced the front of the barn towards the road and connected it to the main house by a series of farm buildings. This protected their dooryard from the harsh north and west winds that blew off Twenty-Five-Mile, or Unity Pond (Winnecook Lake). Eli and Clarissa later erected stone walls, planted apple trees, and refined the landscape around their farm, making it "one of the finest situations in town."[22] The Vickery family's choice of a connected "big house, little house, back house, barn" design for their farm was common throughout northern New England because it allowed many different industries to coexist under one roof. This architecture reflected the small family farm economy that required families to grow a variety of crops, produce diversified animal products, manufacture crafts and clothing, harvest lumber, store firewood, and find innovative ways to use resources throughout the year in order to succeed.[23]

Now that they had their own home, Eli and Clarissa began to fill it with children in rapid succession. While the birth rate had begun to decline for middle class families in the urban northeast, children were still economic assets on rural family farms.[24] Eli and Clarissa's son James Berry was four and daughter Lydia Bartlett was two when their son Newman Whipple was born in 1836, then a daughter Martha Gilkey in 1837, and another daughter Olive Jane in 1838. According to the census there were ten people living on the Vickery family farm in 1840; two men, two women, and six children under ten. One boy in the census under the age of five is never mentioned again. Considering Eli and Clarissa's fertility history and the wide spacing of years before their next child was born in 1846, it is very probable this was a child born to them in the early 1840s who did not live long. It was rare that a woman in the nineteenth century did not lose a child at birth or in the early years of childhood.[25]

Apart from Clarissa, there was one woman living with the Vickery family who was between twenty and thirty years old. This could have been a woman hired from the neighborhood, or perhaps Eli's sister Damaris (who remained single) or Clarissa's sister Hannah (who did not marry Reuel Mussey until 1842), who could help Clarissa with the household work and the children. The one man between fifteen and twenty listed in the census might have been one of Eli's brothers, David or John, or a young man in the community who might have been hired by Eli to work with him planting and harvesting Chenango potatoes, his principal crop.[26] Another daughter named Clara Philena was born in 1846, making Eli and Clarissa's home a very crowded and busy place in the 1840s.[27]

Combined with the tension and stress that could come from life on a farm, large households like the Vickery family's often seemed, in the words of historian Christopher Clark, "hard, cramped, and fraught with conflict."[28] The descriptions in family lore of Eli and Clarissa Vickery's personalities suggest how they each might have coped with these conditions. Eli was considered one of Waldo County's best farmers. He was described as a "kind and good man," although he "had a quick temper." Clarissa, "a woman of much energy," was remembered as

*Eli Vickery (1807–1877), c. 1850. "One of the best farmers"
in Waldo County, he was a "kind and good man," although
he "had a quick temper."*

"a religious woman" who "attended church regularly." She was seen as having "a mind of her own"—which in the era of the "true woman" was probably frowned upon. Having a mind of her own and Eli's quick temper might help to explain why it was also said that Clarissa had a "very trying life with Eli Vickery." In spite of quick tempers and trying times, Eli and Clarissa managed to unite their stronger attributes of competence, kindness, energy, faith, and autonomy in order to create a thriving farm business and family. They did this skillfully enough to allow Eli to take time to participate in town and state governance, now that he was in his thirties and had some status in his community.[29]

Eli Vickery was a Democrat, earlier called a Democratic Republican, which would be expected considering his political heritage. As a Democrat before the Civil War, he believed in the egalitarian philosophy earlier espoused by Thomas Jefferson and later, the democratic reforms of Andrew Jackson. Eli would have been apprehensive that the wealthy Whig Party would try to centralize the federal government, lessening the autonomy and authority of Maine's government and community banks. He would also worry that if Whigs were in power, they would enact policies and tariffs to promote manufacturing and commercial interests at the expense of agricultural interests.[30] Eli must have felt strongly enough about these issues to become officially involved in protecting his and his farming community's livelihood. Using the experience he gained as a Unity town selectman in the 1840s—a civic job that required him to do everything from "going to the south part of town to carry a coffin" to "attending to draw jury men" to "making warrant for the collection of taxes" to finding someone "to take care of the Widow Douglas"—Eli turned his focus on state government.[31]

Eli Vickery served in the Maine legislature as a representative from Waldo County in 1850, 1851, and 1852, and was a delegate to the state, county, and senatorial conventions in 1859. Slavery would have been the most consuming matter for discussion in both state and national governments during Eli's terms. The Maine Antislavery Society constantly petitioned Maine's legislature. This petitioning surely escalated in 1850 after the federal government passed the Fugitive Slave Act, requiring all citizens in the United States to return runaway slaves.[32] Eli no doubt heard Hannibal Hamlin's heated speeches in the Maine legislature condemning the Compromise of 1850 that allowed more slave states into the Union. Though a Democrat, Eli would have been listening carefully, as well, to the rhetoric of those who would go on to form the new Republican party. No doubt, Eli would identify with the Republicans' fear that low-cost slave labor in the south threatened the economic independence of northern farmers.[33]

During the years that Eli Vickery was a representative in the legislature the governor in Maine was Doctor John Hubbard. Hubbard was, as a biographical sketch states, "the earnest supporter of every cause which he thought would advance the moral, social, or personal welfare of the people." He advocated for the establishment of an agricultural college, a female college, appropriations for supporting education, and maneuvered the purchase of land for the State of Maine. Hubbard set a progressive tone in Maine government at this time, capping—some say ending—his term as governor by signing the controversial Maine Law.[34]

As a good Congregationalist, Representative Eli Vickery probably voted in 1851 to enact the Maine Law making Maine the first state in the nation to prohibit the manufacture and sale of liquor. Representative Vickery would have had other progressive legislative concerns to address as well, such as the Maine State Prison in Thomaston that had been established in 1824, the Maine Insane Hospital that opened in Augusta in 1840, and the building of the new Maine State Reform School in Cape Elizabeth for which the legislature voted in 1850. He would have had to face the growing ethnic tensions in Maine caused by the surge of Catholic immigrants into the state from Ireland, and later from Canada. During all these years Representative Vickery would also have had to endure constant factional bickering for control of the Democratic Party in Maine. It must have seemed a relief to Eli to return to Unity where governance problems revolved around such matters as "going to see the Road made by Edmund A Mussey" and spending half a day "repairing graveyard fences."[35] Eli continued to serve as a selectman in Unity throughout the 1850s and 1860s, along with his brothers John Vickery and Nelson Vickery and brother-in-law Samuel S. Berry.[36]

Clarissa Berry Vickery, of course, could not become involved in town or state governance because she did not have the right to vote. Most people at this time believed that politics was outside a woman's proper "sphere" of activity. The workings of politics, like business and commerce, were too sordid and ruthless for a "true woman" who should give full attention to activities within her proper sphere—her home and family. In the nineteenth century Eli would represent his wife Clarissa at the polls, much as his great-great-great-great-grandfather George Vickery had represented his wife Rebecca in the seventeenth century.

But there was change in the air. In the July heat of 1848 a group of men and women from the rural farming communities around Seneca Falls, New York, gathered to hold the first public meeting in the United States demanding the rights of full citizenship for women. These included the right to own property in their own names, the right to be educated as doctors and lawyers, the right to earn the same pay as men for the same job, and the right to vote. It would take a while for the news of the Seneca Falls Convention to reach Unity, Maine, but by the

Clarissa Berry Vickery (1809–1886), c. 1855.
"A member of the Congregational church," she
"lived a life consistent with its teachings" but
had "a mind of her own."

mid-1850s a number of women's rights conventions had been held throughout New England and in 1857 activist Susan B. Anthony would speak in Bangor and Ellsworth, Maine.[37] The Maine legislature had already passed a bill granting married women the "privilege of holding their own property" in 1844 and in 1854 they legislated that a married woman had the right to control her own wages. Clarissa Vickery would have been aware of this new legislation and the controversy that the beginning "Women's Rights Movement" had sparked. It would take, however, almost seventy-five years before the Nineteenth Amendment was passed in 1920, allowing Clarissa's granddaughter Josie Vickery's generation of women the right to vote.[38]

In 1847 Eli's sixty-seven-year-old father David Vickery III died. David III had sold some of the original Vickery farmland to his son (and Eli's brother) Nelson Vickery only the year before his death, with the stipulation that Nelson would "take care of them [David III and Lydia] in old age," which apparently Nelson did.[39] David III's body would have been taken care of after death, as well. His wife Lydia, or his daughter Damaris, and perhaps neighbor women laid out David III's body, washing and dressing him in burial clothes or a shroud of white cotton. Windows were covered and sheets draped over any mirrors, making the busy farmhouse dark and silent. The body was placed in a pine coffin, probably made by one of David III's sons, and the open coffin was displayed on a table in the best room. Until David III was buried, a son or even a neighbor would sit "watch" with his body until the funeral, which would be in some haste, as bodies were not embalmed at this time. Family, friends, and neighbors gathered for the funeral at the Vickery farmhouse where the minister read passages from the Bible and prayers were said. Then David III's coffin was carried on the shoulders of his sons to Unity's new graveyard, the fences of which his son Eli as selectman was careful to keep repaired. The rest of the funeral procession followed on foot (returning later to the farmhouse for refreshments) and David III was laid to rest — "Earth to earth, ashes to ashes, dust to dust; in sure and certain hope of the Resurrection unto eternal life."[40]

Between the time that David III and Lydia Bartlett Vickery started farming and his son Nelson and his wife Isabella Cornforth Vickery took over the original Vickery family farm, much in farming had changed. Isabella was now spared some of the drudgery of housekeeping with which Lydia struggled. Isabella did not have to haul heavy buckets of water from outside because she could have a water pump in her kitchen. A new iron cookstove kept her home warmer and made cooking easier than an open hearth. There was a better design for butter churns, brighter oil lamps replaced dim candles, and tinware replaced the old heavy iron pots.[41]

When David III started farming he used a wooden plow; his son Nelson now used iron and steel plows, and harrows and seed drills that made the work easier and faster. David III had concentrated on subsistence oriented mixed husbandry, trading or selling any products left over; Nelson and Eli's generation began to grow more cash crops in order to buy the new home and agricultural innovations. It might have been too costly for David III or taken him too long to transport his crops in a wagon over muddy, rutted roads to more distant and lucrative markets, but now improved roads and railroads swiftly carried crops to the markets in Augusta and Waterville.[42]

The role of the family in the United States had changed from the sixth generation of Vickerys to the seventh generation, as well. The nuclear family had always been the center for the production of food and clothing, the place children were educated and disciplined, and the only place people were cared for when they were ill. Cloth for clothing was now made in factories and grains for bread were ground in automated flour mills; the family produced less and bought more. By 1850 the state of Maine had established institutions that took over other family responsibilities. Troubled children were disciplined in the Maine State Reform School, the mentally ill were cared for in the Maine Insane Hospital, and children were educated in district schools that were supported by local and state taxes. The Maine legislature had even intervened in the private realm of the family itself by passing the Maine Law that prohibited the manufacture and sale of liquor in the hope of protecting women and children from poverty and domestic violence.

As the nation and its public institutions expanded in the mid nineteenth century, so did the markets for Maine farm products, but competition from farmers on the newly opened western lands also increased. Farming in Maine's changeable climate and hard soils had never been easy, and western competition was the final straw for some frustrated Maine farm families who either left the state or went into other commercial ventures. In 1862 Nelson and Isabella Vickery sold the original Vickery family farm to Nelson's brother and his wife, John and Abigail Murch Vickery. Nelson then became a merchant, "conducting a small store" first in Unity, then later in Pittsfield, Maine, where he and his family moved in 1866.

"After 1820 few new names appeared [in Unity]," observed historian James B. Vickery III. "The general increase in population came from the fecund pioneers."[43] Unity's population of 1,557 at mid-century was the largest it would ever be and farming in Central Maine was at its most fruitful. In September 1851 Unity was called "the garden of Waldo [County]" by the county's largest newspaper the *Republican Journal*, published in Belfast. "There is a look of freshness and neatness about this village," the paper stated, "and there is every where fine farm

houses, about which there is good evidence of neatness and care." [44]
The extended Vickery family was a sizeable part of Unity's population at this time and the owners of a number of Unity's "fine farm houses." All but one of David III and Lydia's eleven children had married and started their own families in the area, and the next generation followed suit. In 1857 James Berry Vickery I and Mary True Ayer were married, creating the next generation of Vickerys and building another Vickery family farm. As was common in many rural families, Eli and Clarissa Vickery's oldest child, twenty-five-year-old James I, was married just three years after the birth of their youngest child, Eli, Jr.

T H R E E

The Montana Families

1860–1900

JAMES BERRY VICKERY I (1832–1911)
and
MARY TRUE AYER (1835–1922)
Married 1857
Unity, Maine

CHILDREN:
1. Eli Ayer (1859–1914) m. Carrie Jerusha Brandenburg
2. Mary Josephine "Josie" (1862–1946) never married
3. David Ernest (1865–1911) never married
4. John Ayer (1868–1924) m. Emily Shepard Nickerson
5. *James Berry II (1872–1960) m. (1) Annie May Stewart,
(2) Cassie Hillman Hunt*

RALPH BERRY (1850–1911)
and
EVELYN "EVIE" CRIE KELLEY (1857–1940)
Married 1875
Unity, Maine
Winnecook Ranch, Montana
Redlands, California

CHILDREN:
1. Lottie (1876–1877)
2. Samuel Stillman III (1887–1984) never married
3. Samuel Stillman III Twin Brother (1887)

94

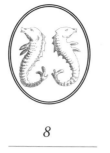

8

Gripped by Fever

THE EIGHTH GENERATION

AS I THINK MORE ABOUT IT *I can recall more of your family but my recollection centers around your grandfather, James B. Vickery [I] and your great uncle Newman who was somewhat of a wag and said funny things that became current jokes in the town and probably beyond it. I remember also your great grandfather Eli Vickery who, however, was quite an old man in my childhood. The Vickery Hill was one of the finest situations in town and I suppose you are living on that same hill. I remember the row of maple trees that ran along in front of your grandfather's house.*
—James E. Kelley to James Berry Vickery III, 16 January 1934[1]

JAMES I AND MARY AYER VICKERY married in the spring of 1857, then moved into a house they built at the foot of Quaker Hill within sight of his father and mother's farm. James I and Mary were third cousins; her grandfather Lemuel Bartlett and his grandmother Lydia Bartlett Vickery were brother and sister. Mary was the daughter of Peter and Jane Bartlett Ayer, and she was born and raised with her three brothers and four sisters in neighboring Freedom, Maine. Her father Peter Ayer, who died in 1852, had been a prosperous farmer and prominent citizen in Freedom, a leader of the Temperance Movement in Waldo County, and had been "everywhere known for his integrity, sound judgement, and sterling character." Mary's mother Jane Bartlett

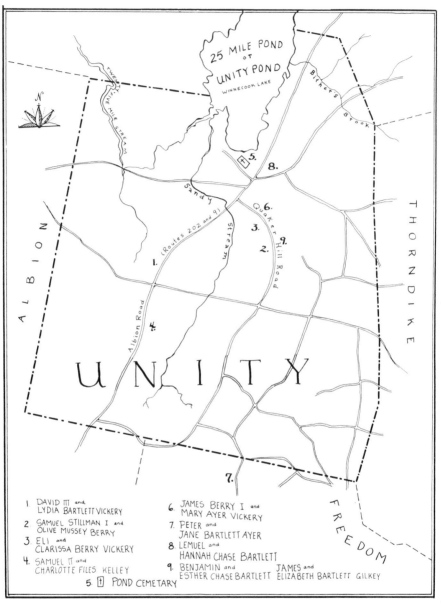

1. DAVID III and
   LYDIA BARTLETT VICKERY
2. SAMUEL STILLMAN I and
   OLIVE MUSSEY BERRY
3. ELI and
   CLARISSA BERRY VICKERY
4. SAMUEL II and
   CHARLOTTE FILES KELLEY
5. ⊞ POND CEMETARY

6. JAMES BERRY I and
   MARY AYER VICKERY
7. PETER and
   JANE BARTLETT AYER
8. LEMUEL and
   HANNAH CHASE BARTLETT
9. BENJAMIN and   JAMES and
   ESTHER CHASE BARTLETT ELIZABETH BARTLETT GILKEY

MAP BY BERRY MANTER

Ayer was described by a granddaughter as being "tall and stately, universally honored and respected," and "invariably carried herself with a serene and gracious dignity." Although Jane came from a Quaker heritage, she and her husband Peter were principal members of the Methodist Episcopal Society. They had donated land on their farm to the Methodists for the construction of the first church in the community in 1826. Peter Ayer was known as "a devout and very religious man." This resulted in the Ayer home becoming "the center and meeting place of the church ministers, and Bishops from far and near" throughout Mary Ayer Vickery's childhood.[2]

Education had been as important as religion in Mary's upbringing. Her father had helped to found Kent's Hill Seminary in Readfield, Maine, and Freedom Academy in Freedom, Maine, which Mary attended. Mary's brother Nathan Ayer had taught in the local district school before he moved to Bangor, Maine, and went into business. (Nathan's son Fred Rollins Ayer would graduate from Harvard in 1902.) According to the inventory taken when Peter Ayer died, a significant library was found in the Ayer home.[3] New printing methods had precipitated an outpouring of publications by the mid nineteenth century, and a collection of books was a symbol of refinement and the mark of a respectable household. Books showed that a family was committed to "mental culture" and wanted to better themselves.

It is clear that the Ayer family valued orderliness, temperate habits, religion, and education. These were basic values of the coalescing middle class at this time and families like the Ayers, as historian Mary Ryan suggests, formed an incubator, or "cradle" where their children were instilled with a middle-class character. While Mary might expect to become the wife of a farmer, it did not preclude her as the daughter of a prosperous farm family from becoming a woman of refinement, intelligence, and conviction. In family notes, Mary Ayer Vickery was described as "a good woman, *proud* & with a dominating personality, People who remember her, speak of her great proudness ... [she had a] Quick temper, & [she] like[d] to have her own way." Mary's parents instilled in her an appreciation for middle class amenities as well. Family lore states that Mary "always dressed well," her father Peter Ayer "ate only with silver utensils" and her mother Jane Bartlett Ayer's silk wedding dress came from Boston.[4]

Education was also important in the Vickery family. Clarissa and Eli Vickery had paid tuition for both James I and his sister Lydia to attend Unity High School when it first opened in the fall of 1851. The catalogue of the school stated that students would acquire both the "practical knowledge" for the "every-day business of life" and the "finished education" that was taught at "boarding schools and higher seminaries."[5] James I and his cousin Hepsibah Bartlett were vice-presidents of the debating society of Unity High School that fall. This was a long way from the simple reading, writing, and arithmetic skills taught in the one-room schoolhouse that Clarissa and Eli attended.

Eli and Clarrissa's progressive belief in education and its value shaped the lives of their youngest daughters as well. In 1857 Olive Jane Vickery and Otis Cornforth were married. Cornforth would become one of Unity's leading and "greatly beloved" teachers. Clara Philena Vickery would become such a fine teacher and would be held in such high esteem in Unity that she would be elected the supervisor of schools in 1875. This was possible because the Maine Supreme Court had ruled in 1874 that it was legal for women to hold public offices not mentioned in the state constitution. The irony was that Clara still could not vote for the office she held. Yet Clara's new position as supervisor of schools represented an important step for women—they were now given public leadership roles and were paid for their work and responsibilities. Women's previous roles in public service were usually in reform and church organizations and solely on a volunteer basis. Clara would be the supervisor of schools until she married in 1878. Obviously, both the Vickery and Ayer families believed in the dignity of teaching as a profession and saw the need for founding and supporting higher education in rural Maine. This shared intellectual background must have been important in bringing James Berry Vickery I and Mary True Ayer together—indeed, family notes state that James I "taught school where he met Miss Mary Ayer."[6] They would pass this appreciation for learning and teaching on to their five children, the first of whom, Eli Ayer Vickery, was born in 1859.[7]

The improvement of one's self and a passion to reform American society were imbued in the spirit of the times in the decades before the Civil War. The Temperance, Anti-slavery, and Woman's Rights Movements all flourished between 1820 and 1860. There was a proliferation in the establishment of public schools, colleges, seminaries, and academies for men and women, though they were rarely educated together. Public libraries were founded, and even in the smallest villages people gathered in associations called lyceums to hear famous speakers lecture on science, history, and literature. There was a great sense of optimism and faith that if committed and aware people came together in associations, they could effect change that would improve society. Temperance organizers reasoned that if liquor was outlawed, husbands would stay sober and working, and there would be no domestic violence or family poverty. Prison reformers were sure that law-breakers kept in solitary confinement, away from evil influences, could be rehabilitated. Advocates for the mentally ill believed that if they were separated from law-breakers and given proper care in hospitals, they could be cured. The American Colonization Society thought if slaves were sent back to Africa, the problem of slavery would disappear. Those in woman's rights organizations were convinced that if women could own property, keep the wages they earned, had the right to vote, and "all the avenues to wealth and distinction" were open to them, they would have equality.[8] While no one can doubt the compassion and determination of antebellum reformers, their thinking was often too oversimplified for complex social problems.[9]

The West Side of Main Street, Unity, Maine, c. 1868.
COURTESY OF MAINE HISTORIC PRESERVATION COMMISSION.

Agriculture in the United States was greatly influenced by the spirit of reform as well. The sight of deserted farms throughout the New England countryside at mid-century and the reality that more and more young men and women were leaving their family farms to work and live in cities or go West worried many.[10] Agricultural reformers claimed that if farmers made better use of their land, educated themselves, and made their farms and farming more attractive, profits would increase and this trend would end. Because there had always been so much land, when the soil lost its fertility most farmers just cleared and planted new fields and left their old fields to lay fallow for up to twenty years until the soil had recovered. During fallow times fields became overgrown with shrub and trash trees, making the rural landscape appear cluttered and untidy. The cluttered rural landscape was an affront to new middle-class sensibilities of efficiency and orderliness and the reformers thought it exemplified the coarseness of farm life.[11] They called for more intensive use of land, encouraging farmers to rotate their crops, use fertilizers, and experiment with new crops and technology. Repeatedly, newspaper and journal articles told farmers that if they expected to keep young men and women on the farms, they needed to make the farm landscape and farm life more appealing.[12]

The business of farming had also changed since the time veterans of the Revolutionary War had rushed into Central Maine to establish their independent family farms. Farmers could no longer survive by producing crops and raising livestock on marginal land for their own use; they had to earn cash as a cash-based economy had begun to replace the farmers' local exchange system of goods or labor and long-term credit. There was also the added competition from farmers in the West who could now ship their crops cheaply on an extended railroad system to eastern markets. By mid-century if a farm family did not make their farm profitable, they left to find work that paid better. Those who would increase their profits, contend with western competition, and keep the next generation on family farms looked for new ways to make better use of their farmland and make farming more attractive to their children.[13]

Agricultural societies, which were organized as early as 1820 in Maine, were the most effective means of promoting innovative, more efficient and productive farming methods that would increase profits and refine rural landscapes. Eli Vickery, his brother-in-law Samuel S.

Berry I, and his daughter-in-law Mary Ayer Vickery's brother Peter Ayer II helped to found the North Waldo Agricultural Society (NWAS) in March 1861. Eli was elected the first president of the NWAS and would serve another term in 1862. Later he was secretary for a year and then treasurer for fourteen straight years from 1864 until his death in 1877. His son James Berry Vickery I would serve as president of the NWAS from 1881 through 1886. The Society's purpose was "wholly for the advancement of agricultural and mechanical arts," and the main venue for this was an annual fair held in Unity starting in October 1861. At the fair farm men exhibited their produce and livestock and women displayed their handiwork and baked and preserved goods, while members of the Society judged the exhibits and gave premiums to the best entries. Horseracing became a permanent addition to the fair in 1862, even though some felt it overshadowed the progressive purpose of the fair.[14]

Agricultural journals like the *Maine Farmer* and Waldo County's principal newspaper the *Republican Journal* reported regularly on the meetings and proceedings of the North Waldo Agricultural Society, wrote reviews of the Unity Fair, and listed the winners of the premiums. They delivered news about the Farmers' Club organized by the NWAS in 1870 and published the club's polemics about the "evil" of horse trotting at the Unity Fair—an evil they were compelled to sponsor after crowds dwindled the one year they banned horse racing.[15] NWAS also connected Central Maine farmers to other farmers in the state and the nation by publishing letters and articles that farmers sent to them on the results of agricultural experiments and new farm equipment, as well as reprinting letters and articles from national sources.

The Maine Farmer and the *Republican Journal* aggressively promoted progressive farming and new institutions that helped farmers expand their markets. The most notable of these institutions was the Maine State College of Agriculture and the Mechanical Arts, later called the University of Maine, that opened in the fall of 1868 in Orono. Established under the Morrill Land Grant Act of 1862, it was one of seventy colleges in the United States that was devoted to teaching agriculture, engineering, and home economics. The Maine State College helped Maine farmers accept and adapt to the inevitable—in order to prevail

Mary True Ayer Vickery (1835–1922), c. 1865. "People who remember her, speak of her great proudness."

they could no longer just farm for a living; they had to farm competitively for a profit.[16]

The agricultural newspapers and journals in Central Maine also featured descriptions of area farmers and their farms, presenting them as models of progress. Sixty-nine-year-old Eli Vickery would be featured in the *Maine Farmer* in the spring of 1876:

A WALDO COUNTY FARMER

I SAW AT THE FARM of Eli Vickery of Unity, (who is one of the best farmers in this county), some fine grade Durham stock, prominent among them a high grade Durham bull one year old this spring, which is a fine animal. He is the handsomest yearling I ever saw. I also saw some very fine lambs. Mr. V. has taken special pains with his cattle and sheep, and they show what good care and good feed has done for them. Mr. V. has one of the best wheat farms in Waldo County. He believes in farming, even in Maine, and is making it pay.[17]

This description in the *Maine Farmer* of the Vickery farm on Quaker Hill was not quite accurate. Eli's son and daughter-in-law James I and

James Berry Vickery I (1832–1911), c. 1860s. "The said James B. Vickery shall well & truly maintain & support his father the said Eli and his mother Clarissa Vickery during the remainder of their days and provide them with food & clothing suitable to their condition of life provide suitable medical attention for them if sick either of them pay all suitable & proper funeral expenses & charges for each after his or her decease and at all times behave & demean himself to & towards his said parents as a dutiful son should do."

Mary Ayer Vickery should have shared some of the credit for this fine farm because by this time they owned and operated it. James I's youngest brother Newman Whipple Vickery had been set to take over the farm on top of Quaker Hill from Clarissa and Eli, but in 1869 James I and Mary decided to legally trade farms with Newman who then moved into their farm at the foot of Quaker Hill Road.[18] Both Clarissa and Eli had strong personalities, and they surely had powerful opinions and exacting methods of farming that had contributed to their success. Newman was known as "somewhat of a wag"; maybe his witty remarks and jokes took energy away from his farm work and profits. Perhaps James and Mary were better suited than Newman to meet the needs of their parents. As was the custom, when James I and Mary took over the family farm they were not only morally, but legally bound to take care of Eli, Clarissa, and James I's sister Clara who still lived at home, according to a "Mortgage Life Lease" provision in their deed:

THE SAID JAMES B. VICKERY shall well & truly maintain & support his father the said Eli and his mother Clarissa Vickery during the remainder of their days and provide them with food & clothing suitable to their condition of life provide suitable medical attention for them if sick either of them pay all suitable & proper funeral expenses & charges for each after his or her decease and at all times behave & demean himself to & towards his said parents as a dutiful son should do. and Clara P. Vickery daughter of said parents and sister of said James B is to have a home & maintainance with said James B during her life in case she remains single & unmarried & to have proper care & treatment of sick and in case of her decease the said James B is to defray all proper funeral charges & expenses necessary for her said maintainance & support of father & mother & sister is to be given & rendered on the homestead this day deeded to me by the said Eli Vickery[.][19]

This new arrangement between the two Vickery farms implies that the desire and necessity for profits on farms affected family dynamics and undermined traditions. Newman would later sell the farm at the foot of Quaker Hill Road out of the family and move to Hampden, Maine, with his wife Sarah Sidelinger Vickery and their son Fred. The house that Newman sold and James I and Mary Ayer Vickery built at the foot of Quaker Hill Road in the late 1850s is now owned and occupied by Unity College.[20]

The 1860s brought more changes to the Vickery family, as well as to Unity, Maine, and the nation. From 1861 until 1865 the Civil War destroyed cities and farms, killed 620,000 soldiers, and brought suffering and death to countless American families. Out of the 73,000 soldiers that Maine sent to fight in the Civil War, 9,000 men died and 11,000 were wounded or disabled. In 1862 Eli Vickery and his brother-in-law Alfred Berry served on the committee responsible for making sure that Unity met its quota of men for the war, as well as seeing that the men got to their regiments and were mustered into service. Eli again served as a recruiting officer in 1865. Out of a population of approximately 1,300, Unity sent over 120 men to fight in the Union army.[21]

Neither of Eli and Clarissa Berry Vickery's sons fought in the Civil War. Thirty-two-year-old James Berry Vickery I found a substitute to go for him in 1864. Apparently his brother Newman had been drafted in 1863, but he did not serve either. It was legal for a man who had been drafted to hire a substitute to go to war in his place, or to pay a $300 commutation fee, and more than 118,000 northern men did so. Certainly, the need for enormous amounts of food to feed the Union army would be justification for some farm owners like James I and Newman Vickery to stay on their farms during the war, especially since almost half of Union soldiers had left farms to fight.[22]

While none of their immediate family members went to war, the Civil War certainly touched the Vickery family. Clarissa's nephew Reuel Berry fought in the Seventh Battery, Mounted Artillery and her nephew John F. Berry served as a lieutenant in the 81st U.S., a regiment of black troops.[23] John Berry's cousin James Edwin Berry summed up the attitude of some concerning segregation in the army when he wrote to his brother Ralph Berry: "John Berry has gone to the war, then—'Bully for him' … I do not think that I would want to be an officer in a colored Regiment. Had rather be a private in a white."[24] Many white men were willing to serve in black regiments, however, as historian James M. McPherson suggests, because a white man had a greater opportunity to become a commissioned officer. Fewer than 100 black men were ever commissioned officers, although close to 200,000 blacks fought as soldiers and sailors during the Civil War. Twenty-Six-year-old Lieutenant John F. Berry died of yellow fever in New Orleans in 1865. Most Unity families who lost men in the Civil War—such as the Berrys, Kelleys, Murches, Mitchells, and Rackliffs—were all related to the Vickerys in some way and their deaths touched everyone. In 1934 James E. Kelley wrote to his cousin James Berry Vickery III that when he was a boy living in Unity he

> SAW THE BOYS IN BLUE march away to war in 1861—Went with my father to my Aunt Martha (Stone) Kelley's to break the news of the death of her son Jonathan from starvation in a rebel prison. Her cry of grief and anguish rings in my ears to this day. [25]

Martha Stone Kelley had already lost one son and a son-in-law during the war. While historians have suggested that the Civil War had little impact on the daily life of rural northern communities, clearly they have not taken into consideration how constant anxiety and sorrow marked everyone's lives as they went about "as usual."[26]

Throughout the 1860s the Vickerys endured a number of deaths in their immediate family that were not war related, but they also celebrated several births. On 19 May 1862 Eli and Clarissa's eight-year-old son Eli Vickery, Jr., died of diphtheria. Diphtheria is an infection usually located in the throat. Childhood immunizations make it a rare disease today, but in the nineteenth century it was often fatal and there were frequent epidemics. Two days after Eli and Clarissa's youngest son died, their granddaughter Mary "Josie" Josephine (James I and Mary's second child) was born. That next summer in 1863 Clarrisa Berry Vickery's eighty-three-year-old mother Olive Jackson Berry died and in October 1865 Eli's seventy-nine-year-old mother Lydia Bartlett Vickery died, just a few months after the birth of James I and Mary's third child David Ernest Vickery. Then in July of 1868 Mary gave birth to their fourth child John Ayer Vickery. Their last child, James Berry Vickery II, was born on 6 May 1872. Life went on even in the face of death, and the births of James I and Mary Ayer Vickery's children must have been some solace as members of their family died.

At the time of her death in 1865, Lydia Bartlett Vickery had been living with her son Eli and daughter-in-law Clarissa on Quaker Hill. She probably moved there after 1862 when her son Nelson sold the original Vickery family farm on the Albion Road that she and her husband David III inherited from his father and mother. Lydia's son and daughter-in-law John and Abigail Murch Vickery had bought the farm from Nelson, but apparently John was not a contented person. He and Abigail sold the oldest Vickery farm out of the family within a few years and moved to another farm down the road, near the bridge that crossed Sandy Stream. In the spring of 1870 forty-six-year-old John Vickery, who was "a highly respected citizen and one of the Selectmen of the town," took his own life by drowning himself in this stream.[27] Perhaps inheriting his father David III's "black" turn of mind, the notice of John's death in the *Republican Journal* stated that he was "supposed to be insane." He left his wife Abigail with three young daughters.[28]

John Vickery was not the first of Eli's siblings to die. In 1858 his youngest brother Albert Vickery had died from tuberculosis, then called consumption, at the age of twenty-seven. Albert's young wife Louisa

Craig Vickery had also died from consumption soon after they were married.[29] Eli's brother Benjamin Bartlett Vickery was listed in the 1870 census as a grocer in Corinna, Maine, with his second wife and children, but family tradition says shortly thereafter "he moved West and was never heard from"—not a rare occurrence in Maine in the nineteenth century. Before the 1870s many Maine men and whole families were gripped by Western "fevers," went West, and sometimes disappeared.

The "Ohio Fever" between 1810 to 1820 had started the emigration of thousands of people out of Maine to the Midwest. In the 1840s "Oregon Fever" pulled lumbermen from Maine to the Northwest in search of fabled fir trees three hundred feet tall, while later other Mainers joined an estimated 11,500 emigrants in wagon trains on the overland trail to Oregon's abundant farmland. Thousands more Mainers rushed to California in the late 1840s, then to Colorado and Nevada in the late 1850s when they caught "Gold Fever." Of course, all along Maine seamen had been going around Cape Horn to the West Coast and into the Pacific Ocean to the Hawaiian Islands and Asia, as well as to places closer to home, transporting cargo, trading, and hunting for whales. Many Mainers had traveled West to make "quick" money and return or to find a better life and settle permanently. Local and national newspapers and magazines reported on their achievements or misadventures. Speculators, boosters, novelists, poets, folk singers, and the federal government had been promoting western settlement for decades. Journalist Horace Greely's advice in the 1850s to "Go West Young Man" was heeded with gusto. The West was a powerful symbol and myth in American society. It was seen by some as a "safety valve" that allowed industrial workers and immigrants to escape the perceived social and economic ills in the East. The West also gave frustrated farm families and failed businessmen a chance to start over, and provided new opportunities for young people. By 1870 going West had become commonplace.[30]

A number of Vickery-related young men and women from the Bartlett, Berry, Fowler, Kelley, Mitchell, Mussey, Rackliff, and Trueworthy families in Unity went West to the gold fields and mining camps in 1849 through the 1850s and 1860s. The words of one of Eli Vickery's cousins writing from California to Unity in 1864 gave a sense of the relentless optimism that kept so many going out West:

James Edwin Berry (1838–1899), c. 1890, brother of Reuel, Ruth, Ralph, and Sam Berry and Mary Berry Cook who left Unity and settled in California. "Everything I hear from home is interesting to me though I may never see the land of my birth again."

TIMES ARE VERY DULL here right now, more so than I ever saw them, but I think we have a chance to do pretty well this winter. Crops were a failure here this year. Everything is very high. I have now been at home [after visiting Unity] about six weeks. I have lost considerable by being gone so long. I found my claims sold and I have to start anew as you might say, but there is gold here yet and I know how to find it.[31]

Eli and Clarissa Berry Vickery's nephew James Edwin Berry took up mining in the Sacramento area of California in the early 1860s. He was the son of Clarissa's brother Samuel Stillman I and Olive Mussey Berry, and one of four of their six children who left Maine to go out West. His letter home to Unity in 1864 has a pragmatic tone about his experience:

I AM AT WORK IN THE MINES yet but do not think that I shall work at mining much longer unless my luck changes. It seems as though the longer I mine the less I have. I feel the force of the suggestions in your last [letter] that some other kind of business or some other place would be beneficial, but it is an old adage that a "rolling stone gathereth no moisture," therefore I have stuck to this place almost three years & shall stop here this summer & then if I do not find a "turn in the road" I will have to travel.[32]

James Edwin Berry later traveled about the West Coast looking for lucrative work, though he never seemed to find anything that gave him satisfaction. He finally took up teaching, settling with his wife Mary Jane Adler Berry and their four children in the San Francisco area. In a letter to his brother Ralph Berry in 1892 he put his life and aspirations in perspective. His sentiments speak to the prevailing middle-class values and highlight the subtle change in thinking about how virtuous teaching or farming with its manual labor was at the turn of the century:

I NEVER EXPECT TO get ahead in the world and shall be satisfied to earn a good living and give the children a good education thus giving them the means by which they will not be obliged to rough it through the world. If they were dummies I would not care about trying to educate them to any great extent but being capable of receiving an education and being of a class not overburdened with muscle I want to educate them for the business of the world rather than for manual labor. What they will be adapted to is yet to be seen and determined. There is one thing they shall not follow, if I can prevent it, and that is teaching.[33]

James Edwin and Mary Jane Adler Berry kept close ties with their Berry and Vickery relatives all of their lives, though apparently they never returned to Unity. Writing to his mother Olive Mussey Berry in Unity in November 1888, James captured the feelings of a displaced person:

EVERYTHING I HEAR FROM HOME is interesting to me though I may never see the land of my birth again. Nothing however would afford me greater pleasure than to visit the scenes I first beheld, I fancy the rocks and trees, the hills and streams are the same, but the people, of course, are all changed.[34]

While mining enticed many of Unity's young people West, it was ranching in the 1870s and 1880s that offered them the greatest opportunities. In 1862 Charles W. Cook of Unity read an account in a newspaper about the opportunities in the Montana Territory written by Captain James Liberty Fisk. Captain Fisk led military escorts for settlers to Montana's mining camps from 1862 to 1866. Congress funded these escorts in order to protect settlers from attacks by Native Americans and Fisk's reports to Congress were published in newspapers. Motivated by this simple newspaper article Cook impetuously left his home, took a train to St. Joseph, Missouri, then a boat to Omaha, Nebraska, traveled with a team to Denver, Colorado, and finally drove one hundred twenty-five head of cattle for four months until he reached Virginia City, Montana. No one could have imagined at the time that Cook would begin a remarkable exchange of people, culture, and capital between Unity, Maine, and Montana that would last for one hundred and thirty-five years. Helping to lay the foundation and forming the heart of this exchange were the eighth, ninth, and tenth generations of the Vickerys and the Berry branch of their family tree.[35]

Symbolically, as this new generation left farming in Central Maine and moved West, Eli Vickery died. It is clear after examining the inventory of Eli's estate that he still practiced a local exchange system of goods or labor and long-term credit because at the time of his death in the spring of 1877 he held outstanding notes from family members and neighbors that amounted to $4,000.00 (about $64,000 in 2001 dollars).[36] Eli was an economic, as well as political power in his community and many depended on him for financial help, especially during the mid-1870s when the nation was in an economic depression.[37] Even so, Eli was a shrewd businessman and protected himself from inflation by charging 8 percent on many of his loans. The kind of economic power that individual farmers like Eli had in their community, however, was steadily eroding as more banks and other corporate financial institutions were established to service a cash-based economy. Eli Vickery's death marked the end of "The Farmer's Age" in the United States.

JAMES BERRY VICKERY II (1872–1960)
and
ANNIE MAY STEWART (1880–1933)
Married 1902
and
CASSIE M. HILLMAN HUNT (1903–1997)
Married 1940
Montville, Hartland, and Unity, Maine

CHILDREN:
With Annie May Stewart:
1. Everett Stewart (1903–1986) m. Ethel M. Willsey
2. Eric Arthur (1907–1991) never married
3. *James Berry III (1917–1997) never married*

ELI AYER VICKERY (1859–1914)
and CARRIE JERUSHA BRANDERBURG (1869–1960)
Married 1889
Unity, Maine
Shamrock, Missouri
Hunter Hot Springs, Big Timber, and Columbus, Montana
Clark, Wyoming

CHILDREN:
1. Edgar Ayer (1890–1918) never married
2. Mary "Allie" Alverda (1893–1984) m. James O'Shea
3. Emma Christine (1894–1932) m. David Parker
4. Dorothy Brandenburg (1895–1979) m. (1) L'Roy Buck, (2) Lawrence
Simon, (3) Harry Brumpton
5. Carol Louise (1897–1991) m. (1) Edward G. Townsend, (2) Fred Myers
6. Elizabeth Chase (1899–1975) m. Lawrence B. Swain
7. William Theodore (1901–1984) m. Margaret Sandilands
8. Elsie Belle (1902–1982) m. (1) John Cunningham, (2) Lee Shockey,
(3) Frank Liston
9. Frederick Brandenburg (1903–1992) m. Helen Louise Sparhawk
10. James Vincent (1905–1950) m. Alice Irene Smart
11. Jack Mason (1908–1982) m. Ferne Clements

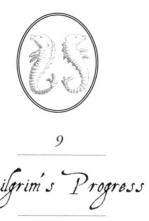

9

Pilgrim's Progress

THE NINTH GENERATION

IF I RECOLLECT RIGHTLY *Thomas and Bethiah Hussey were ancestral not only to the Montana Husseys, but to the Thomas Cook family as well. I think Mrs. Oscar Mueller at Lewistown [Montana] could, however, furnish you with much more complete and reliable records of all this than I could. You certainly should have a portrait of Thomas Cook in your History, as well as a full account of him. He was the one who started Unity's Montana hegira.*
—S. Stillman Berry III to James Berry Vickery III, 29 March 1950[1]

$\mathcal{I}$ N 1950 S. STILLMAN BERRY III wrote to his "kinsman" James Berry Vickery III that the migration of young men and women from Unity, Maine, to Montana in the 1870s through the 1890s was a "hegira." This was a reference to the flight of Mohammed from Mecca that has come to mean an exodus or departure from one's country and friends in order to escape an undesirable situation. For some in Unity, moving West was a hegira, or exodus from difficult and changing economic times on Maine farms in the last half of the nineteenth century. Exhausted soils, competition from western farmers for the same markets, fewer opportunities to supplement farm income, and rising debts caused a "period of crisis" in Maine agriculture and those who could not or did not want to adapt left.[2] However, this migration to Montana also represented new opportunities and choices for ambitious young men and women in rural Maine where once farming had been their destiny. Montana's rich deposits of gold, silver, copper, and coal as well as its vast stretches of rangeland for cattle and sheep offered them great opportunities to make fortunes.

The saga of the Vickery family members and their Berry relatives who went to Montana from Unity tells two different stories of family. Members of the Berry family went West in the late 1870s, and their story is one of an interdependent community of men and women from Unity and Waldo County who went to the Great Plains region of Montana to establish and work on sheep ranches. In one way or another they were usually related and they thought of themselves as one large family of "pilgrims." Their ties to Maine were strong as people, culture, and money flowed continuously back and forth between the two locations in an exchange that extended and connected families and community over 2,000 miles. Their ties remained strong because they continued their Maine heritage of family farm mutuality on sheep ranches in Montana. Historian Thomas C. Hubka has described this tradition of farm mutuality as networks of family and friends in a community who "assisted each other through a wide variety of work and social activities" in order "to facilitate their farming operations and thereby improve their overall quality of life." Like the farm family mutuality that Hubka studied in rural Maine, ranch family mutuality for Mainers in rural Montana in the late nineteenth century gave "a distinctive character ... to everyday work and family life."[3]

The sons of James Berry Vickery I and Mary Ayer Vickery went west in the1880s and 1890s, a bit later than their Berry cousins and their story is one of an independent family. The Vickery men did not travel or live with sisters or wives from their Maine community and there is no sense that their journey was any sort of pilgrimage, nor were they pilgrims. James I and Mary's younger sons David Earnest Vickery and James Berry Vickery II went to Montana at different times, spent only a short time there, and returned to their home in Maine before the turn of the twentieth century. James I and Mary's eldest son, Eli Ayer Vickery, first emigrated to Montana with at least one other Unity man (some sources say twenty-six other men), but he married and settled in the boarderland region of Montana and Wyoming apart from the Unity community. Eli Ayer's connections to Maine were not as strong as the community of Berry pilgrims because he married a western woman, and together they created their own family and community "out West" with their eleven children. There was communication with family "back East," but there was no overt exchange of people, culture, or monetary investment that connected those in Maine with Montana. In many ways the independent family that Eli Ayer Vickery and his wife Carrie Brandenburg Vickery created out West in the 1890s was similar to the independent family that the Vickery ancestors George and Rebecca Phippen Vickery created in Massachusetts Bay Colony in the 1650s. It was the center for the production of the food they ate and the clothes they wore, the place their children learned to read, and the only place all were born and cared for in sickness and old age.

There were a number of factors for the Vickerys and Berrys that made going West particularly attractive in the second half of the nineteenth century. The Homestead Act of 1862, granting one hundred and sixty acres of public land to anyone who paid a small registration fee and lived on the land for five years, was a powerful incentive for Unity's young men and women to look West—as powerful as the allure of land in Maine had been to their Revolutionary ancestors. The young men from Unity who served in the Civil War might now feel freer to leave since ties to their village had already been loosened.[4] Those who had not served in the war might look to the West as a place where they could find adventure and test their manhood. Montana was, as the *Atlantic Monthly* called it, "the haven and heaven of adventure" where one could develop "a splendid type of rugged American manhood."[5] In 1869 railroads connected the East Coast to the West Coast of the United States, making the journey West easier, and providing an option to slow, tedious, bulky, and expensive covered wagons. A devastating economic depression engulfed the United States in the mid-1870s, frustrating farmers, bankrupting businesses, and triggering social unrest and violent urban protests by exploited and unemployed workers. In Waldo County one report during this depression stated that "teeming fields that bore bountiful harvests now show[ed] a deplorable state of deterioration."[6] These deteriorated fields represented both those who were barely holding on to their family farms and those who had abandoned them for opportunities elsewhere.

While owning land, finding adventure, and making money were important motives for Unity's young people to heed "the call of the

West," there were important cultural factors as well. The image of the Wild West was a powerful symbol and was mythologized in the collective consciousness of nineteenth-century Americans and Europeans. For many the American West was not just a geographic place of boundless economic and social possibilities, it was an idea that affected them emotionally. Freedom to escape from society was one of the more common feelings associated with the West. As late as 1898 people claimed that "The Treasure State [Montana] is still the haven of runaways from everywhere else ... [and] it is still thought bad form to ask a man what his name was back East."[7] As more and more people settled the West, popular authors like James Fenimore Cooper, Caroline Kirkland, and Walt Whitman, and heroes like Daniel Boone and Kit Carson fostered "a romantic love of the Vanishing Wild West," according to historian Henry Nash Smith, that helped to perpetuate the western myth.[8] Novelists Owen Wister and Willa Cather and artists Charles M. Russell and Frederic Remington kept the romance and fascination with the American West alive long into the twentieth century.

Americans also felt a historical and spiritual connection to the West. In her memoir "Reminiscences of My Trip across the Plains and My Early Life in Montana, 1863–1879," Harriet Sanders, a founding member of the Society of Montana Pioneers, actually compared the arrival of her group of pilgrims at Bannack to the landing of the Pilgrims at Plymouth in 1620.[9] The Berrys and their ranch family community who went to Montana also called themselves "pilgrims," and this characterization was significant because it carried centuries of meaning and was a familiar allusion in New England.[10] These nineteenth-century pilgrims from Maine were not afraid to confess fear for their future—"that they were strangers and pilgrims on the earth." They had faith that God had prepared a "better country" for them in Montana, as God had earlier prepared for their seventeenth-century Pilgrim fathers and mothers in the New World.[11] And like their Pilgrim ancestors to whom many in Waldo County could trace their roots, God would prepare a "city" for them as well—not on a hill, but in another sacred American place—the Wild West.[12]

The celebrated Lewis and Clark Expedition from 1804 to 1806—which happened while David II and Sarah Stone Vickery were clearing land in Unity, Maine, to establish the original family farm—first familiarized Americans with the area of the Northwest Territory that would become Montana. President Thomas Jefferson commissioned Meriwether Lewis and William Clark to detail the natural resources in the new lands west of the Mississippi acquired in the Louisiana Purchase and to explore possible trading routes. They traveled from St. Louis, up the Missouri River and westward to the Rocky Mountains, along the Salmon, Snake, and Columbia Rivers all the way to the Pacific Ocean. Their maps and reports about the opportunities for wealth were widely copied and published, and excited adventurers and investors throughout the United States and Europe. Until the early 1860s, however, fur traders were the only whites who exploited the resources in the Northwest. They built trading posts and introduced steamboats for navigating the upper Missouri River, readying the territory for future white settlements in Montana.

The fur traders also brought diseases and alcohol with them that killed thousands of Native Americans and accelerated the disintegration of their way of life. Much like the Native Americans in Maine, Native Americans in Montana became dependent on trade items and would be forced into "trading land for a living."[13] In the early 1860s Montana was still the home of more than a dozen Native American communities that included the Sioux, Arapaho, Crows, Assiniboine, Atsinas or Gros Ventres, Mandan, Arikarees, Blackfeet, Shoshonis, Bannocks, Salish or Flathead, Nez Percé, Kutenai, and Kalispel or Pend d'Oreille. After the Civil War the Cheyennes, Chippewas, Metis, and Crees would move into Montana.

The great discoveries of gold in the early 1860s started the flow of fortune hunters—black and white Americans, Asians, and Europeans—to Montana, later called the "Treasure State."[14] While the gold found there was equally as rich, the rush to Montana was never as frantic as it had been to California in 1849 or Colorado in 1859, in part because the United States was in the middle of the Civil War and getting to Montana was difficult. The real importance of the gold rush and all the ensuing reports and newspaper and magazine articles was that it focused more attention in the late nineteenth century on Montana, which was made an official territory in 1864. In the August 1866 issue of the *Atlantic Monthly* Edward B. Nealley enthusiastically wrote about the year he spent traveling throughout the gold fields of Montana Territory.

Only four years earlier, he declared, "all this region was *terra incognita* ... a country unexplored and unknown, and held by the various Indian tribes in the Northwest as a common hunting-ground," but it was now "welcoming all changes tending towards refinement and a higher civilization." Nealley's description of the white people who chose to settle there—"their frankness and honesty of purpose, their love of justice, and their sturdy democracy"—assured potential pilgrims that core Anglo-American values flourished out West.[15]

THE WESTERN BERRYS

I THINK I WILL LIKE *my new home and know I shall be contented here. It is the* <u>pleasantest</u> *place I have seen in Montana ... I presume Ralph wrote you all about the wedding &c. Ben went down the river and met us at Carol. He was going to Bismark but got delayed. I had a long journey but a very pleasant one, And have not yet regretted the step I have taken, and I have no fear that I will.* <u>Ben is just as good to me as he</u> *can possibly be. And Mother I* <u>guess I won't want a divorce in five years</u>*. We don't go in for style out here.... Ben sends his love (and thank[s] for letting me come out here), and will do everything in his power to make me happy & contented. After I get settled will write a long letter about everything.*

—Mary Berry Cook, Camp Baker, Montana Territory, to Samuel Stillman I
and Olive Mussey Berry, Unity, Maine, 9 June 1878[1]

*I*N 1862 TWENTY-SIX-YEAR-OLD Charles W. Cook was the first of Unity's young men to go to Montana.[2] After driving cattle to Montana, he tried mining. But by the late 1860s sheep and cattle ranching had eclipsed mining as the way to get rich in Montana because it had become more difficult and expensive to mine the deeper gold, silver, and later copper deposits. Many men rushed off to easier digging in the Black Hills of Dakota Territory. After he explored what is now Yellowstone National Park where Cook Peak is named for him, Charles Cook decided to try ranching, and he traveled to California and then to Oregon where he purchased a large band of sheep. Charles's younger brother, twenty-five-year-old Benjamin "Ben" Bartlett Cook had tried working in a factory in Maine, but left for the West in 1870 where he

Charles W. Cook (1838–1927), c. 1860s. "He was the one who started Unity's Montana hegira."

spent some time working in the first flouring mill in the Montana Territory and mining at Diamond City before he decided to join Charles in his sheep venture.[3] Together they drove the sheep from Oregon to Montana, and established a sheep ranch in the Smith River Valley near White Silver Springs.[4]

The Cook brothers from Maine were among the first people to bring sheep into Montana, and according to one published account, "so well did their business thrive that in ten years their flocks had increased to 15,000."[5] Not including the public land that they used for grazing, their ranch "Willow Lodge" covered ten thousand acres at one time. Needing labor, the Cooks soon encouraged young men from Unity to come West, work for them, learn the sheep business, and then start ranches of their own. These men, often accompanied by wives and sisters, thought of themselves as a family, and they helped each other financially and emotionally to get ahead, practicing a continuation of the "democratic collectivism inspired by mutual need and mutual assistance" that they practiced in Maine farm communities.[6]

The Cook ranch was thus the impetus and the first stop for most of the Maine pilgrims who came to Montana in a chain migration. This chain migration of industrious Berry family members and others from the Clark, Files, Fogg, Fowler, Harmon, Hunt, Moulton, Stevens, and Webster families from Unity (surprisingly no Vickerys) and other neighboring towns in Waldo County whose work ethic the Cooks knew, was surely one important reason that their business thrived. As late as 1959 young men in Maine were still recruited to work at the Berry's Winnecook Ranch (founded a few years after the Cook ranch), as evidenced in a letter written by James Berry Vickery III to his cousin S. Stillman Berry III, the president of the ranch corporation:

> I REGRET THAT the boys that I recommended to you and Thayer [Stevens, manager of the ranch from 1943 to 1975 whose own heritage could be traced to Maine] decided to stay and work here this summer. They are ambitious brothers and among the few who are serious and conscientious. Now that they are out of college and working for the summer, they wish that they had taken the ranch jobs.[7]

The post office on the Cook ranch, the crucial link between Maine and Montana, was symbolically named "Unity."

Twenty-two-year-old Samuel "Sam" Stillman Berry II was the first in the Berry family to go to work on the Cook brothers' ranch. Throughout 1877 he wrote to his family in Unity from Montana declaring that there were great opportunities "for doing things in a ranch way" in Montana. Sam II was sure that if his brother Reuel "would put his money into the sheep business out here he could make more in five years than he could there [in Maine] in a lifetime, and not work as hard as he does in the potato business."[8] Having failed to excite Reuel, Sam II hoped his father Samuel Stillman Berry I might invest some money in ranching. "You think that I am all taken up in the sheep business,"

Ralph Berry
(1850–1911), c. 1890. "Pioneer
Ranchman of White Sulpher Springs
and Winnecook, Montana."

Evelyn "Evie" Kelley Berry
(1857–1940), c. 1890.
"I have got to be a regular old
ranchwoman."

he stated. "Well, I think there is lots of money in it. Anything will suit me if there is money in it…. If father would put some of his money into sheep [in Montana] it would pay more than one-fifth of that in the bank."[9] Sam II was finally able to convince his brother Ralph Berry to come West. With what funds he had, twenty-eight-year-old Ralph joined Sam II on the Cook brothers' ranch in May 1878 with hopes that they would later buy their own ranch.

Ralph Berry left his twenty-one-year-old wife Evelyn "Evie" Kelley Berry in Unity when he went to Montana with his sister Mary Berry in 1878. Ralph and Evie had been married for three years and had had one child, a daughter named Lottie, who died in 1877 when she was only eight months old.[10] The youngest of five children, Evie Kelley Berry, who was married at the age of eighteen, was the daughter of Samuel II and Charlotte Files Kelley of Unity. Her great-grandfather Aaron Kelley had fought in the Revolution, and he and his wife Mary Kennedy Kelley and their five children had come to settle in Unity from Boothbay, Maine, about the same time as David II and Sarah Stone Vickery and their family. Aaron and Mary Kennedy Kelley's son Samuel I, and

Ralph and Evie Kelley Berry's marriage certificate, 25 November 1875.
COURTESY OF UNITY HISTORICAL SOCIETY.

David II and Sarah Stone Vickery's daughter Sarah were married in 1800 and had twelve children. (This was the Sarah Vickery Kelley who had so "vehemently" defended her home from looting during the War of 1812 that she frightened away the English soldiers.) Thus, Evie Kelley Berry was the great-granddaughter of David II and Sarah Stone Vickery. This made the Vickery family and the Berry family related in "two different ways," as S. Stillman Berry III would later tell his young cousin James Berry Vickery III. First, Clarissa Berry married into the Vickery family, becoming the wife of Eli Vickery in 1831. And then Evie Kelley, David II and Sarah Stone Vickery's great-granddaughter, married into the Berry family in 1875.[11]

S. Stillman Berry III, who was Ralph and Evie Kelley Berry's only surviving child, once described his mother Evie and her middle-class progressive belief in education:

> SHE DIDN'T finish high school. She was ill, what they called lung fever, in high school. Lost her hair and her teeth and they despaired of her for a while. But she came out of it. She never had any more education but what she gave herself by reading good books. She always had the passion for literature, and she read Dickens and things like that early, and everything she could get her hands on. And she had an almost pitiful passion for educating. She always thought that was the solution to all problems, and when she wasn't educating herself, she was trying to educate someone else, and often it was just thrown away, but she did that all her life.[12]

While Stillman "adored his mother Evie," his reference to her "almost pitiful passion for educating" hints at his frustration concerning the energy and money Evie invested in the education of several of his cousins that he apparently felt was "just thrown away."[13] Although self-taught, Evie Kelley Berry was certainly considered educated enough to teach school in Unity while Ralph went to Montana and no doubt, she felt she was fulfilling her civic duty in "trying to educate someone else." Ralph and Evie apparently planned for her to join him when he was settled.

Nineteenth-century women's diaries, letters, and memoirs suggest that most married women were not unwilling or reluctant to go West—husbands and wives usually made this decision together.[14] But that did not preclude the loneliness, isolation, fear, and exhaustion women often felt on the western frontier. Women especially missed other women. "I had company last week…. They were the only ladies I had seen for three months," Mary Berry Cook would write to her sister-in-law Evie Kelley Berry in Maine after living in Montana for a few months. "What do you think of that—three months & not see a woman," she exclaimed.[15] This would seem odd to Mary and Evie because nineteenth-century women often formed close emotional relationships with other women and counted on other women for help and support, in part because men and women's roles and activities in American society were so rigidly separated.[16] For Mary, Evie, and many women who went West where there was "no one at the ranch but men" and no sight of a woman for three months, writing and receiving letters kept their supportive female networks of family and friends back East intact regardless of the distance between them.[17]

Twenty-five-year-old Mary Berry accompanied her brother Ralph Berry to Montana in 1878.[18] Mary had decided to come West to marry her fiancé Ben Cook and settle on the Cook ranch, even though her parents S. Stillman I and Olive Mussey Berry seemed to have some doubts about the marriage.[19] Ben and Charles Cook were related to the Berry and Vickery family network through marriages within the Bartlett, Chase, and Hussey families in Unity, and Mary was the niece, and Sam II and Ralph were the nephews of Eli and Clarissa Berry Vickery. Even though they knew Ben Cook and his family, Mary's mother and father might have had legitimate concerns about her marriage to him because she became engaged on the rebound. Before Mary and Ben's betrothal she had been engaged to Charles Taylor. According to the family story Taylor "went to Bangor [Maine] to work for his Uncle Jonathan Parkhurst & met another girl who was quite wealthy & [from] a good family…. He married her—Ben came from [a] good family—had been West, made some money & came back[.]"[20] Going West to marry Ben offered Mary the opportunity to begin a new life far from hurtful and embarrassing gossip about her previous love life.

Mary Berry and her brother Ralph left Unity in the spring of 1878, leaving their thirty-one-year-old sister Ruth Berry to care for their aging parents. Mary would have had to wait until her brother Ralph was ready to go West as nineteenth-century propriety required women to be accompanied by men when they traveled. They took trains as far as Bismark, North Dakota. On one leg of their journey Mary rode with General Philip H. Sheridan, the famed Civil War hero. Sheridan was now the commander of the United States Army's Missouri Division that had just won his "total war" against Native Americans in the Northwest Territories. Mary later wrote her family about her traveling experience with the general:

From Chicago to St. Paul I had the honor of riding all day and sleeping at night in the next section to Gen. Sherridan. He is an inveterate tobacco chewer. [My brother] Reuel's quids are nothing in comparison to the ones Sherridan chews. His spittoon was enough to turn a hog's stomach. He is rather stern looking with dark piercing blue eyes. Rather good looking when he smiles, but by no means handsome.[21]

Upon reaching Bismark Mary and Ralph took a steamboat up the Missouri River to Fort Benton, Montana, which was established by the American Fur Company at the headwaters of the Missouri in 1850. Ben Cook met them along the way, and he and Mary were married at Fort Benton. The three of them rode in Ben's "nice easy" buggy to Helena, then on to Camp Baker (later called Fort Logan) in the Big Belt Mountains near the Smith River Valley. The roads from Fort Benton were, according to Mary, "in a terrible condition. Mud—Mud & water—I never saw [such] mud before. I don't think I could have stood the journey from B. [Benton] if I had been obliged to have taken a coach." The "long journey" from Unity, Maine, to Montana took about five weeks.[22] This journey and her marriage transformed Mary as her closing words in a letter to her sister Ruth made clear: "I remain Your Sister Maym [Mary] Berry; she that was, Maym Berry; formerly of Unity Maine now of Smith River Valley Montana Territories. Soon to be a State."[23]

For many women like Mary Berry Cook, the West was a Garden of Eden of fertile fields and abundant wildlife where they could begin anew. They had an image of this garden as a domestic space where they could cultivate a home and a community and felt it was their duty to tame and bring order to the Wild West.[24] They brought domestic possessions and cultural items with them from the East to help them carry out their civilizing mission. They made household pets of jack rabbits, wild birds, antelope, and coyotes.[25] Even in the most rustic living situations they paid great attention to propriety, manners, and to setting a moral tone in their new western communities by establishing churches, schools, and libraries. But even women who stayed back East were expected to exert a civilizing influence on men who went West, as Mary Berry Cook clearly affirmed in a letter from Montana to her mother back in Maine in 1879. "It is well for a young man here to have a girl back there that they think a great off," stated Mary, "for it keeps them from yielding to many a temptation which they might if there was no one that [they] thought cared for them."[26]

One of the strongest advocates in the nineteenth century of the ideology that it was women's duty to be carriers of civilization, agents of order, and keepers of morals was Catherine Beecher, daughter of the esteemed minister Lyman Beecher. She actively promoted the training of young women as teachers so they could go West and act in her words as "a new source of moral power."[27] By 1880 32 percent of all college students in the United States were women. Nearly half of these newly college-educated women consciously decided not to marry and became career teachers, librarians, doctors, lawyers, and social workers. Teaching as well as tending to the poor, nursing the ill, and in general redeeming American society with their moral leadership outside the home had become accepted as appropriate occupations for women because they were seen as natural extensions of mothering. These expanded public roles gave many women unprecedented power to shape and lead their communities, especially out West.[28] In a deliberate strategy to tame society some western states even gave women the right to vote in the latter half of the nineteenth century.[29] Hundreds of women did go West and like the Montana teacher Mary Berry Cook described to her sister in 1880 many of them were trained at Mount Holyoke College. "Our school teacher is a young lady just from the States[,] Holyoke, Mass.," Mary wrote. "[She] Is not pretty but good looking & of course smart or she would not come away out here a stranger to everybody[.]"[30] A "young lady" teacher would have to be "smart" to survive out West as Mary stated, because she usually arrived alone (fulfilling her moral duty mitigated the propriety of traveling alone) and did not have a family of "pilgrims" to sustain her.

"I suppose you notice the heading [Pilgrims Rest] of this letter," Mary Berry Cook wrote her sister Ruth Berry in Unity soon after she settled on the Cook ranch. "Well yesterday some one suggested this be called that, as every pilgrim that comes to this country makes for this place and makes it their headquarters."[31] While it must have been comforting to be among familiar people in a new land, it could also be overwhelming, as evidenced by Mary Berry Cook's words to her mother in July 1878. "I shall be so glad when we have a smaller family, and all these pilgrims get settled," she wrote, "Not that I have to work very hard—but I don't like so many in a family, it seems more like a hotel than anything else."[32] Clearly, Mary's definition of family here included all the pilgrims who arrived from her community in Maine.

Though the men who came to work on the Cook ranch slept down in the wool house, they ate in the main house and at times there could be twenty-five or more at the table.[33] Room and board was often part of their wages and preparing food to feed them was a constant chore. "They eat out here in this country about four times as much as they do east," exclaimed Mary. "Everyone is blessed with an appetite if they haven't got anything else they can call their own."[34] The smell of so many sheep men at the table must have been overwhelming. Wool is oily and after working with sheep, as someone who grew up on a Montana sheep ranch stated, "your clothes collected a thick layer of grease that smelled like the floor of a well-used sheep shed."[35] Fortunately, Mary did not have to do "any of the washing," she told her mother, because "the men all wear woolen and do their own washing. They all sleep in colored blankets so ther is no bed clothes except pillow slips."[36]

Necessity often made men feel obliged to help women with housework out West. While there were defined roles for men and women as there were back East, the "rules" for behavior were relaxed because of the extraordinary circumstances of settlement.[37] There is ample evidence in Mary's correspondence that her husband Ben and her brother Ralph helped with the food preparation on the Cook ranch. "Ben & Ralph got dinner and washed the dishes"; "Ralph and I got dinner"; "Ben is a very nice cook, and if I fail on anything he can tell me what the matter is with it"; "Ben & I made a keg of preserves"; "We—Ben and I have been making mincemeat today"; and "We churned [butter] for the first time since I've been here, last Saturday, that is Ben done the work and I told him how to the best of my ability."[38]

There were examples of women helping men with outside ranch work as well. "Went out herding with Ben yesterday.... Expected I would be lame today as it was the first time I have ridden horseback, but I feel all right today," wrote Mary to her sister Ruth.[39] Another Maine woman, Sadie Lord Webster, whose husband Frank worked on the Cook and Berry ranches wrote that she "went after the cows on horseback" with her husband, and she, too, was surprised that "the rid-

Mary "Maym" Berry Cook (1853–1935), c. 1885.
"I shall be glad when we have a smaller family, and all
these pilgrims get settled."

ing didn't hurt me, I couldn't tell by my feelings that I had been [riding]."[40] Both women seemed relieved that stepping outside their proper sphere did them no harm.

Most people believed that the West was a better place for the soundness of their bodies and minds. Mary Berry Cook (who had not yet experienced a Montana winter) said that she felt healthier out West:

> [I] AM MUCH BETTER THAN USUAL in the Summer[.] We don't have such very warm weather as you have there [in Maine]. The hottest day here the themomiter was only 87 and they said that was the warmest they had here for several years and then no matter how warm, we get a nice breeze here from the mountain. The nights are always cool about like your nights in September. Oh! It is a delightful climate, and this is the prettiest valley in the whole Territory.[41]

Mary encouraged her family and friends in Maine who had lung afflictions or a general malaise to visit her. "I feel very much worried

*Benjamin "Ben" Bartlett Cook (1848–1920), c. 1885.
"Ben is a very nice cook, and if I fail on anything he can
tell me what the matter is with it."*

about Sade," she wrote. "I wish she would come out this Aug.... I know this mountain air would help her if anything will."[42] Mary's sister-in-law Evie Kelley Berry felt the same way, and wrote her mother in 1882 that, "We are all well. Neither Ralph or I have been sick a day in the Territory. This is very healthy country, and on that account, as well as many others, we have both become much attached to it as a place in which to dwell."[43] Writing to the *Republican Journal* in Belfast, Maine, from Montana in 1881, Flora I. Black exclaimed, "I think this must be a beautiful country for people in poor health, the air is so pure and invigorating."[44] Future president Theodore Roosevelt, who went West in the early 1880s after the death of his wife, also recognized its regenerative powers. He stated that out West he could lead "a free and hardy life, with horse and with rifle" and feel "the beat of hardy life" in his veins and "the glory of work and the joy of living."[45]

After working for Charles and Ben Cook the first few months following his arrival in Montana, Ralph Berry and his brother Sam II decided to "take up" a ranch of their own and wrote to their father in Unity, Maine, for financial help.[46] Samuel S. Berry I, who was a shrewd

1860 – 1895

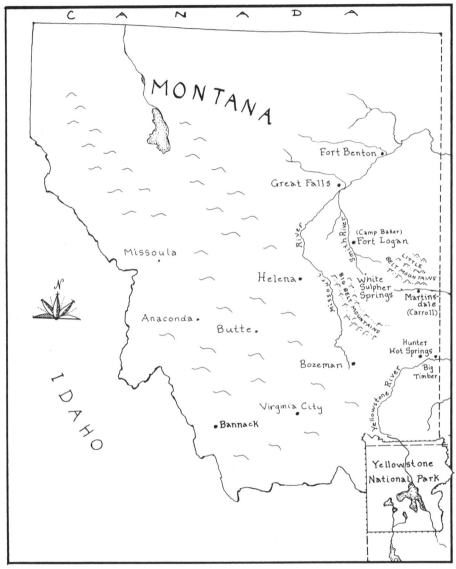

Map by Berry Manter

The Montana Families

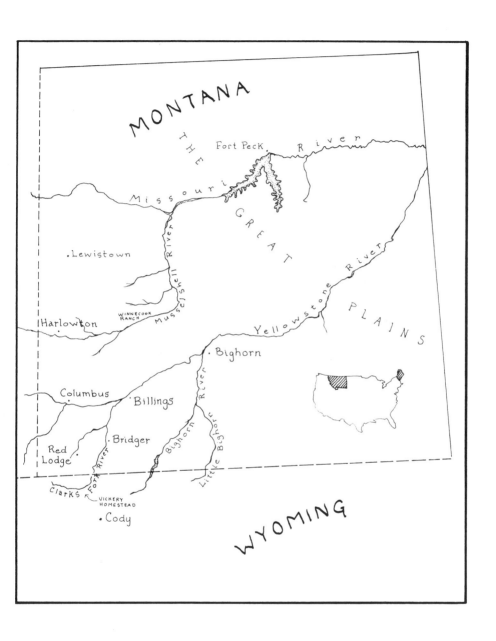

*Samuel Stillman Berry I (1814–1890), c. 1875, father of James,
Reuel, Ruth, Ralph, and Sam Berry and Mary Berry Cook. "If father
would put some of his money into sheep [in Montana] it would pay
more than one fifth of that in the bank."*

and successful farmer and businessman, replied that he wanted a financial "statement" of what his sons "could do in the sheep business."[47]

There had been a "Golden Era" of sheep raising in the hill country of New England from 1830 to 1840, but lowering of the protective
tariff on wool, increased wool production in the West, and attacks on
flocks by the rising population of dogs had caused its decline.[48] Most
farms in Maine that kept sheep after the Civil War had only small flocks
of ten to thirty sheep, and while they were raised for wool, sheep were
primarily used for mutton and breeding stock by this time.[49] In the late
1870s Maine farmers were concentrating on increasing their dairy herds
because they could make more money by producing milk, cheese, and
butter. Because cows live off clover and sheep destroy it by cropping it
too close, it is difficult to raise the two animals together on small farms.
So, father Samuel I might have needed some assurance concerning
large-scale sheep ranching and the wool-growing industry out West.

Montana has a diverse geography. The western one-third of its
147,138 square miles is covered by the rugged Rocky Mountains. The
eastern two-thirds of Montana is comprised of lush valleys fed by

Olive Mussey Berry (1812–1896), c. 1875, mother of James, Reuel, Ruth, Ralph, and Sam Berry and Mary Berry Cook. "And Mother I guess I won't want a divorce in five years."

mountain rains, punctuated by smaller mountain ranges, and crossed by small rivers and streams that flow into the Missouri and Yellowstone Rivers. From these valleys roll the vast grassy, semi-arid range lands of the Great Plains. While historian Stuart Bruchey describes the Great Plains as "an area of devastating blizzards, hailstorms, and high winds sweeping uninterruptedly over the treeless grasslands" with an "ever present threat of economic ruin to man, beast, and crop," the high altitude where the Unity pilgrims settled kept the climate and soil dry and the grassy ranges were ideal for wool growing, unlike Maine where sheep fleece and hoofs took longer to dry out when wet, making them susceptible to disease and foot rot.[50] Another advantage of this particular region, as Mary Berry Cook pointed out to her mother, was "the strong wind which blows the snow off, and gives the sheep a good chance to winter well. They have here what is called a 'choneuk' (a warm strong wind) which will carry off a body of snow in a few hours."[51] The "choneuk," or chinook was important because sheep were herded to the mountains for summer grazing and spent the winters pastured in the valleys and foothills. The sheep most commonly used in Montana was a cross between the Merino and Cotswold breeds that grew a heavy fleece of good quality wool and could withstand the severe winters.[52]

Mary Berry Cook's brother Ralph was "much taken up with the sheep business" after they arrived in Montana, and he confidently wrote to his father:

> WE HAVE NOT GOT ENOUGH money to get a good start, so would like for you to loan us enough to make up with what we have. Chas. and Ben will help us and they say the sooner we start in, the better. We have got together $1,500 and if you will let us have as much more, we will pay you all the interest you ask and they say if we do not have more than ordinary luck we can pay you in two years, so you see it is good business.[53]

Sam II wrote to his father as well, highlighting those from Unity who had done well like the Cooks and the Husseys; he could also have mentioned the Severances. "I do not know of anyone here that has made a failure of the business," he said.

> RALPH AND I SHALL START this fall in the business and would like your assistance to start with [and] we will give you 8% for the amount we wrote for which I know is safer in sheep here than in a bank.... Ralph sent a statement to Evie which is lower than I shall give for I know that we can do better than that with ordinary luck. He called wool 10 cents per pound which is not half what it is selling for in Helena and the lambs 50 cents per head lower than they are bringing.[54]

Ralph and Sam borrowed some money in Montana, but that December father Samuel I came through with a check, though with some uneasiness, as Ralph's acknowledgment shows:

> I CAN NOT FEEL BUT I AM under great obligation to you & how to extend my heartfelt gratitude is more than I can tell but feeling is beyond expression. I realize & appreciate the fact that it is giving us a good start and giving us a lift that will be remembered for all time to come. If we have good luck, we can pay it all back in

one year from next shearing time & have a fine start. You may not think so but sheep will pay, more than pay, for themselves clear from all expenses in two years.... We had to run in debt some and pay big interest but as it is only a short time, we can pay every cent next shearing & have some left.[55]

Telling his father that two neighboring sheep ranchers were going back to Maine to "hire all the money they can get there to buy more sheep," Ralph assured his father that others saw the profit in wool growing, too. Evidently Ralph's assurances were convincing and the Berry brothers established their first ranch called "Meadow Bluff" in November 1878 near the Cook ranch in the Smith River Valley and stocked it with two thousand sheep. Since Ralph and Sam's "wool clip and lambs" made them "a good little income of $4,521" that season it can be presumed that they paid back the loan from their father on time.[56]

In April 1879 Ralph's wife Evie Kelley Berry arrived in Montana at, "just the right time to escape the mud," said her sister-in-law Mary Berry Cook, no doubt remembering her own trip. "If she had been one week later she would have had a hard journey by coach as the rain this week and last would have made it very muddy. She had a short pleasant trip. Said she was not any tired when she got here—I never saw her looking better."[57] Evie and Mary both acted as agents of order, bringing from Maine to Montana domestic and cultural items that conveyed familiarity and refinement to their new homes.[58] "You should have seen the smile on Ralph's countenance when I unpacked the clock," wrote Evie to her mother, "and he gazed on its homelike face and then how that smile deepened into a broad grin when the cigars were brought to light."[59] At Mary's request Evie also brought ferns and colorful autumn leaves from Maine with which Mary trimmed her lace curtains. "They look very pretty and people often ask where they come—if they are real or painted," Mary wrote her mother. "We don't have such leaves out here—the trees being all spruce pine & cottonwood."[60] When Mary came West she had brought flower bulbs from Maine that she planted in Montana soil, and had her organ shipped from home—the only such musical instrument for miles around. True to her mission to bring civilization to the west, Mary hoped later to teach a few "music scholars."[61]

"Mr. Cook's Ranch, Unity, Montana,"
called Willow Lodge, c. 1896.

Evie arrived in Montana at the beginning of the most labor-intensive time on the sheep ranches, and Mary had written to Evie preparing her for what she could expect: "The lamb season is at hand. We shall have eight or ten men employed, on both [Berry and Cook] ranches. This is the busy time of the year and the men have to work very hard."[62] Lambing was the most crucial period in the sheep industry and ideally it began in April when the range grasses had come in and the weather was mild. While a couple of herders and their dogs could graze bands of sheep that might expand to 4,000 or more, extra men were needed during lambing and shearing times. Many of the young Maine men who came to Montana worked on the sheep ranches as itinerant laborers, going from ranch to ranch. Lambing was a twenty-four-hour event, and plenty of skilled hands and constant attention were required—weather conditions, difficult deliveries, predators, and failure of ewes to claim their lambs being persistent threats to the lamb crop that ranchers needed to make a profit.[63] As Mary wrote her sister Ruth in May 1879, lambing was exhausting work.

SAM GOT ALL TIRED OUT through lambing. I was afraid he would get sick: but he had a few days of rest and is now better. He is a great care <u>taker</u>, and his work frets him if it don't go just to suit him. He is anxious to get ahead. He had care of the dorsets, and for a few days they did not get milk enough from the cows [to supplement the shortage in the ewes' flow] to feed all of them and some of them died. From starvation Sam said. It made him feel so badly to see some die after he had taken so much pains to make them live.[64]

Floor plan of Willow Lodge, Montana drawn by Evie Kelley Berry, 1879:
"In the plan I have left all the doors open so you may find your way. In the sitting room are pretty green holland curtains at the windows with green tassles. On one side of the room middle way of the wall is a bracket a home made one with a red lambrequin. This is filled with beautiful specimens of wool & some dried flowers. Above the brackets hangs a picture in a large oval frame of the five Cook boys. Above that a motto with a silver background "He leadeth me." On either side hang pictures of Uncle Daniel and Aunt Lizzie Cook. Then there is a large picture of Diamond City a music rack and several small pictures. Maym's room is fixed up real pretty. All the windows in the house are very large & she has a curtain for her's made of unbleached muslin trimmed with a wide band of red. It loops back on each side and has a very pretty red lambrequin. Her dressing table has muslin drapery trimmed like the curtain & the cover is burlap fringed all round and worked with red worsted. There is one carpet on the sitting room and it looks up to the rafters just as we imagined it did only not half so funny. The bedrooms are ceiled overhead."

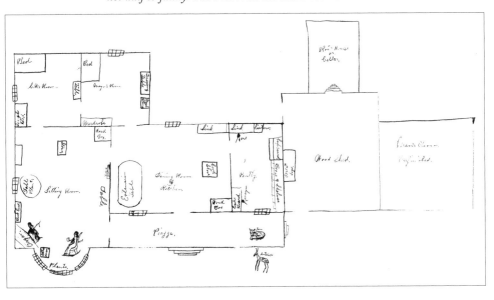

When the weather was particularly harsh the lambs were even brought into the house to keep them alive. "A housefull of lambs makes it harder for me," Evie Kelley Berry wrote home during lamb season, "but I don't mind it much after all, for I have got to be a regular old ranchwoman."[65]

Sheep shearing happened in the dusty heat of June and July and was grueling piecework. Holding a squirming sheep between his legs the shearer clipped the fleece off using large-bladed shears, trying to work as fast as possible without cutting the sheep—an experienced shearer might only take five minutes—then he deposited the sheared fleece, or "wool clip" as it was called, for credit and ran to the pen for another sheep. "Sam I find, is working too hard, is getting too ambitious," said his sister Mary Berry Cook. "Yesterday he sheared sixty-five sheep. They have 10 cts per head, and of course the more one shears per day the more pay they get. But he was pretty well used up."[66] Evie described the routine of shearers working in Smith River Valley:

THE BOYS HAVE FINISHED shearing the home band and have gone home to prepare to shear their own. The men are nearly through down to Hussey's and will get here the last of the week. Then Ralph & Sam are coming back here again & will not begin on their own before the 20th. Ralph shears fifty per day & Sam & Ben some over sixty. They can turn off a thousand pretty quick.[67]

Sam himself wrote his mother that he "got really beat out" lambing and "worked very hard" shearing, but it was worth it. "I got good pay for it," he said. "I sheared some over 1,200 [sheep] which brought me over $120.00 for one month's work. That is more than I could make in Yankee land in one year working on a farm."[68]

The shearing crews that were in most demand were Australian, Mexican, Native American, and American, though there were Irish, English, Scotch, Scandinavian, and Chinese crews as well. The crews usually followed a seasonal shearing circuit starting in Arizona and California, moving into Oregon and Washington, or into Idaho and Wyoming, then Montana and Canada. Then they went back to where they started in Mexico or Arizona and started the circuit all over again.[69] On the whole itinerant shearers were a "rough lot," frequently drinking quantities of whiskey and smoking marijuana.[70] There is no evidence that the Maine crew was a "rough lot," but it was mean and dirty work. Unfortunately, though it paid well, when too many men arrived in the area they caused wage deflation, as Mary Berry Cook pointed out in 1878. "Sam is making his five & six dollars per day through shearing. I don't know what the boys will do after shearing. There is so many pilgrims that wages is much lower than formerly."[71]

After shearing the sheep there was still plenty of hard work to do. The fleeces had to be put into sacks. While cattlemen could just drive their herds to the railroads, sheepmen had to haul the wool sacks on wagons to the steamboat landing at Fort Benton or to railroad stations in wool centers like Helena, Billings, Carroll (later renamed Martinsdale), or Big Timber. "Bull teams" were needed to pull these long processions of wagons piled high with wool sacks that could weigh two to three hundred pounds each. Getting the bull teams ready was dangerous, as Mary Berry Cook explained to her Maine farm family who surely could visualize this work.

The Winnecook Ranch crew atop bags of fleece, c. 1917.
S. STILLMAN BERRY PAPERS, 1880-1984. SMITHSONIAN INSTITUTION ARCHIVES,
RECORD UNIT 7335, BOX 47, FOLDER 1. NEG.#2003-228.

I WENT DOWN TO THE carell this morning to see the men yolk the teams for hauling the wool to Carroll. They call them Bull Teams. But they are wild steers that never had a yoke or rope near them. Have a few trained oxen to put with them. The cattle here are turned out when calves and are not got up until they are four or five years old. Then they yolk them up and put them on a team and work them, no training at all, and the first time they attempt to yolk them is a sight worth seeing. Tis very exciting & dangerous work, for they will take right at a man and tear him into pieces if he is not mounted on a horse. One of them (the wildest) killed his mate, it took them several hours to get him under control. No one dared approach him, even with a horse near.... They got him yolked after a while. Then when they unyolked him he put for Ben, but he was on top of a pile of logs in an instant. They make nice oxen after they are broken if they are not injured during the process of yolking. First they throw a lasso and draw them into a little open made of ropes, and get them where they can't help themselves, then yolk.[72]

Between 1875 and 1878 the number of sheep in Montana increased from 20,000 to 100,000 and in 1879 more than 50,000 fleeces were sent down the Missouri River on steamboats from Fort Benton. The final destination for most of the wool grown in Montana was Boston. In 1880 there were 185,000 sheep and almost a million pounds of wool was marketed. Nearly one-half of the sheep were in the Smith and Musselshell Valleys where the pilgrims from Unity settled.[73]

Many Maine men had come to Montana to make quick money, and they fully intended to return to Maine, sooner rather than later if the wages on sheep ranches were too low. After they had earned some cash they went back East in the fall, often returning the next spring. "Many of our Waldo county young men who have been employed on ranches in Montana may be expected home this fall," reported the Belfast, Maine, *Republican Journal* in 1884. "They have been earning $500 or $600 a year this way, but farmers [ranchers] generally are cutting down expenses and will try to get along with less help."[74] Some men who returned from Montana during the winter "bought themselves fine sleighs, and sporting a great buffalo robe, took keen pleasure in taking young ladies for rides, always driving up the street at break-neck speed."[75] One of S. Stillman Berry III's early memories in Unity was "being in a sleigh bundled up" in a "beautiful buffalo robe" that his father Ralph Berry had sent to the family in Maine from Montana.[76]

The men who were committed to staying after lambing and shear-ing, and who hoped to establish their own ranches someday continued to work around on area ranches. They hayed, built corrals, herded, rounded up horses, managed livestock, cut wood in the mountains, worked in mills in the region, and contracted to construct bridges and other public projects. A number of Maine men did start their own ranches, often forming partnerships and remaining in Montana for the rest of their lives. Yet many still kept abreast of life back in Maine. "The good old [*Republican*] Journal comes regularly every week," wrote one pilgrim to the newspaper in Belfast, Maine, "and I can assure you it is a welcome visitor to all the Waldo county settlers who have homes in this far away country."[77]

The plentiful grass and open, unfenced range in the public domain of "this far away country" proved ideal for ranching. But to take advantage of the land out West, the white settlers had to eliminate the buffalo and Native Americans who were already living on it. Most of the thirteen million buffalo that grazed on the land were eventually killed off by epidemics of contagious diseases carried by imported cattle. Pro-fessional hunters got rid of the rest, slaughtering hundreds of buffalo a day and leaving the carcasses to rot on the Plains. By 1883 there were only two hundred buffalo left in the entire West, and they troubled ranchers no more.[78] Removing the Native Americans from the land, many of whom had already been removed from their homes to Mon-tana, was more difficult, and settlers turned to the federal government for solutions. As anthropologist Peter Nabokov states, the government's answers "came down to the old options—wipe out Indians, segregate them, or somehow blend them into society at large."[79]

Like their colonial ancestors, the Montana pilgrims understood it was their Biblical duty to tame and cultivate the wilderness, and civilize "heathen" Native Americans. By the mid nineteenth century this belief had evolved into the philosophy of Manifest Destiny which claimed that it was the special mission and responsibility of Anglo-Saxon Americans to expand their advanced and civilized way of life across the continent.

So even while they idealized Native Americans in poems, novels, and art as "noble savages" who were closer to nature and more virtuous, they energetically worked to make them conform to "civilized" white middle-class values. If Native Americans were to blend into society at large, they had to become individual landowners, convert to Christianity, and adhere to rigid social roles for men and women as defined by whites.

Some Americans lamented that "every step of the white man's progress has been a step of the red man's decay."[80] But when faced with Native Americans as neighbors, white settlers felt somewhat differently. "Five Indians came to this Ranch last Tuesday. They pretended they were looking for some of ther horses which had strayed away, but I guess that was only an excuse to look around and see what they could steal," claimed Mary Berry Cook about Native Americans in central Montana. "I wish you could see a lot of these wild indians after you had seen ther corse countenance once you would have but little sympathy for the 'Poor Indian.'"[81]

Many of the Native Americans who lived in Montana at this time or came in the later years of the nineteenth century were pushed there from their original homelands in the eastern and southern parts of the United States by continuous Euro-American expansion. While some Native Americans like the Crows welcomed whites into the territory because they brought guns to trade, others like the Sioux were distressed that white settlers disturbed their buffalo hunting grounds, laid railroad tracks through their land, and disrupted their way of life. The varied communities of Native Americans were not united, and some fought one another for control over their diminishing lands. Attempts by the United States government to negotiate treaties only aggravated tense relations between competing Native American communities.[82] Contention among Native Americans, however, did make some white settlers feel safer, as these words from pilgrim Mary Berry Cook suggest: "There is no danger," she wrote to her sister in 1879, "as long as the Indians are fighting among themselves."[83]

Horse theft was the main source of conflict between the Montana pilgrims and Native Americans.[84] The federal government's "Indian Wars" after the Civil War had already killed a good portion of the Native American population. General George Armstrong Custer's "Last Stand" at Little Big Horn River in southeastern Montana during the nation's centennial anniversary in June 1876 outraged the public. Newspapers as far away as the *Maine Farmer* demanded that "this army of hostile savages must be broken up at whatever the cost."[85] With an increase in cavalry, funds, and intensity in fighting, the federal government did finally "break up" and segregate most Native Americans on reservations by the early 1880s. But some Native Americans continued acts of defiance like stealing horses. Mary Berry Cook related one such episode to her sister Ruth:

> WE HAVEN'T HAD ANY trouble from hostile Indians thus far this Summer. There has been several parties out stealing horses. One party of five stole twenty seven horses from the Muscleshell and Missouri Valleys. The citizens went after them and got the horses back. They killed two Indians and wounded the other three. One of the citizens was badly wounded. The fight was right back of the Cook ranch in the mountains.... Sam & Ben went to the scene of action with the Soldiers. Ben brought me part of a war bonnet that was left on the field and Sam found a bullet that went right through one indian. That was all the trophies they brought back. That night Evie was <u>scared</u> I can tell you. She and Charlie Moulton was up about all night fortifying the house and getting all the lamps & [illegible] in readiness for an attack.[86]

Mary was not scared—or so she insisted. She "was asleep in five minutes ... and slept quietly until morning." Native Americans rarely harmed settlers, and aside from horses they were usually looking for food, as Mary had earlier told her mother:

> SOME INDIANS WENT through the Muscleshell two weeks ago. Stole some horses and frightened the settlers. Six went into a house [and] ordered Mrs. Hall to get them some supper. Took the cartridge out of Mr. H['s] gun and "<u>bossed</u>" the family around and left without doing any harm beyond taking the horses.[87]

Mary documented violent acts and thefts that were committed by white men too, but as she recognized, whites were quick to blame Native Americans first.

THERE WERE SOME MEN murdered and their horses run off between the Muscleshell and Yellowstone last week. It was at first laid to the Indians, but it proved to be white men, the ones that robbed the mail at Boseman.[88]

Judge L. E. Munson, who was one of the first United States judges appointed by Abraham Lincoln to bring the rule of law to Montana in 1865, had a deeper understanding of the situation. "Whites would murder whites for plunder, scalp and mutilate their victims, and then report it as an Indian massacre," he stated, "to be followed by similar outrages by whites upon the Indians."[89] Of course, using race as a screen to perpetrate brutality was not unique to the West in American history.

There were also times of reciprocity when ranchers and Native Americans came together. In July 1880 Ralph Berry and four white men drove two bands of Merino sheep that included over two thousand sheep and nineteen hundred lambs from southwestern Utah, through Idaho and Wyoming to the Musselshell River Valley in Montana. Just outside of Salt Lake City, Utah, they were approached by a group of Ute Native Americans, no doubt because Ralph was driving the sheep through their reservation, as he wrote to his wife Evie:

WE HAD TO CROSS THE Ute Reservation [and] while we were crossing a creek some Indians came in site on a little round butte at which time they discovered us & after holding counsel a short time fired one shot which struck in the bank ahead of us. We paid no attention to it & in a while they came down to us so I gave them a wether & lamb & they helped us cross & then went on their way rejoicing. I knew very well that they done it to scare us.[90]

One wether (a castrated male sheep) and one lamb seems a small price for Ralph to pay for the privilege of crossing Ute land, probably letting the sheep graze there as well, and then for the Utes' help in getting nearly four thousand sheep across the creek. Better grazing was often found on reservations and in the late 1800s many ranchers in the Northwest leased Native American land.[91]

Whites of course fought among themselves over control of the plentiful grass and open, unfenced range in the public domain out West.

There were violent conflicts between cattlemen and sheepmen, but rarely in Montana, because usually the same people who invested in cattle also invested in sheep, and boundless land for ranching alleviated problems in conflicting grazing patterns of cattle and sheep.[92] The *Rocky Mountain Husbandman* reported that the sheep men and the cattlemen got along "harmoniously."[93] In the Smith River Valley area where the Berrys ranched there were sixty thousand sheep and fifteen thousand head of cattle that grazed together in 1879. There were, however, distinct cattle and sheep cultures. Sheep herders never captured the imagination of Americans like "cowboys," according to historian James McClellan Hamilton:

THE SHEEP HERDER and his faithful dog were interesting but not showy like the cowboy and his trained horse. The sheep herder had nothing to match the saddle and chaps of the cowboy. His clothes were plain in comparison with the flaming flannel shirt, the red handkerchief, and the ten-gallon hat of his rival on

A sheep herder and his precious dog herd sheep in the mountains of Montana during summer grazing, c. 1900. "We think more of our dogs out here than you do there [in Maine] of the hired men."

horseback. Sheep had to be tended in the daytime and corralled at night to protect them from predatory animals, while cattle roamed at large. Lambing and shearing were tame exhibitions compared with the excitement of cutting out steers and branding calves on the roundup.[94]

Much has been made about the relationship of a cowboy and his horse, but the relationship between a sheep herder and his trained dog was just as special, as Mary Berry Cook made poignantly clear to her sister Ruth:

WE HAVE JUST HEARD of the boys [Ralph and Sam] loss. They have lost their dog and are feeling badly about it. He was about the nicest dog in the valey, and they won't be able to get another. He was worth fifty dollars to them for He was the best trained dog around here, and they can not replace him. They have a pup but he is not going to make as good a herder as the other. Has not the <u>sence</u>. Spot understood everything that was said to him. He had the prettiest fur—long and as fine as silk—We think more of our dogs out here than you do there [in Maine] of the hired men.[95]

Winnecook Ranch, c. 1890. The year the Berry family began what would become the Winnecook Ranch Corporation, the census in the Musselshell Valley, Montana, showed that twenty-five percent of the population had come from Maine, the most from any state.

THE MONTANA FAMILIES

Ironically while wild dogs could devastate the sheep industry by attacking bands of sheep, domesticated dogs that herded and guarded sheep were crucial to its success.

By the fall of 1880 Ralph, Evie, and Sam Berry had sold Meadow Bluff Ranch in the Smith River Valley and had moved into the neighboring Upper Musselshell Valley where they established the Berry Brothers' Ranch. Later called Winnecook Ranch in honor of Winnecook Lake (Unity Pond) located in their birthplace of Unity, Maine, it would stay in the Berry family for the next one hundred and twelve years. The previous year Ben and Mary Berry Cook had also made changes in their lives by selling out their share of the Cook ranch. While the family back East was surprised, Evie Kelley Berry seemed to understand Ben and Mary's motivation.

> [BEN] HAS BEEN contemplating a change in his business for some time. There is too much care on a sheep ranch for Maym too, and even if one has help about the general housework there is much to see after and care for. When men do the work they do not save much, they rather let things go but a woman with any ambition at all cannot do so and the care on so extensive a ranch as Cook's is not small.[96]

From the time Mary first arrived in Montana she had written home about the overwhelming family of pilgims living on the Cook ranch, but in the spring of 1879 the situation reached a crisis point. "There is a crowd at the ranch as usual," she wrote to her mother, "[but I] shall not stay there through the busy season, as I can not do the work, and it will be unpleasant where there are so many men. Ben thinks of changing his present location & perhaps his business."[97] No doubt for the health of their marriage they did sell most everything they owned on the Cook ranch in 1879, and Ben and Mary planned to set up housekeeping alone, as Mary wrote her sister Ruth:

> AS I HAVE WRITTEN you several times the Cook ranch is always crowded with commers and goers beside all the regular herders & workmen and we thought it much pleasanter to have a home by ourselves, beside I couldn't stand the housework, and it is impos-

sible to get anyone but a china man[98] to cook. Then I don't like to live in a place like a hotel where you are never alone, and when we settle and have a home of our own there will be <u>one</u> Cook house that won't keep open doors for everybody and everything, if I am mistress of it: I like company but to be over run with Tom, Dick and Harry I will not. Don't let anyone out of the family read this.[99]

Mary and Ben never did "settle and have a home" of their own, as Mary's mother's prophecy that their marriage would only last five years seemed to come true after all.

The family story claims that Mary Berry Cook "never cared for life on [the] ranch."[100] That may be true insofar as her life on the ranch with all those pilgrims never gave her privacy or enough time alone with Ben to forge a solid marriage in the crucial first year. Apparently they traveled some together for the next couple of years and "spent considerable money," but Mary and Ben "never lived together much after awhile."[101] The family story contends that Ben eventually "took to drinking" and Mary "came home [to Maine] and lived with her people."[102] In the fall of 1880 Ben and Mary were in Unity, Maine, together and their only child Harold Berry Cook was born there in February 1881.[103]

Maine women who went to Montana often came home when they gave birth for the first time, returning West when their babies were older and stronger. There is no evidence that Mary ever returned to Montana after her son's birth. Ben did return and continued in the sheep business into the 1890s, although there is no mention of who did the work in Mary's absence. Then Ben opened a "furniture and undertaking business," and from 1900 to 1906 he was the chief of police in Great Falls, Montana, dying there in 1920.[104] Mary Berry Cook lived in Unity with her sister Ruth until the age of eighty-two. Her cousin James Berry Vickery III who was eighteen at the time of her death in 1935 wrote that Mary "always seemed to me a very beautiful old lady. Her white hair curled in front, and a black velvet choker ab[ou]t her throat, beautiful large brown eyes, was a romantic person, like to talk of [the] past, was rather sad looking at times—I always liked her very much."[105] Ben and Mary's son Harold or Hall apparently continued the tradition of living an itinerant ranch life and died in Great Falls, Montana, in 1936.[106]

Mary's brothers continued ranching in Montana, although Sam

Sisters Ruth Berry (left) and Mary Ellen Berry Cook (right), c. 1930, Unity, Maine. "Mary E. Cook always seemed to me a very beautiful old lady ... liked to talk of past, was rather sad looking at times."

sold his share of the Berry Brothers' Ranch to Ralph and Evie for $10,000 in September 1882. In January 1883 Sam Berry II and Florence Ellen Bartlett were married in Unity, and Sam appeared to settle for a while in Maine. He still had investments in sheep ranching in Montana, however, and while visiting there in the spring of 1885 he died of complications from pneumonia at the age of twenty-nine. He never knew his daughter Sybil Samuel Berry who was born later that fall.[107] Ralph Berry's summation of his brother Samuel Stillman Berry II's life captures the essence of nineteenth-century New England values: "There is no consolation in death, but there is consolation in knowing that he lived an honest, honorable and upright life and that his years

*Husband Samuel Stillman Berry II (1856–1885) and wife
Florence Bartlett Berry (1856–1899), c. 1883, Maine. They
represent the unfathomable mixture of joy and despair that is
the meaning of life across time and place.*

were years of industry. I hope that when I am summoned, I shall be as
well prepared."[108] Ralph need not have worried; the next twenty-six
years were remarkable years of industry.

In 1887 Ralph took on Frank Webster as his partner at Winnecook Ranch. Frank was a Maine man and a relative of sorts since he
was a nephew of Charles and Ann Kelley Webster, Evie Kelley Berry's
sister and her husband who were also ranching in Montana. Evie was in
Unity, Maine, at this time where she gave birth to twin boys in March
1887. Only one of the boys survived and he was named Samuel Stillman Berry III, and was called Stillman. Because he was so frail he and

Evie stayed in Maine until he was two years old. When Evie finally returned to Montana, she and Stillman lived in White Silver Springs and not on the ranch sixty miles away from town, presumably because of Stillman's health. Or perhaps like her sister-in-law Mary Berry Cook, Evie did not relish living in the hotel-like environment of the ranch with her young son. Winnecook Ranch was a gathering spot for pilgrims from Maine much as the Cook ranch had been, according to Frank Webster's wife Sadie Lord Webster.

THIS LAST WEEK we have had a houseful.... Last Friday night there were fourteen of us and it has been from ten to that number ever since ... Neva [Stevens Clark] and Frank Clark, Lizzie [Webster] and Sam [Kelley Webster], Nell [Hamilton?] and Ben Stevens.... Yesterday after dinner they went away[.] Lizzie went home with Neva on the roadcart, Frank Clark and Sam went away on horseback each leading a horse with the girls saddles on them; we were all out to see them off. Mr. [Ralph] Berry said add a few Brayleys and Reynolds to the crowd and it would really be a Unity outfit.[109]

In 1894 Ralph Berry bought out Frank Webster who established his own ranch nearby. With nearly 25,000 sheep Ralph was now, in his own words, "the largest [single] sheepman in Montana."[110] At the turn of the century he entered into a successful partnership with Melzer Stevens, another Maine man, and the number of their sheep reached 40,000. In 1900 there were six million sheep in Montana, making it the number one wool-growing state in the country.[111] By this time Evie and Stillman had moved to Redlands, California, in the San Bernardino Valley for both Stillman's health and his education. Early in their son's life it became clear to Evie and Ralph that he was not suited for the rigors of ranch life in Montana. Indeed, they never even took Stillman to visit the ranch until he was twenty-two years old, though he lived only sixty miles away in White Silver Springs when he was a child.[112]

Stillman had serious ear and throat problems that left him partially deaf and his general health, as his personal physician described it, was "never robust."[113] A great part of Ralph Berry's drive in the sheep business came from his concern for his son Stillman's future. "You know

Samuel "Stillman" Berry III (1887–1984), c. 1897.
Early in their son's life it became clear to Evie and
Ralph that he was not suited for the rigors of ranch
life in Montana.

how anxious I am to reach the $200,000 mark within the next year and therefore have sufficient means to take us through and have enough left for Stillman in case he should always be in poor health," wrote Ralph to Evie in the late 1890s. "If he was all right, I would not feel that way for I know his intellect is a fortune in itself."[114] Despite his poor health it was obvious to his family when Stillman was still a boy that he would become a scholar.

While Ralph worked to provide for Stillman—and to provide for his mother and sister in Maine, and his brother James Edwin Berry and his family in California, as well as managing the Montana investments of his widowed sister-in-law Florence Bartlett Berry—Evie dedicated her life to tending to Stillman and guarding his health.[115] Ralph was spending much of his time in St. Paul, Minnesota, which had become the center for doing business in the sheep industry out West. Thus Evie and Ralph lived apart a good part of their lives after Stillman was born, and one might speculate on the strength of Evie and Ralph's marriage to withstand such long separations. On a quest to consult an ear specialist in Switzerland, Evie even took Stillman on a trip around the world in the early 1900s. At the same time Ralph was absent during most of Stillman's youth, and Stillman was never able to resolve the hurt he felt from the lack of his father's attention.[116] By the time that Stillman graduated from Stanford University with a bachelor's degree in zoology in 1909, and then his master's degree from Harvard University in 1910, Ralph was spending more time in Redlands with Evie. He had incorporated the ranch, sold stock in the Winnecook Land and Livestock Company, and hired Ben Stevens (another Mainer) as the general manager in 1906, making it possible for him to leave Montana for longer periods. It also freed capital for Ralph to invest in real estate in Redlands and Cuba.[117]

Evie Kelley Berry (far left) and Ralph Berry (far right) in front of Winnecook Ranch, 1909. Ralph Berry incorporated the ranch, sold stock in the Winnecook Land and Livestock Company, and hired Ben Stevens (another Mainer) as the general manager in 1906.

Evie Kelley Berry (center), c. 1909, Winnecook Ranch. In the years after Ralph's death Evie and her son Stillman gained controlling interest in the ranch and were both elected to the Winnecook Board of Directors.

Sixty-year-old Ralph Berry died in June 1911 in Redlands, California, from what started as an ear infection and culminated in a diabetic coma. Evie and Stillman brought his body back to Maine, and the "Pioneer Ranchman of White Sulpher Springs and Winnecook Montana" was buried in Unity Pond Cemetery with his ancestors.[118] In the years after Ralph's death Evie and Stillman gained controlling interest in the ranch and were both elected to the Winnecook Board of Directors, though they continued to live together in Redlands, California, until Evie died in 1940. After Stillman completed his Ph.D. in marine zoology at Stanford in 1913, he began to spend longer periods at the ranch in Montana and became the president of the Winnecook Ranch Corporation in 1917. Stillman loved to roam the ranch lands looking for flora, fauna, and artifacts, but he did not like working the sheep. In the 1930s he delegated the day-to-day ranch operations and entrusted the ranch finances to a series of resident managers. Henceforth, S. Stillman Berry III only visited the ranch to attend the annual corporation meet-

The Berry Family, Unity, Maine, 1910. Left to right front row: unidentified girl, S. Stillman Berry III, Sybil Samuel Berry ("the other SSB"). Left to right back row: Ann Kelley Webster, unidentified woman, unidentified man, Ruth Berry, Mary Berry Cook, unidentified man.

ing each summer, although he would remain its president and most earnest guardian for the rest of his life.[119]

In 1880, the year the Berry family began what would become the Winnecook Ranch Corporation, the census in the Musselshell Valley showed that 25 percent of the population had come from Maine, the most from any state.[120] Many of these Maine pilgrims were from Waldo County and they formed a significant segment of "the Maine colony in Montana," as the *Republican Journal* described it.[121] Rather than a colony, however, these "pilgrims" saw themselves as an interdependent family of relatives, neighbors, and friends, who gave and expected mutual support in a new country. But, there was a downside to this interdependent ranch family mutuality. As historian Michael Zuckerman points out in his eighteenth-century community study *Peaceable Kingdoms*, mutuality also occasioned the "self-suppression of individualism."[122] There was certainly some repression of individual aspirations for the sake of the common good in ranch family mutuality in Montana. One example was the ending of Ben and Mary Berry Cook's marriage, which might have flourished if they had more privacy from "pilgrims" and freedom from ceaseless ranch family responsibilities. Ruth Berry— Ralph, Sam II, and Mary's sister who was left behind in Maine to care for their parents and never married—was another example. What yearnings and plans did she put aside so that her brothers and sister could go West?

The western Berry family story challenges the notion that "family" has only meant the nuclear family throughout history, and it encourages us, as historian Linda Gordon suggests, "to examine families both as having collective interests and as battlegrounds for competing interests."[123] The Berry family experience was in contrast to the experience of their cousin Eli Ayer Vickery who went West in the late nineteenth century and created an independent family community with his western wife and their eleven children.

THE WESTERN VICKERYS

I KNEW JAMES VICKERY [I] *and his brother Newman and their father Eli. I went to school with James Vickery [I]'s son Eli [Ayer] who, I think, went West and died there. We were very good friends in those days and I admired him as a jolly joker.*
—James E. Kelley to James Berry Vickery III, 4 December 1933[1]

$\mathcal{E}$ LI AYER VICKERY, the eldest son of James Berry I and Mary Ayer Vickery, was twenty-four years old when he first went to Montana in 1883. At the age of seventeen he had taught school for seven terms in Unity in order to earn enough money to attend Kent's Hill Academy, the school his grandfather Peter Ayer had founded.[2] But evidently Eli did not want to make teaching his career after leaving Kent's Hill. This is understandable; by this time most teachers were women and the pay was low. When his grandfather Eli Vickery died in 1877 his parents had gained complete control of the family farm on Quaker Hill in Unity, and Eli Ayer Vickery and his brothers David Earnest Vickery and John Ayer Vickery probably expected that their youngest brother James Berry Vickery II would inherit the farm, as had become the Vickery family custom.[3] Thus, the older sons Eli Ayer, David, and John pre-

The Vickery Homestead, Quaker Hill, Unity, Maine, c.1880.
"One of the finest situations in town." Left to right: David Earnest
Vickery, John Ayer Vickery, Mary Josephine "Josie" Vickery, Mother
Mary Ayer Vickery, Eli Ayer Vickery, James Berry Vickery II.

pared to make their own ways away from the Vickery family farm, albeit
with some help from their father.

David Earnest Vickery visited the West, but decided to spend most
of his life in Unity, later becoming the proprietor of a general store in
Pittsfield, Maine. He never married, though apparently he was engaged
at one time. John Ayer Vickery became very successful in the shoe business, one of Maine's most important industries after the Civil War. He
and Emily Shepard Nickerson from Brewer, Maine, married and settled
in South Brewer. The Vickery brothers' only sister Mary Josephine
Vickery, who was called "Josie," never married, though family papers
note that she had a "romance with Lou Sherman." Daughters who did
not marry were expected to stay home and take care of their parents in

Left: David Earnest Vickery (1865–1911), c. 1890. The proprietor of a general store in Pittsfield, Maine, he never married, though apparently he was engaged at one time.

Right: John Ayer Vickery (1868–1924), c. 1920. A civic and social leader who was "a valued and highly esteemed member" of his community of Brewer, Maine, he was also "one of the foremost individuals having to do with the business of the State" having helped develop the important shoe industry in Maine after the Civil War.

old age. In the same family papers the words "mentally ill" beside Josie's name suggests that she may have needed to be taken care of herself.

Unlike his brothers, Eli Ayer went West and stayed. One account says he left for Montana in 1883 with twenty-six men from Unity. Another says that just he and Elisha Clark left together that year.[4] One way or the other, once he arrived in Montana he set out in a separate direction. Contrary to the rest of the Unity community Eli Ayer did not make a pilgrimage to the Cook ranch in White Sulpher Springs. While Ralph Berry was his second cousin, he did not join him on the Winnecook Ranch in the Musselshell Valley either, nor is there any evidence that the Berry family and Eli Ayer ever had any contact out West.[5]

Eli Ayer came back to Unity briefly in 1886, then returned to Montana to settle permanently. After some time in Montana, he must

*Left: Mary Josephine "Josie" Vickery (1862–1946),
c. 1885. Josie never married, though family papers note
that she had a "romance with Lou Sherman."*

*Right: Eli Ayer Vickery (1859–1914), c. 1889.
Unlike his brothers, Eli Ayer went West and stayed.*

have decided that becoming a merchant offered him the best opportunity for success, because he went to Big Timber, Montana, about seventy miles southeast of White Sulpher Springs and southwest of the Musselshell, and with two people who did not seem to have Unity connections, he opened a general store under the name of "Budd, Kellogg, and Vickery." Perhaps he returned home to secure the capital to invest in the store and to ask advice from his family, as two of his brothers were businessmen. Considering the travel pattern of most of the Montana emigrants who came back to Maine in the fall and returned West in the spring, Eli Ayer could well have been home in Unity when his seventy-seven-year-old grandmother Clarissa Berry Vickery died in November 1886. Family notes maintain that she had a "bad heart," although the notice of her death in the *Belfast [Maine]City Press* stated that she died "very suddenly of heart disease."[6] Clarissa was buried next to her husband Eli in the Unity cemetery encircled by the fences that he had so carefully kept in good repair during his years as a selectman. To affirm that Clarissa's eternal life was assured the *Belfast City Press* also put on record that, "Mrs. Vickery was a member of the Congregational church, and lived a life consistent with its teachings."[7]

In 1882 the Northern Pacific Railroad reached Big Timber, Montana, making it an important wool market and shipping point. It would have been a favorable place to open a general store to sell necessities to sheep ranchers after they hauled thousands of pounds of wool into town. The Budd, Kellogg, and Vickery general store would have sold all sorts of goods like groceries, hardware, tools, and dry goods such as bolts of cotton calico, linen, and silks, laces, and sewing needs. Prices in Eli Ayer's store would have been high, as it was expensive to ship goods from the East to stock the shelves of stores in Montana. One of the first things that Mary Berry Cook wrote home about was the high prices merchants commanded for simple items:

> THE MOST ONE NEEDS here is a good supply of calico dresses, and one nice dress to wear when one goes into Helena, as there people are very dressy. I am going to get some calico and go over to Mrs. Lewis and make it up. Little things costs everything I paid 75 cts for two papers of pins & one of hairpins. So when Evie comes out [West] she wants to get a good supply of such articles, for here they don't sell anything for less than seventy five cts.[8]

The Budd, Kellogg, and Vickery general store also stocked bustles, a kind of pad or framework that women wore below their waists to give fullness to their skirts. In 1889 Eli Ayer Vickery met his future wife Carrie Jerusha Brandenburg when he sold her a bustle.[9]

Carrie Jerusha Brandenburg was born on a farm in Shamrock, Calloway County, Missouri, in August 1869. According to family legend Carrie's great-great-great-grandfather Solomon Brandenburg was a member of the royal Hohenzollern family in Germany. Because he married a Jewish woman "against the family wishes" he was "disinherited and his heritage confiscated." Solomon's only son Matthias emigrated to Virginia and settled on the Potomac River with his wife, probably sometime in the first half of the eighteenth century. Their son Joseph Brandenburg and Delilah Vesser married and moved west to Kentucky. Joseph and Delilah's son Jonathan Brandenburg and a woman named Smith married and moved even further west to Missouri. Their son and his wife Samuel and Alverda Murray Brandenburg were the parents of Carrie Brandenburg.[10]

When Carrie was ten years old her mother died. Alverda Murray Brandenburg had given birth to at least seven children in sixteen years beginning in 1863. The average two-year span between her pregnancies

---

Carrie Jerusha Brandenburg (1869–1960), c. 1888. According to family legend Carrie's great-great-great-grandfather Solomon Brandenburg was a member of the royal Hohenzollern family in Germany.

suggests that she died in 1879 giving birth. In a letter that Carrie wrote to her nephew James Berry Vickery III in 1936, she explains succinctly what happened after her mother died: "In less than a year my father too, died. Then our home was broken up—the farm sold and we children brot to Montana."[11] Carrie and the other children were brought to Montana in the spring of 1881 by her seventeen-year-old brother Jay to live with their mother's sister Sue Murray Hunter and her husband Dr. Andrew Jackson Hunter.[12] The Hunters had taken "squatters rights" to the hot springs area about twenty miles west of Big Timber in the early 1870s and developed it into a well-known health resort called Hunter's Hot Springs.[13] Carrie lived with her aunt and uncle at the springs for two years, attending school in nearby Bozeman. In 1883, however, she returned to Missouri to attend Christian College in Camden Point, just outside Kansas City.[14] Early frontier colleges were really equivalent to high schools and considering Carrie was about fourteen years old at this time, Christian College probably gave her a high-school education.[15] After five years away, following a visit to cousins in Missouri and Kentucky, Carrie came back to Montana once and for all in 1888. She settled this time in Big Timber where her married oldest sister Mary Susan "Mamie" Brandenburg Yule and her youngest sister Emma Brandenburg lived, and she began to teach school.[16]

As the family story goes, one auspicious day Carrie rode "sidesaddle" to the Budd, Kellogg, and Vickery general store to buy a bustle to finish a dressmaking project on which she and her aunt had been working, and "met there her future husband" Eli Ayer Vickery.[17] Marriages on the Western Frontier, as historian Lillian Schlissel has found in her research of women's diaries, "arose out of a sense of mutual congeniality and the conviction that a man and a woman together were necessary to do the work of living on the frontier." Thus, men and women were "free to follow their inclinations, and weddings were made expeditiously."[18] Eli Ayer and Carrie obviously felt this "mutual congeniality," followed their inclination, and were married on 20 November 1889 in her sister and brother-in-law Alec and Mamie Brandenburg Yule's home. Shortly after their wedding Eli Ayer and Carrie traded his interest in the general store for rangeland located between Big Timber and Columbus, Montana, on White Beaver Creek not far from the Yellowstone River.

Eli Ayer and Carrie Brandenburg Vickery with their first child Edgar Ayer Vickery, Montana, c. 1890. Family papers state "Edgar's birth was assisted by Dr. Craig, another Unity man."

Echoing the pioneering days in Unity, Maine, of Eli Ayer's great-grandparents David II and Sarah Stone Vickery, he and Carrie built a ranch house of logs from the surrounding wooded hills. They bought a small herd of cattle and awaited the birth of their first child. When Carrie's time came in August 1890, they traveled twenty-five miles back to Big Timber "over rough roads in a lumber wagon," surely a painful journey for a woman about to give birth. But Carrie would have wanted to be with her sisters, no doubt, when her son Edgar Ayer Vickery was born. Family papers state that "Edgar's birth was assisted by Dr. Craig, another Unity man."[19]

Eli Ayer next invested in a band of sheep for the Vickery ranch with the encouragement of a banker in Big Timber who promised to "loan him all the money he needed," using the ranch as collateral of course. "With the good range he could just as well run both sheep and cattle," advised the banker, and Eli Ayer surely knew that he needed to invest in the ranch if it were going to expand and make a profit.[20] There is no evidence that Eli Ayer Vickery ever wrote home to borrow money. Reminiscent of small farms back in Maine, many small ranch operations out West like Eli Ayer and Carrie's were just making ends meet, however, and had no cash reserves to survive economic downturns or extreme weather conditions. Thus, after a particularly harsh winter, followed by a financial depression in the early 1890s, the bank foreclosed on the Vickery ranch, or so the official family version reads.[21] "However," wrote James Berry Vickery III, "my father [JBV II] told me that he watched his brother play poker one afternoon, and [he] lost [the ranch] in this card game. (This was never mentioned by the family.)"[22] Regardless of how, Eli Ayer and Carrie lost the ranch. One of the appeals of the West was the ease with which people could remake themselves. In that spirit, Eli Ayer and Carrie, who were expecting another child, loaded up a wagon and moved with their toddler Edgar down the road to Columbus to start over.

Columbus is close to both the Yellowstone River and the Stillwater River and like Big Timber it was a major wool-shipping destination. It was in the Columbus/Stillwater area in January 1893 that their daughter Mary Alverda who was called "Allie" was born, quite possibly in the tent in which the family now lived. Giving birth in a tent, in a wagon, or by the side of the road during storms or the bitter cold of winter was a commonplace event for settlers in the West, and many women delivered their babies alone or only with the help of their husbands.[23] Yet, while this was part of everyday life, one cannot help but imagine the risks of giving birth in a tent in January "in a cold blizzard and way below zero," and the anxiety Carrie must have felt.[24] There is no mention of a doctor attending Allie's birth.

Eli Ayer and Carrie did whatever they could around Columbus to support their growing family. Eli Ayer cut and put up hay. Then he harvested timber for the first bridge built across the Yellowstone River. While caring for two small children, Carrie cooked for the crews of men wherever Eli Ayer worked, catching trout in the nearby rivers to feed them. In April 1893 Eli Ayer's twenty-one-year-old brother James Berry Vickery II arrived from Unity, Maine, to join them. One of James II's first jobs in Montana was to tighten the bolts on the newly constructed Yellowstone Bridge. It seems, however, that Eli Ayer might have asked his brother to come out West because he wanted or needed James II, or "Uncle Jim" as he was called, to help him with a new scheme for making money—placer mining for gold.

In essence, a "placer" is the place, usually a stream or creek, where a glacier has deposited particles of the gold it has eroded from large disintegrating veins of ore. "Placer mining" is the process of digging placers with a pick and shovel, or scooping sand on a stream bottom, then washing the dirt in a flat pan or dredging it in a sluice box in order to

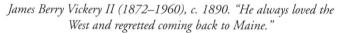

James Berry Vickery II (1872–1960), c. 1890. "He always loved the West and regretted coming back to Maine."

separate the dust, flakes, or nuggets of gold. Although it demanded persistence, placer gold was called "poor man's diggings" because it took little investment or special skills to mine it.[25] Often others in better financial positions furnished supplies or funds called a "grub stake" to mining prospectors for a share in the gold they discovered. In 1893 Eli Ayer and Carrie Brandenburg Vickery were grub staked for a placer mine claim on the Clark's Fork River just across the border in Wyoming. It is not clear how Eli Ayer and Carrie came to own this claim. One source said Eli Ayer had invested in it when he owned the general store in Big Timber.[26] Another said he paid someone fifty dollars for it.[27] And still another states that "one of the prospectors that Eli Ayer had grub staked while in the store, offered to trade his gold claim over on the Clark's Fork in payment of his debt."[28] That fall Eli Ayer, Carrie who was expecting another child, three-year-old Edgar, and baby Allie, along with "Uncle Jim," a "cow puncher" named Dan Doty, and another married couple Tom and Abbie Sawyer Trial, loaded up the wagon and headed for Clark's Fork River.[29] "Tho it was the beginning of long years of pioneering," Carrie sentimentally wrote years later, "our hearts were young and hopeful and nothing daunted [us] as we faced the future."[30]

It was unusual for Eli Ayer's family to join him working a placer claim. Because placer mining was cheap and easy it attracted mostly young single men with a get-rich-quick attitude who stampeded from one temporary placer town to another when new gold was found, or even rumored to be found. Mining camps and towns also attracted a good number of dubious characters, thieves, and crooks; crime and murder were common; and violent gangs of bandits on the open road called road agents followed the gold rush from placer to placer. In the early years before organized federal and local law enforcement, vigilantes who were in turn gangs of citizens attempted to provide order by tracking down criminals and hanging them on the spot. By 1893 the state of Montana was governed by the United States Constitution and depended on courts of law and trial by jury to keep the peace and citizens safe and vigilantism was not sanctioned.[31] Sometimes, however, away from settled areas people still had to protect themselves. It took the Vickery family and their traveling companions two weeks to reach Clark's Fork River. They camped along their way south and stopped at several ranches of acquaintances, one of whom was Frank Clark, another

"Unity man." Somewhere along their route they were accosted by a road agent who demanded to see their "passports." At that point, according to the legend, Eli Ayer Vickery pulled out his Colt 44 and countered, "Here it is!" The Vickery entourage continued its journey unscathed.[32]

Reaching the placer claim on Clark's Fork about sixty miles north-west of Yellowstone Park, the Vickerys and their group set up tents and proceeded to build more substantial shelter. They constructed one-room dugout cabins with walls made from drift logs collected in the river. These cabins had dirt floors coated with black sand and covered with "gunny sacks" and ceilings roofed with canvas.[33] Resonating with historic overtones, the family story contends that the dugout cabins were ready for the Vickery family to move into on Thanksgiving Day 1893, and they celebrated the occasion with "a wild goose dinner." The rest of that first winter at Clark's Fork they lived on "jackrabbits and sage hens."[34] While Eli Ayer and Carrie and their children lived in one dugout cabin that would be their home for the next seven years, "Uncle Jim" had his own dugout. There were probably several more such cab-ins, as there were a number of others who joined the Vickerys at or near the same placer claim.[35] Placer mining was impossible to do in winter and high-water times, but since it was a mild fall the claim was "work[ed] some before it froze up."[36]

Next the Vickerys and the other miners built sluices in the river. A sluice is a long inclined wooden trough that holds quicksilver and catches the gold in sediments as water flushes through it when a flood-gate on one end is opened. Quicksilver or mercury helped to collect the gold by amalgamation. While others washed the dirt in the sluices, Car-rie Vickery shifted the gold particles into small bottles that were later taken to Helena, Montana.[37] Gold dust was the circulating medium at this time, and each place of business had its own scales where it would be weighed and then used to make purchases.[38] This inexpensive method of placer mining had mostly been abandoned by this time as the mining industry invested in heavy machinery and mills to extract the larger and more lucrative "mother lodes" of silver and copper found deeper in the earth. Most of the men who were looking for get-rich-quick diggings went on to the Black Hills in Dakota Territory when gold was discovered there in 1876, and then later to the Yukon in 1897.

The Vickery family would soon turn away from placer mining as well—high water that washed away their mining equipment helped to make that decision—and they took up homesteading.[39]

Wool growing was still one of the most important industries in Montana and its Wyoming border in the early 1890s, but agricultural homesteading was steadily increasing.[40] Since Eli Ayer and Carrie had decided to settle permanently at Clark's Fork, they established a homestead, or farm—returning to the life in which they both had been raised.[41] They filed a homestead claim on 160 acres adjoining their placer claim, and later filed for another 160-acre claim (another source says three hundred and sixty acres[42]) under the Desert Land Act of 1877. This act sold western desert or dry land for $1.25 an acre with only a twenty-five-cents-per-acre down payment to those who promised to irrigate part of it. The land in this area had only recently opened for homesteading, having been ceded by Crow Native Americans. The Vickerys dug irrigation ditches from Bennett Creek, cleared sagebrush, fenced in fields, built barns and corrals, and planted oats, alfalfa, and vegetables, which Eli Ayer took north to Red Lodge, Montana, to sell. All the while Eli Ayer and Carrie continued to add to their family. When Emma Christine was born in April 1894, Eli Ayer went ten miles down the Clark's Fork River to get an early homesteader named Mary Coates "Ma" Sirrine to help with her birth.[43] The next April Dorothy Brandenburg was born. As an adult Dorothy Vickery recollected what her mother Carrie told her about this time:

> [MOTHER] WAS ALWAYS READY to let any of us go when a call for help came … no doubt recalling the many times when she so sorely needed someone to see her through a very trying experience…. How many times she bore the pain of childbirth with all its attendant demands, and with so little compared to today's supplies for need, and for comfort. I recall her saying after my premature birth she lay 27 days without her hair being combed. Father was building sluice boxes preparatory for the "gold rush" days before high water, and could spend little time with her…. So difficult to find anyone to come in but finally got a 16 year old girl to look after the children and stand by to call Father when changes were needed for mother or babe. Neighbors were so few

and far in those days, no telephone, and the nearest woman neighbor 12 miles down and across the river so that the horses had to swim across at the fordable times of the year. It was 25 miles to town [Red Lodge] up and over a narrow mountain, taking two or three days to make the round trip.[44]

Eli Ayer and Carrie's next child Carol Louise was born in May 1897, and then Elizabeth Chase was born in April 1899. When Elizabeth, the fifth Vickery girl was born her sister Dorothy said she remembered seeing her "Papa" standing with the newborn in his arms. "We've got a baby," he said, "She should have been a boy."[45] Carrie had a different view of the matter and wrote, "each year a pig, chickens, more cows, and another baby girl."[46] These were the last of Eli Ayer and Carrie's children born in the dugout cabin at their old placer-mine claim.

By the turn of the twentieth century placer mining was a part of Eli Ayer and Carrie Vickery's past. They had put down firm roots literally and figuratively on their farm in what was now called Clark, Wyoming. "Uncle Jim" had gone back to Maine to help his and Eli Ayer's father and mother with the Unity family farm in the fall of 1895. In the spring of 1900 Eli Ayer and Carrie moved their family into a new and "better" home they made of logs about one-half mile from their dugout cabin. It had "a tiny kitchen, a large living room where they all ate, played, studied, and many of them slept at night," and "a tiny bedroom" that was Carrie and Eli Ayer's. Later they added a new room that became the "boys' room."[47] About every two years until 1908 another Vickery child was born. William "Ted" Theodore, named for William McKinley and Theodore Roosevelt (Eli Ayer was a staunch Republican) was the first born in their new home in June 1901 and according to his sister Dorothy it was an unforgettable event, no doubt because "Papa" finally got another boy:

THEN TED DECIDED to join the family and that was one time Father's prayers were truly answered. Both Ted and Mother had a very difficult birth unfoldment because Ted attempted coming through hind-foremost. A doctor was sent for from Red Lodge [Montana]. He brought his pretty nurse along and they got lost in the hills somewhere near Clark's Fork Canyon, finally reaching the ranch near 4 A.M. In the meantime Father, with God's help, persuaded the long-looked-for boy to reverse itself enough to get through the doorway and be spanked into breathing and a lusty yell…. Well, you know Mother. She finally relaxed and was beginning to recover her valiant spirit when the doctor arrived. Nothing for him to do but look at her and marvel that Father had accomplished everything in perfect order and cleanliness, but was pretty beat out by the experience. The Doctor? Oh, he took himself off for home and sent a bill for $25.00 for the call.[48]

Dorothy Vickery's story about her brother Ted's birth hints at changing experiences with childbearing in the United States and changes

Eli Ayer and Carrie Brandenburg Vickery Family, Wyoming, c. 1902.
A group of Mormon men from Utah ribbed Eli, assuring him that with such a large family he would be made bishop in the Mormon Church. Left to right: Mary "Allie" Alverda, Emma Christine, Papa Eli Ayer with William Theodore, Dorothy Brandenburg (back), Mother Carrie with Elsie Belle, Carol Louise (front), Elizabeth Chase, Edgar Ayer.

THE MONTANA FAMILIES

especially on the Western Frontier at this time. First, when Carrie sensed that Ted's birth had complications, there actually was a doctor and a nurse close enough to summon.[49] After attending the birth of six children Eli Ayer would have had enough experience to "accomplish everything in perfect order and cleanliness," and indeed not so many years before a husband might have been expected to be prepared to deliver his own child out West regardless of the complications. Yet the doctor who would have needed the assistance of a "pretty nurse" marveled at his capabilities. The professionalization of medicine gave doctors more authority now in childbirth and while this doctor might have felt his importance diminished he still expected to be paid for his time.

In rapid fire after Ted's birth the rest of Eli Ayer and Carrie's eleven children were born: Elsie Belle in September 1902, Frederick Brandenburg in September 1903, James "Jim" Vincent in September 1905, and finally Jack Mason in May 1908. When baby Jim was born Allie said it was a "hot September and flies were bad.... We girls took turns waving flies from Mother." When Jack, the last Vickery child was born Allie recalled that, "some neighbor woman came one day and said, 'Where will you put another baby?' Mother replied, 'The Lord will provide a way.'" Allie remembered her father as well saying one day "how thankful they should be for babies strong, bright, and perfect in body," and he planted a cottonwood tree to celebrate the birth of each Vickery child.[50]

With eleven children Eli Ayer and Carrie were certainly not following the birth control trend in the United States. Since the middle of the nineteenth century the drop in fertility rates in all parts of the country made it apparent that couples were consciously limiting the number of children to whom they gave birth. By the end of the century the average urban middle-class white family had only three or four children, down from the mid-century total of five. Families wanted fewer children so that they could spend more quality time and finances on each child's development.[51] Eli and Carrie Vickery's family planning strategy, however, still made sense in rural America when as many children as one could have were welcomed and needed to work on the family farm. Not far from the Vickery farm at this time lived a group of Mormon men from Utah who apparently ribbed Eli Ayer about having such a large family and tried to convert him, assuring him that with such a large family he would be made a bishop in the Mormon church.[52]

There is no denying the hard work of taking care of eleven children, but Carrie did have some help. The Vickery family had hired a girl to help with the cooking and the children at least until the first Vickery girls were old enough to help care for the younger ones. While the Vickerys' was a loving home, Eli Ayer and Carrie ran a disciplined household where each child knew his or her duty and place. As Carol explained, "The razor strap in our home was never used for anything except keeping father's straight-edged razor sharp" because a frown from Papa Eli was enough to make the children behave.[53] Dorothy remembered that the Vickery dining table

Eli Ayer and Carrie Brandenburg Vickery, Wyoming, c. 1900.
"In looking forward too much to the 'Tomorrow of Happiness'
that may never come we are apt to overlook many of the
little joys of life that [are] ours today."

WAS ALWAYS DRESSED UP same as for company every day with Mother's silver service…. Only fine china was used … and white linen table cloth. Father always served the plates from his side of the table after prayer had been said all around…. Mother at the opposite end of the table attending to the service of the beverages, teas, coffee, milk, and fruit juices, and the youngest children sat on either side of her so that she might keep them in order, and teach them the fundamentals of correct dining…. And woe be to any one who spoke out of turn or misbehaved in any way. They had to take their plate and eat their meal in the kitchen, company or not, for strict discipline was the order of the day, every day, year round, and blest was the family because of it.[54]

Carrie, like so many other western women, was fulfilling her duty in taming the Wild West by using the family's finery everyday and insisting that the children learn proper middle-class etiquette. Company was always welcomed at the Vickery table, and after church services as many as twenty-five people would show up at the Vickery home for Sunday dinner. The family joked that the final hymn after the Sunday service "On to Victory" was often paraphrased "On to Vickerys."[55]

Meals at the Vickerys' included "gallons of fresh spinach from the garden" prepared with whipped cream and newly churned butter, topped with sliced hard-boiled eggs; parsnips cooked with fresh pork slices; "large kettles of corn on the cob, potatoes in the skins"; and large loaves of homemade bread, "crusty and brown." On the table "there was always a salad or cottage cheese garnished with watercress from the spring house 100 yard from the house" and "a gallon or so of rich buttermilk for fresh drinking." In March and April donuts were fried in a "kettle nearly full of smoking hot ranch fat," part pure lard from their own pig and part sweet suet from a "young cow critter" butchered on the ranch. Next came "early rhubarb for sauces and pies," and in summer "the favorite meat dish was roasting spring fryers" and "hot biscuits turned out at the last minute," and of course trout caught from the nearby river. The Vickery children were "trained to eat everything that was put on" their plates and of course at an early age, the Vickery girls helped gather vegetables, make butter, and prepare the large meals.[56]

The meals had not always been so bountiful, however, and as one of the eldest children Carol remembered, when "grace was said over meager meals, and [while] there was conversation, never was there complaining, or mention of lack."[57]

Although the Vickery girls did hire out, helping neighbors when babies came, at threshing time, doing cooking and "anything there was to do," said Allie, there is no evidence that the Vickerys hired labor to do the agricultural work on their farm.[58] The Vickerys were their own labor force and as Carol claimed, "There was much to learn right there on the ranch and each child was placed in the making and keeping of the home[stead] according to their aptitude and abilities."[59] Allie recalled that Carrie taught the girls to sew, knit, crochet, and piece quilts, but Emma was the most talented seamstress and "was constantly sewing," helping to keep the children clothed. Both the boys and girls helped clear the land for planting, "grubbing out" sagebrush and making piles to burn, as well as collecting "light sagebrush sticks" to fuel the cookstove.[60] They all helped Papa butcher pigs. "Each of us," explained Dorothy, "was given something to scrape with and a cleaner, whiter pig skin has never since been found throughout the universe. No wonder we all enjoyed bone-rinds. All the highchair babes cut their teeth on them. The breakfast bacon plus rinds came from the brine well seasoned and luscious."[61] Allie remembered learning to dress chickens as well.

MY BROTHER AND I would scald one [chicken] each and then see who could get the feathers off the quickest.... We both got so we could pick a chicken a minute. Then we cooled them and dressed them (took out the entrails). It took three or four for our family, according to size. Father told me if I took all the care of the chickens, he would give me a third of what he made when he took the chickens to town. It was quite a job dressing out what he took. Anyway, when he came home he gave me a $10.00 bill as my third.[62]

The children also were taught to mend harnesses, shoe horses, and resole their own shoes. Dorothy remembered how they drove the "stacker team so the hay would roll just right for the buck rakes and the stacker," shaping the piles with their hands into a "well rounded load," sometimes weighing two hundred tons, and leaving the finished stacks

Elizabeth Chase Vickery (left), Emma Christine Vickery (center), Carol Louise Vickery (right), 1907. "Each year a pig, chickens, more cows, and another baby girl," declared Mother Carrie.

"right there in the field to hold firm through the winter."[63] They also stacked grain and fed "shiny bundles" of it into the threshing machine that separated the oats and wheat from the fodder. They worked in the "dark, earthy-smelling root cellar sprouting potatoes in the spring … one of the more unpleasant tasks" and scraped and cleaned the chicken house.[64] They gathered wild berries for jam, and Edgar and Allie as the two eldest took care of several beehives.[65] They all fed the chickens, lambs, and calves before milking their cow "Old Rose." While "there was no end to hard work both outside and in … it was more fun to do the outdoor farm work," said Carol.[66] The girls all clearly loved to be with Papa Eli.[67]

The Vickery children's academic education started before they were old enough to attend school. Allie said that her father "made a blackboard and Mother taught us our letters and numbers on that."[68] Later the older Vickery children attended school held in different homes in the area. In time Eli Ayer helped to build a log schoolhouse, becoming one of its trustees, and teachers were hired; the first boarded with the Vickery family for ten dollars a month. The schoolhouse was located about three or four miles from their home near Bennett Creek, and sometimes as Edgar, Allie, Emma, and four-year-old Dorothy walked to school "over rocky hills" and "sage and cacti land," and "across creeks," coyotes and wolves followed them at a distance.[69] Rattlesnakes were also a concern and according to one story, before the children were allowed to go out mornings, Carrie would take a "six shooter" to shoot the snakes after the family dog Kaiser rousted them.[70] Later the Vickery children traveled to school by buckboard pulled by their donkeys Mamie and George. School terms were usually three months long and were held during the winter and summer so school would not interfere

The Vickery children traveled to school by buckboard pulled by their donkeys Mamie and George, c. 1910.

with planting and harvest times when the children's labor would be needed at home.[71] This did not mean that their studies stopped though, as Carol described:

> MY PARENTS WERE NATURAL TEACHERS, they taught us chil-
> dren the foundations of all that we know, not only the three r's,
> but truth, honor, and fineness. After a long day's work was done
> and the chores finished by lantern light, we gathered around the
> long table and studied by the kerosene lamp. We took turns read-
> ing aloud books our parents provided for us. I vaguely remember
> them reading *A Tale of Two Cities* and *Les Miserables* at an early
> age, stories that were "clear over my head" but beloved by all.[72]

The children's religious education began at home as well. "We all knew a little bit about the Bible as Mother had taught us the Lord's Prayer, the Twenty-third Psalm and many other verses," said Allie.[73] Church services on Sunday were held in area schoolhouses with or without an itinerant minister. Many Protestant churches back East sent missionaries to "destitute frontier communities" out West to help women settlers establish a religious culture.[74] Because there might not be a specific church building, camp meetings, "love feasts" (a celebration of the Last Supper), revivals, and prayer meetings were often held outdoors or in schoolhouses. In 1901 a missionary family came to Clark's Fork and organized a Sunday school in the new one-room schoolhouse.[75]

Along with Sunday church services, the schoolhouse was also the site of other community cultural and social gatherings. The schoolhouse served as the voting booth, a dance hall, a theater where Christmas programs were presented, and a lending library. The lending library was one of Carrie Vickery's special projects, as it would be since as a woman her responsibility would be setting a moral tone for the community. To raise money for buying books "basket socials" were held where picnic baskets of prepared foods were auctioned off. "Carrie's box always took 'top honors' as every man would bid as high as he could afford to get Mrs. Vickery's box," wrote Carrie's granddaughter Eileen O'Shea Hyem relating a family legend.[76] "When we got ready to drive over to the schoolhouse for one of these events," remembered Carol, "Father would fill the wagon box with hay and all the children sat in the hay with

Father and Mother up on the one spring seat of the wagon. When we arrived the dear old team would be unhitched and tied at the end gate so they could munch hay while waiting for the return trip."[77]

The events of daily life were often turned into festivities at the Vickery homestead. In the summer and fall Papa Eli would take several of the children with him to Red Lodge, Montana, twenty-five miles away to trade garden produce for flour, sugar, lumber, and other supplies that might have to last for months. The trip took two days and it was a treat to stay at the Pollard Hotel, Red Lodge's first brick building. Their arrival back home was always a cause for celebration and the family "dressed up & went down the road to meet" them.[78] Carrie ensured that the children knew the meaning of national holidays and commemorated them. She made their first American flag from scraps of red, white, and blue fabric. One February a "patriotic party" was planned to celebrate the completion of a new room addition to the house. The children recited poems about Lincoln and Washington and neighbors joined them to dance to fiddle music on the new floor. The party turned into a three-day affair as a not uncommon sudden blizzard snowed in the guests. But one of the most memorable occasions on the Vickery homestead was the celebration in absentia of Papa Eli's parents James I and Mary Ayer Vickery's golden wedding anniversary on 18 March 1907. "Mother" Carrie "made the house festive with yellow crepe paper decorations, made golden corn bread, tied a yellow ribbon on the cat" and the Vickery children "wrote letters to their grandparents" in Unity, Maine, "describing the party."[79]

The party was all the more remarkable because except for Carol, who made a visit to her Vickery grandparents in Maine while she was working in Washington, D.C., during World War I, and Ted, who went to work on his "Uncle Jim's" Maine farm briefly in 1920, none of Eli Ayer and Carrie's other children ever met their grandparents.[80] Carol said "it was a source of grief to my Mother that none of the relatives ever got to see her babies."[81] There does seem to have been regular communication between eastern and western Vickerys. Grandmother Vickery sent a subscription of the *Youth's Companion* to the family, as well as a yearly "Missionary Barrel." Allie fondly recalled her father reading the *Youth's Companion* as they got ready for bed at night and the contents of the "Missionary Barrel" that they received from their family back East.

Grandfather James Berry Vickery I (1832–1911), c. 1900.
He was "an honored and respected citizen of Unity."

THE HIGH LIGHT of each year was the "Missionary Barrel" (as we called it), from Maine. Grandmother Vickery always fixed so many things. Also, it was half full of apples. No apple since has tasted or smelled so good. We never had much fresh fruit. There were sacks of dried apples, knitted things, and clothes my cousins had outgrown. I was so proud to dress up in them.[82]

One letter between the eastern Vickerys and the western Vickerys written by "Mother" Mary Ayer Vickery to her "Children" Eli Ayer and Carrie does indicate that there was talk at least of getting together:

I WILL NOW FINISH this letter which I commenced I think nearly two weeks ago, as I have just finished the little dresses, I wanted to send…. [I would like to join one] of the love feasts with

*Grandmother Mary Ayer Vickery (1835–1911), c. 1910,
Unity, Maine. "It [is] best [not] to make any effort
towards going West for I guess I am not strong enough."*

Elie and Carrie, but do not know of anyone I can go with, and my
health has been poorer than common all the Spring. 4 or 5 weeks
ago I had the grip not so very bad ... [and then] I took cold, and
had tonsilitis ... and I was quite sick last week, but last Monday
was sitting up reading when I took the iodine, so I have been quite
poorly this week. I may be real well after I get over my cold &c,
but don't think it best to make any effort towards going West for
I guess I am not strong enough. I have my dreams and my antic-
ipations and I am going to be cheerful & happy about it, and perhaps some sweet day you can visit us, and in the mean time, I will
like Dorcas of old, I will make garments for the little children, and
when Jesus call me home, perhaps it will be said of me, "she too
hath done what she could.[83]

Mary Ayer Vickery was almost seventy years old when she wrote this letter in May 1903, but unlike previous Vickery generations, she and her husband James I had had no grandchildren growing up in their home. Their son David and daughter Josie never married, and while their son John Ayer and Emily Nickerson Vickery had four children by this time, they lived about thirty-five miles away in South Brewer, Maine. This would change for the Unity grandparents within a few days of Mary's letter though, when James Berry II and his wife Annie Stewart Vickery's first child Everett Stewart Vickery was born.

Carrie Brandenburg Vickery had tried to stay in touch with her Brandenburg relatives through the years as well, but letters were sparse. Carrie finally decided to remedy the situation by writing a long letter and sending it to her oldest sister Mamie Brandenburg Yule, asking her to add to it and send it on to the next relative. They were to do the same until it made a full circle back to Carrie who wrote and sent out a new letter. Carrie called it the "Big Letter" and it started a family tradition. According to Allie when the "Big Letter" arrived back in the Vickery home it was a "big event" and "kept the family close for years."[84] In one of these surviving "Big Letters," thirty-three-year-old Carrie wrote a poignant summation of her life's philosophy to her sister Mamie:

IN READING OVER some of your letters I notice you so often speak of our happiness in the future. But long ago I ceased to make plans in that way. One's dreams are so seldom ever realized and I think the best way is just to get all the comfort and pleasure out of each day as it comes. In looking forward too much to the "Tomorrow of Happiness" that may never come we are apt to overlook many of the little joys of life that [are] ours today. As for those of us with large families, all babies at once almost, there is much hard work and many cares. But the real comfort is now, I think, and not by and by. Now I have them always near with their sweet baby chatter, I know their whereabouts at all times, see each and every one tucked in with their good night. We know all their lessons and they repeat after me the little verses they learn to recite. They are all as capable of being smart in school and of doing things in the world, as the average and if I may only live to see them grow up I know there are many proud and happy days to come. But in a different way than now. For all that we see & know is that families grow up, separate and drift apart. When they grow up away from my arms and out into the world, they have interests and <u>loves</u> of their own. I may see them sometimes and maybe not. I so often think of Eli's mother who works and prays for us day after day and how her heart yearns for her first born whom she has not seen in twenty years. Even the love of his little children she is not permitted to share. So dear I could talk on & on and the more I should convince myself that 'tis best to "take no thought of the morrow" but be gloriously glad in all the joy of today.[85]

On 10 November 1911 Eli Ayer Vickery received a Western Union wire from his brother James II in Unity: "Father passed away yesterday forenoon of Heart failure. Service Sunday at One PM."[86] By this time Eli Ayer himself had suffered heart problems. The oldest girls Allie and Emma had moved to Cody, Wyoming, to work for their room and board while they prepared for high school, but when their father's health began to fail, Edgar was sent to bring them home.[87] In May 1914 Papa Eli died at the age of fifty-four "after a losing four year battle with hopeless, pernicious anemia," and Emma and Allie never returned to school.[88] Their sister Carol later recounted the day Eli Ayer died: "As my mother and the older ones did the final, necessary things, I took my three young brothers for a long walk along our river bed, and explained to them as best I could what had happened."[89] Eli Ayer Vickery, like his grandfather Eli in Unity, was well respected, had been appointed a justice of the peace, and "people all came to him for advice when they were sick and in trouble."[90] In his obituary he was described as "a man, stalwart and true, a good neighbor, a faithful husband and a kind and exemplary father."[91] "At the funeral service," recalled Eli Ayer's son Fred, "there was a big crowd. The house was filled with people and the yard was filled with people standing."[92]

Eli Ayer's forty-five-year-old wife Carrie persevered on the farm after his death. By 1917 Carrie's daughters Allie, Emma, and Dorothy had married and left home, and her daughter Carol was working at and attending the Polytechnic School (now called Rocky Mountain College) in Billings, Montana, sending "part of her pay to help out home finances."[93] Even though Carrie found it financially difficult to stay on the homestead with her other seven children, she was characteristically hopeful in a letter to Carol:

> YOU SPOKE OF sending home some of your money, but don't send any, dear child until you have the things you need to be neat and comfortable. Of course, we need many things here but some how we have always managed to get along. We are all hoping to get a hundred dollars together as soon as we can to pay in on the mortgage, and it will save renewing and keep up the interest, Ted and Edgar both working now and think we can manage it.[94]

If not for World War I Carrie and her sons Ted and Edgar might indeed have been able to "manage it."

Americans had tried to stay neutral in the European war that had begun in 1914 between Germany and Austria-Hungary, who were called the Central Powers, and the countries of Britain, France, and Russia. But American economic interests, the loss of American lives and property at sea from German submarine attacks, and Germany's proposed alliance with Mexico that calculated to give Mexico back its former territory of Texas, New Mexico, and Arizona finally forced the United States into World War I in 1917. In 1918 Carol went to Washington, D.C., to work in the War Department. While Carrie was sad to see her go, she saw her departure as an opportunity. "I just must not be sorry about your going dear, for it may mean so much to you and all of us," Carrie told Carol. "I can't help thinking about the lines," she continued, "something about the tide in the affairs of men & etc. Seems as if something leads us on, and God knows best."[95] While Carrie could not know the historical consequences of Carol's government job during the war, her sense that it might "mean so much" to Carol and "all of us" was accurate. Because of the war, women were able to enter occupations in war industries and government bureaucracy from which they had previously been excluded. While their hard work, valiant support of the war effort, and patriotic citizenship helped to win the war, it also changed the way the public thought about working women and helped to win them the right to vote two years after the war ended.[96]

Later in 1918 Carrie's oldest son Edgar was drafted and sent to

Europe to fight with the American Expeditionary Forces. After Edgar entered the military and the older children departed, Carrie realized she could not afford to stay on the homestead. Moving from the home for which she and her family had worked so hard was not an easy decision for Carrie to make as she wrote Carol in September 1918:

> EVEN THO THE ALLIES are victorious, no one can see when the end will be. I wrote you of the plans we were making about moving, but it just nearly kills me to think of it. But the start will have to be made some time. I was counting on the pay from Edgar making our house payments. But I have not rec'd any yet and I have heard that so many others have not, that I have begun to worry and it frightens me terribly for fear I have made a mistake [in not moving earlier]. I am going to the Bank again this week and see what I can do.[97]

Edgar was very concerned about helping his mother hold on to the homestead, but besides sending his pay home there was not much he could do about the situation.[98] Understandably, he also was grappling with some of the deepest moral issues of war, as a letter home from Camp McArthur in Texas reveals:

> THEY PUT A LOT of stress on the importance of being able to handle the bayonet well and there they sure work a man to see that he can handle it. I can learn it all right, but I would much rather take my fighting out in shooting. This idea of running up and poking sixteen inches of cold steel through some guy I have never met, just to keep him from doing the same thing to me, don't appeal to me much I can tell you, but if I ever get where I have to do it I sure will.[99]

Edgar would never get the chance to test himself during World War I. Less than a month before the Armistice that would end the war, Carrie's son Private Edgar Ayer Vickery of Company F, 329th Infantry died on 15 October 1918 in an army hospital in France, having contracted influenza or flu on the troop ship.[100] More American soldiers were killed by the Great Flu Epidemic in 1918 than were killed in bat-

Edgar Ayer Vickery who died during World War I was buried first near the coast at La Mans, and his body was later moved to the Oisne-Aisne Cemetery in France. His mother Carrie later said, "We could have requested the army to send him home, but I thought it over and decided to leave him with his comrades."

tle during World War I. Before it ended, according to Gina Kolata in her book *Flu*, the epidemic killed "more Americans in a single year than died in battle in World War I, World War II, the Korean War, and the Vietnam War," and worldwide the epidemic killed an estimated forty million people.[101] Edgar was buried first near the coast at La Mans, and his body was later moved to the Oise-Aisne Cemetery in France.[102] Carrie later said, "We could have requested the army to send him home, but I thought it over and decided to leave him with his comrades."[103] The family erected a cross for Edgar in the family burial plot at Clark, Wyoming, next to his father Eli Ayer Vickery. In 1930 the French government financed Carrie's trip across the United States and the Atlantic Ocean to visit her son's gravesite in France.

After Edgar's death Carrie moved permanently from Wyoming to Bridger, Montana, where she lived for the next forty years, renting out the homestead in Clark during the school year, and returning with her other sons each summer to "put up hay and work the ranch."[104] Carrie

Brandenburg Vickery never remarried and she never stopped noting each year she was married. When one of her thirty grandchildren was married in 1954, she said her grandmother Carrie reminisced "that if Eli were still alive they would be celebrating 65 years of marriage."[105]

Eli Ayer and Carrie Vickery biologically created a community from their large family in the Yellowstone borderline area of Montana and Wyoming. While they socialized with their far-flung neighbors, the Vickerys were really a tight individual community unto themselves who depended on each other for financial and emotional support. By all accounts they flourished, although it can be argued that like the Berry family's experience with ranch family mutuality, the western Vickery independent family experience might also have suppressed individual aspirations for the common good of the family. That the older Vickery girls ceased their education to return home to care for their father Eli Ayer when he was dying is but one example.

The significant difference between the independent western Vickerys and the interdependent mutuality of the western Berry family had everything to do with the women. Women, as anthropologist Anthony

---

The Eli Ayer and Carrie Brandenburg Vickery Family, June 1930.
Left to right, front row: James "Jim" Vincent, Carol Louise, Emma Christine,
Carrie Brandenburg (center), Mary "Allie" Alverda, Elsie Belle, Jack Mason. Left
to right, back row: Elizabeth Chase, Frederick "Fred" Brandenburg, William
"Ted" Theodore, Dorothy Brandenburg.

F. C. Wallace states, have "often had the responsibility of ensuring the continued solidarity of the 'family connection.'"[106] Indeed, nineteenth-century women believed it was their Christian duty to preserve family connections and when they went West, despite the overwhelming amount of work they did, they always found time to keep in contact with their family (especially their mothers) and friends back East. According to historian Lillian Schlissel, women "simply refused to sever the framework of their old lives as they began to build anew."[107] The Berry women were Maine women, and they had connections in Maine that they endeavored to keep strong with steady letter writing and frequent visits.[108]

Carrie Brandenburg Vickery certainly acted as a "connector" with her brother and sisters through her "Big Letter," but she was a western woman with no family connections of her own to the East. She respectfully acknowledged her husband's parents and her children's grandparents in Maine, and attempted to keep in contact with them, but her attention and energies were focused on her immediate family of eleven children. In the summer of 2001 Nora O'Shea Robertson reflected on her grandparents' lives and their sense of family connection and responsibility: "Eli and Carrie left a great legacy [with eleven children] and right now I am not sure of how many descendants [there are] but they are numerous and spread in many directions. They also left us a legacy of how to live and to always be a 'stick together family.' We were to live so as never to disgrace the family and to remember our roots."[109]

The years 1917 and 1918 marked transitions in the Vickery and Berry families out West and back East. Carrie Brandenburg Vickery moved from the Clark's Fork ranch to town life in Bridger, Montana. S. Stillman Berry III became the president of the Winnecook Ranch Company. And on 23 April 1917 James Berry Vickery II and his wife Annie Stewart Vickery's third son was born in Unity, Maine. Holding fast to tradition they named him James Berry Vickery III.

FOUR

The Twentieth Century

1900–1997

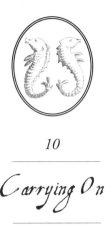

10

Carrying On

THE TENTH GENERATION

COUSIN GERTRUDE FISHER *called on us early last fall and she told us that your wife passed away also what a nice son you have in James B. 3d and of his interest in genealogy. It must be very pleasant for you to have two sons at home and with the family of your nephew you must have quite a house full. At the time I remember the house it always held quite a family. I can see now just how the house & all the buildings looked going up the hill to them. I should like very much to visit the place again.... I wonder what you have in Unity for church services now. We always went regularly as did your family and we are interested in that as everything about yourself and family and things about the town.... We shall be very glad indeed to hear from you or any of your family at anytime. There are not so many Vickery family left and it is pleasant to keep up the acquaintance by letter writing.*
—Claribel S. Vickery to James Berry Vickery II, 2 January 1934[1]

WHEN ELI AYER VICKERY'S twenty-three-year-old brother James Berry Vickery II returned to Unity, Maine, from the borderland of Montana and Wyoming in the fall of 1895—bringing home "a little box of gold dust" to help him tell tales of his Wild West adventures—he settled down back on the family farm on Quaker Hill. Apparently settling down back on the family farm was not entirely his own choice because as James Berry Vickery II's son James Berry Vickery III would later reveal, "He always loved the West and regretted coming back to Maine."[2] However his father James Berry Vickery I was over sixty years old and his older brothers had established their individual careers, so it fell to James II as the youngest son to put aside his personal desires and carry on the family farm.

Throughout the late nineteenth century politicians and the press had bemoaned the sight of abandoned farms in Maine, but in truth, Maine had more farms in the years from 1880 to 1910 than it ever had or would have again.[3] About 900 people lived in Unity at this time. Having dwindled from its peak of 1,557 people in 1850, the population would remain stable until the 1940s. For the time being, at least, the economy seemed stable as well. By the early twentieth century there were four general stores, two hotels, and a telephone company in Unity, making it a center for the wider hinterland. (Electricity did not come to Unity until 1916.) There were a few sawmills in the village that produced shingles, staves, cheese boxes, spools, and excelsior—curled shreds of wood used as packing material and furniture stuffing. The Belfast and Moosehead Lake Railroad stopped in Unity to pick up passengers and load potatoes and pulpwood. There were two creameries that made cheese and butter, and bought and sold milk and eggs. On the banks of Sandy Stream sweet corn was canned at the Portland Packing Company, which would employ 10 percent of Unity's population by 1910.[4]

Meanwhile as the nineteenth century turned into the twentieth, farmers like James Berry Vickery II who patronized the general stores, harvested the timber on their woodlots (an important source of ready cash), kept the cows and chickens, and grew the potatoes and sweet corn "performed their [daily] chores as they had done for years," as his son James Berry Vickery III would later write.

THEY PITCHED DOWN HAY from the mow, watered the cattle, milked the cows, chopped up a few sticks of kindling, lugged a few armfuls of wood for the wood box; then they were ready for a supper of bread and milk, a wedge of pie, two or three molasses cookies; thereafter they removed their heavy boots and toasted their feet before the old Glenwood range, smoked a pipeful, read the *Republican Journal* or *Bangor Commercial* and retired to bed before nine o'clock.[5]

And like generations of farmers had done for years, James II "took a wife" because, romance notwithstanding, it was expected of him—a farmer needed a wife and children to make the farm work and prosper. James Berry Vickery II and Annie May Stewart were married in December 1902 at Belfast, Maine, by the Reverend Walter Edgett.

Annie May Stewart had been born just south of Unity in Montville, Maine, on 15 August 1880. Her father Lafayette Edmund Stewart was a farmer and a machinist who repaired watches.[6] His "people" had settled the Blue Hill, Mount Desert, and Vinalhaven areas of Maine in the eighteenth century before moving to Montville in the 1820s.[7] Annie's mother Abigail Nancy Douglas Stewart's family was from Unity, neighboring Thorndike, and Montville, and Abigail and her older sister Adeline were married to brothers. (Adeline Douglas married Lafayette's older brother George "Avery" Stewart.) Annie was the eldest of Lafayette Edmund and Abigail Nancy Douglas Stewart's four children. A formal studio photograph taken of the Stewarts in the late 1890s presents an image of the ideal middle-class family at the turn of the century—a gentle mother with her hands folded in her lap, her youngest child beside her, and a strong father gripping the arm of the chair with his right hand, a Masonic pin on his lapel, surrounded by his dutiful older children. Photographed against a painted background of an impressive library of a grand home, the Stewart family clearly wished to be seen as educated and committed to "mental culture."

After they were married in December 1902 James II and Annie lived with his parents James I and Mary Ayer Vickery and his sister Josephine on the family farm on Quaker Hill. In May 1903 Annie gave birth to the first of their three sons, Everett Stewart Vickery. Like most rural women, Annie gave birth to her children on the farm. It was not until the 1920s and 1930s that middle-class urban women began to choose to give birth in hospitals where they felt they would be offered the safest and newest technology and scientific methods.[8] After Everett's birth, like the Montana pilgrim women who came back to Maine to have their babies among family, Annie took baby Everett for an extended visit to her parents living in Brooks, ten miles southeast of Unity, probably in part to regain her strength after childbirth.

While visiting with her parents Annie had a photograph taken of ten-month-old Everett and she sent it home. A growing sentimental

Annie May Stewart (left) and her cousin Lucy Stewart, 4 July 1901. They could trace their lineage to Pilgrim John Dunham who came to Plymouth, Massachusetts, during the MAYFLOWER years, and their "people" settled the Blue Hill, Mount Desert, and Vinalhaven areas of Maine in the eighteenth century before moving to Montville in the 1820s.

attachment to very small babies in American culture motivated conscientious middle-class mothers like Annie to photograph their children and then create a family photo album and decorate the home with photographs that documented the growth and accomplishments of their families.[9] Advances in photography that no longer required subjects to sit still for long periods of time also made it easier for Annie to photograph baby Everett. New father James II had yet to see the value in his son's photograph as a visible "testament to ancestry, inheritance, and continuity" in the Vickery family genealogy, however, as evidenced in his next letter to Annie.[10]

HOW IS THE BABY does he sleep good nights. Oh that picture of him was immense his head looked like a big round pumpkin with a small hole in it. I think it must have been taken with a Lick telescope. Mother and Josephine thought it was a little dear but I just took off the stove cover and chucked it in. I suppose

Annie May Stewart "of Montville," c. 1902.
Rural women, still a larger population than urban women in the United
States, rarely complained about their lives of sunrise-to-sundown labor.

The Lafayette Edmund and Abigail Nancy Douglas Stewart family, c. 1898.
Photographed against a painted background of an impressive library of a grand
home, the Stewart family clearly wished to be seen as educated and committed to
"mental culture." Left to right: Annie May, Arthur Gilman, Lafayette Edmund,
Edith, Henry "Bert," Abigail Nancy Douglas.

you are having a good time, well get all the rest you can and a
streak of fat. I am getting <u>some</u> lonesome. When do you want to
come home[?][11]

The description of baby Everett's photograph as "a little dear" is ambig-
uous. Perhaps spending the extra money to have this photograph taken
made its value "a little dear" or too costly to burn. More than likely this
comment was the sentimental reaction of Everett's grandmother and
aunt; his image was precious to them and they thought him "a little
dear." James II's rash destruction of what otherwise would have become
a cherished family heirloom could have been an indication of the frustration that he felt because his wife was away, which he might well have
ascribed to the "little dear."

By the time that James II and Annie's second son Eric Arthur
Vickery was born in May 1907, though he would not be named as such
for almost four months, James II seemed to have warmed to fatherhood.
Again, Annie took the new baby and went to stay with her parents. Having been left with four-year-old Everett, James II clearly enjoyed him.

Everett is getting along fine as a new mitten good as pie he
and I went to church this morning and he gave Mrs. Cooper one
of those beautiful hugs. I thought to myself I wish I was small. I
guess he misses you some but he has not said anything about it
only once. How is the baby getting along where do you get his
milk. How do you like the name of Eric Ayer Vickery. [You] send
me one [name]. We are having a beautiful time.[12]

This time James II had Everett's photograph taken. "Everett and I went
up to Pittsfield last Saturday.... We had his pictures taken but I am
afraid they will be pretty sober," he wrote Annie on 17 September 1907.
"He knew I was writing you and said to send you a kiss.... How are you
getting along[?] I hope your lameness is all right and [you] are feeling
better by this time. When do you want to come home[?]" asked James
II.[13] The resulting "sober" portrait shows Everett on the threshhold of
boyhood; his haircut is decidedly masculine, but in spite of that his
white dress with eyelet flounce, which was the style for both young girls
and boys at this time, defined him as a genderless toddler.

Everett Stewart Vickery, 1907, age four. On the threshhold of boyhood, Everett's haircut is decidedly masculine, but in spite of that his white dress with eyelet flounce, which was the style for both young girls and boys at this time, defined him as a genderless toddler.

The evidence in these two letters hints at a volatile and impetuous element in James II's temperament, one that seems to echo through this male line of the Vickery family from David III's "very jealous temperament" to Eli's "quick temper."[14] This might also have been exacerbated by James II's regret and resulting resentment about having to come back to Maine when he had wanted to stay out West. The private nature of any couple's relationship can never be known, but James II seemed to exhibit a profound insensitivity to his wife Annie's feelings in these letters as well—insinuating in her absence that he wished to be hugged by Mrs. Cooper, and that her son did not miss her. Patriarchal authority and an indifferent or a callous attitude by a husband towards his wife were becoming socially unacceptable in the early twentieth century. Still the ideal model today, "companionate marriages" based on romantic love, sexual pleasure, and companionship—and not just on economic security—had begun to be emphasized by the new professional groups of educators, psychiatrists, and sociologists. It was expected that a husband and wife would be friends and lovers, that parents would be "pals" with their children, and that this new kind of family would live in a single household.[15] Perhaps these letters reveal James II's struggle to balance his new role that called for tenderness as a husband and father with his image of himself forged by his heritage as a brusque, pragmatic, and unsentimental Yankee farmer.

Of course, there were many gaps between what was presented as the norm at any time and the realities of marriage and family life, especially in rural farm households with extended families that usually adhered to traditional family roles. As historians have suggested in the nineteenth century, intergenerational conflict was more likely to occur in these family arrangements.[16] There were seven people living in the Vickery farmhouse in 1907: seventy-five-year-old Grandfather James I, seventy-two-year-old Grandmother Mary, forty-five-year-old Aunt Josephine, thirty-five-year-old James Berry Vickery II, twenty-seven-year-old Annie, four-year-old Everett, and newborn Eric. It must have been difficult for Annie to be the third woman in the Vickery household, having less authority, privacy, and freedom to define her domestic space—the power base for many women. No wonder Annie retreated to the home of her parents after each of her children's births.

In the same 17 September 1907 letter to Annie, James II mentioned that he had "sold 12 Diggers in all so far and think I will sell quite a lot more."[17] This was a reference to the Hoover digger, a new machine for digging potatoes, and it highlights how twentieth-century farmers in Maine still practiced mixed economies in order to keep the family farm in business. Maine farmers learned to contend with western competition in the last half of the nineteenth century by replacing their beef cattle with dairy herds and specializing in crops that grew well in Maine's distinctive soil and climate like apples, pears, wild blueberries, sweet corn, and potatoes.[18] While potatoes had been grown commercially in Maine since the mid nineteenth century, they did not become a principal cash crop in Waldo County until the early 1900s. Only after planting varieties that were less susceptible to disease, parasites, and blight, and using fertilizers and pesticides and more efficient farm machinery like the Hoover digger could farmers increase their potato production with less labor and capital, and central Maine farmers were encouraged to do so by the market price of potatoes.[19] James Berry Vickery II not only planted potatoes on his farm, he diversified his investments and energies by selling the farm machinery that made it profitable as well.

In her book *A Maine Hamlet* sociologist Lura Beam depicted life in the Down East rural community of Marshfield, Maine, in the years 1895 through 1907 that was not unlike the life in central Maine at this time.[20] These were the years during which James Berry Vickery II arrived home from the West and he and Annie May Stewart married,

Potato Fields, Waldo County, Maine, c. 1900. While potatoes had been grown commercially in Maine since the mid-nineteenth century, they did not become a principal cash crop in Waldo County until the early 1900s.
COURTESY OF UNITY HISTORICAL SOCIETY.

began their family, and took over the Vickery family farm from his mother and father James Berry I and Mary Ayer Vickery. In the opening chapter entitled "Man and Woman" Beam described her grandfather and grandmother with whom she lived as a child, and a sense of James Berry I and Mary Ayer Vickery's lives might be gleaned from her description as the context of the two couples' lives were so similar.[21]

Lura Beam's grandparents and James I and Mary, who also had grandchildren living with them, were approximately the same ages. Beam's recounting of her grandparents' genealogy as the "eighth generation from the first English ancestor who came to Massachusetts, and the fourth from the first settled in this Maine spot" described James I and Mary's places in the Vickery genealogy as well.[22] Both sets of grandparents stayed on their respective farms in Maine in the late nineteenth century while other community and family members migrated West, usually never to return. Lura Beam suggests that because of this the "emotions" of her grandparents were "strangely tuned toward places they had never seen."[23] Grandparents James Berry I and Mary Ayer Vickery would also have had a heightened consciousness of the greater world outside Maine from their son James Berry II's western adventures, and son Eli Ayer and daughter-in-law Carrie's letters from Wyoming, although James I and Mary would never see Montana and Wyoming themselves. These examples of James I and Mary, Beam's grandparents, and the countless others in Maine whose children left for destinations all over the world throughout the nineteenth century show that even those who stayed behind were closely connected to and aware of the world beyond Maine's borders.

The daily lives of Lura Beam's grandparents in Marshfield and the Unity Vickerys were probably similar. Like Beam's grandparents, James Berry I and Mary Ayer Vickery would have read *The Old Farmer's Almanac*, the Bible, their local papers, seed catalogues, and no doubt "Dr. Talmadge's sermon from the last Bangor Sunday newspaper." Like Beam's grandmother, Grandmother Mary Ayer Vickery would have made the rag rugs, quilts, and pillows in her home, and knitted socks, scarves, and mittens, sewed frocks for the grandchildren, "baked all the bread, pies, and cake eaten by the family for nearly sixty years, smoked the hams, and made the jellies, jams, pickles, and mincemeat." Like Beam's grandfather, Grandfather James I would have "swung the scythe in the summer and the axe in the winter," built farmhouses, barns, "sheds and poultry houses, sleds and hayracks," and raised the farm produce. And like Beam's portrayal of her grandparents, James I and Mary would have been the last couple in their farm family "to touch rural American life in its undiluted form"—living "by the weather, by whatever came, and by what they could do with the whole body."[24] Yet, however romantic and "pure" life on the family farm might be remembered and portrayed, it was very hard work, especially when many Americans were enjoying physically easier lives.

In November 1911 seventy-nine-year-old James Berry Vickery I, "an honored and respected citizen of Unity, died of heart failure" as had his mother Clarissa Berry Vickery twenty-five years before.[25] Earlier that year James I's son David Earnest Vickery, who owned a general store in nearby Pittsfield, had died "after a short illness caused by indigestion" which indeed may have been heart-related as well.[26] While James I's death came after a full life, forty-five-year-old David's sudden death shocked his family and community. "I dident think it was going to be the last time we was going to see Mr. [David] Vickery[,] dident he pass away sudden Annie and don't it seem odd to you not to see him round," wrote Annie Stewart Vickery's mother Abigail Douglas Stewart, adding with classic Christian reasoning, "But he is Better of[f] Annie haint he[.]"[27] Three years later in 1914 James I's fifty-five-year-old son Eli Ayer Vickery who "had by his industry just gotten to where he could begin to enjoy the fruits of his labors," also died of heart problems in Clark, Wyoming, after lingering for years.[28]

Similar to the experiences of the previous generations of Vickerys these deaths in the eighth and ninth generations were offset by the birth of a new Vickery child in the tenth. James II and Annie Stewart Vickery's third son James Berry Vickery III was born on 23 April 1917. There is no evidence that Annie took her new son to visit her parents, who were still alive. Perhaps in the ten years between the births of her son Eric and baby James III Annie had established her presence in the Vickery household and felt more comfortable staying home. Because there were so many years between his birth and the births of his older brothers (Everett was fourteen years older) James Berry Vickery III continued for many years to be the indulged member of the family.

James Berry II and Annie May Stewart Vickery family, 1918. James Berry II and Annie Stewart Vickery bought their first automobile (a "Chandler") in 1916. They and their sons loved their automobile and they took many auto trips together through the "pristine" countryside during James III's childhood. Left to right, front row: Everett Stewart, James Berry III (center), Eric Arthur. Left to right, back row, Annie May Stewart, James Berry II.

While children were still expected to help with farm chores, ideas about children and childhood were changing in the early twentieth century. It had become the fashion to give children enough freedom from parental control to express their feelings and find their individual ways in life, while providing guidance in an elevated home environment.[29] Finding his own direction would have been made easier for James Berry Vickery III with two much older brothers to lighten his obligations on the farm. James III, who was called "Jamie" as a boy, later reminisced that he had had a "marvelous" childhood "with plenty of books to read and 300 acres of fields to roam."[30] Being "born into a home where the Edison phonograph and books mattered" motivated him to seek "out the best" all of his life.[31] No doubt referring to his own home, James III once stated in a newspaper interview, "I believe in the force of the home, an especially important influence for the development of young people."[32] Snapshots taken throughout the 1920s of young James III at play attest to a childhood that fostered imagination and self-discovery.

In April 1917, the month and year that James III was born, the United States declared war against Germany, and fourteen men from

Left: James Berry Vickery III, c. 1922. This image evoked such fond memories of his childhood on the family farm that James III once sent it as a Christmas card.

Right: James Berry Vickery III, c. 1927. James III, who was called "Jamie" as a boy, reminisced that he had had a "marvelous" childhood "with plenty of books to read and 300 acres of fields to roam."

Below left: James Berry Vickery III (left) with his brother Eric Arthur Vickery, c. 1929. Throughout their lives Eric and James III took pleasure from their times together.

Below right: Boy Scout James Berry Vickery III, c. 1929. No doubt referring to his own home, James III once stated, "I believe in the force of the home, an especially important influence for the development of young people."

Unity fought in World War I. Before it ended on 11 November 1918, over 112,000 Americans died fighting in the war, including two of the Vickery family's young men. Twenty-four-year-old [Samuel] Benjamin Berry, the son of Reuel and Hattie Myrick Plummer Berry and nephew of Ralph and Evie Kelley Berry, Ruth Berry, and Mary Berry Cook, died in France as a "result of wounds received in battle."[33] Eli Ayer and Carrie Brandenburg Vickery's twenty-eight-year-old son Edgar Ayer Vickery contracted influenza on his way to France and died there.

World War I also brought Eli and Carrie Brandenburg Vickery's daughter Carol Louise Vickery to Maine, the first of the western Vickerys to visit those in the East. Working for the War Department in Washington, D.C., as a secretary, and thus living on the East Coast in 1918, Carol planned to make a sojourn to the farm in Unity that her father Eli Ayer had left over thirty years ago. Her mother Carrie, showing a remarkable level of familiarity with Maine and the Vickery family members for someone who had yet to visit, wrote to her from Montana:

> I HAVE JUST THOUGHT so much about you and [am] so anxious to know if your plans [to visit Maine] all worked out. If Uncle Jim met you at Belfast and who else went with him. I know you will tell me all about it, and the old farm, and especially all about grandmother, the baby [James III] and every one of them. You will want to write a big chapter on Boston. Harry brot in a beauty big trout when he came to dinner. How I wish I could pass it over for the supper down in Maine.[34]

Carol's plans "all worked out" and she traveled to Maine that June. Her many cousins "took her canoeing on the Penobscot River, horseback riding in the beautiful Maine hills, and digging clams on the beach at Searsport."[35] Her eighty-three-year-old grandmother Mary Ayer Vickery was delighted finally to meet one of her western grandchildren, and as Carol later reminisced, "She almost killed me with kindness. I never was a big eater, but after tucking me deep in a feather bed she would bring in a big glass of milk and piece of cake for a bed time snack."[36] A photograph of a beaming Carol sitting on the grass under a maple tree holding her fourteen-month-old cousin James Berry Vickery III in her lap captures the joy of this family reunion.

Carol Louise Vickery and her cousin James Berry Vickery III, Unity,
Maine, 1918. World War I brought Eli and Carrie Brandenburg Vickery's
daughter Carol to Maine from Montana, and her many cousins "took her
canoeing on the Penobscot River, horseback riding in the beautiful Maine
hills, and digging clams on the beach at Searsport."

Carol Vickery and her brother Ted, who came to work briefly on the family farm in Unity in 1920, were the only ones of the eleven western Vickery grandchildren ever to see their Maine grandmother Mary True Ayer Vickery.[37] Mary died in 1922 at the age of eighty-seven, "the last of a family of eight, all of whom lived to be long past middle age" as stated in her obituary.[38] When Mary was born in 1835 it was scandalous for a woman to give a public speech, inconceivable that she could vote or be elected to Congress. When Mary died in 1922 women had become accomplished and effective public speakers, they had won the right to vote in 1920 as the result of the Nineteenth Amendment to the Constitution, and in 1917 Jeannette Rankin (who, incidentally, was from Montana) had been elected the first woman to the United States House of Representatives. Nonetheless Mary's obituary presented her as having lived the life expected of a nineteenth-century woman: "She had lived in Unity all her married life, was a devoted mother and a good neighbor, [and] during her active life she was much interested in her church as well as whatever pertained to the welfare of the neighborhood and town."[39]

James Berry Vickery III was five years old when his Grandmother Vickery died and his memories of her were those of a much-loved grandchild. He remembered that she had "beautiful white hair," that she used to read the *Youth's Companion* (the same magazine she sent to the western grandchildren) to his brothers Everett and Eric, and that one morning before he went to school she gave him a "yellow & pink bonbon" from a box of candy Uncle John (who lived in South Brewer) had given her that she kept on top of the organ in her room. This reference to the organ in Grandmother Vickery's room indicates that she probably slept in the parlor—not an unusual arrangement in extended families. James III remembered the poignant story told to him that when he was a baby his mother and father went to the fair with him and that his grandmother was so "lonely" for him that she walked a distance to a relative's house lamenting, "if they had only left the baby," and had to be walked home.[40]

James III claimed that because his grandmother was "born in the age of the horse & buggy" that she did not "quite understand" automobiles. "It was always her impression that the automobile had to be pushed out the garage by hand," he said, because "she didn't think it would back up itself." That Grandmother Vickery might not have had a clear sense of how automobiles worked is understandable, because automobiles were controlled primarily by men on farms and many older rural women never learned to drive.[41] Rural women of her daughter-in-law Annie's generation, however, would embrace the automobile as the solution to the problem of isolation on farms.[42] James III also remembered the day in October that his Grandmother Vickery died:

THE MORNING SHE DIED she came out to breakfast—tho had to be helped—she didn't eat anything—tried to drink some coffee but spilled it—returned to her room[;] sat in a rocker. —Dr. was called Whitney—he gave her a hypo which did no good—she tried to say Jimmy—but only mumbled it. She was dressed & put to bed & died in [the] forenoon.[43]

Left: Everett Stewart Vickery (1903–1986), 1921. Everett, who married Ethel Willsey of Hartford, Connecticut, lived in Hartford, worked in sale, and was an "avid outdoorsman and fisherman."

Right: Eric Arthur Vickery (1907–1991), 1925. Eric, who attended Shaw Business College in Waterville, Maine, decided like his father, grandfather, great-grandfather, and great-great-grandfather that he, too, was a farmer.

The funeral service for Mary True Ayer Vickery, conducted by the Reverend W. Cheever of Pittsfield, was held at the family farm. "Surrounded by a profusion of flowers, she was borne to her last resting place, the bearers being her two sons [James Berry II and John Ayer Vickery I] and her two grandsons [Everett who was nineteen and Eric who was fifteen.]"[44]

Two years later Mary's fifty-six-year-old son John Ayer Vickery I lost his life by falling overboard from the steamboat BELFAST on the way from Boston to Bangor, Maine, on the night of 8 July 1924. John, who was the president and part owner of the J. M. Arnold Shoe Company in Bangor, was returning from a business trip to Boston on the BELFAST accompanied by Walter L. McDonald, a salesman and director of the company. Packet steamboats, or steamers made of iron and later steel were designed to carry dispatches, mail, passengers, and small goods;

since they had coal-fired steam boilers they were efficient and dependable and had replaced wooden sailing ships for such trips.[45]

John Vickery and McDonald shared a stateroom on the BELFAST, and according to McDonald, after eating supper John "was taken with cramps and left the stateroom several times to go on deck. He went out [again] about midnight and did not return." McDonald said he "went to sleep and did not miss Mr. Vickery until the boat arrived at Rockland."[46] The story in the *Boston Globe* maintained that there was "no doubt" that John, "while standing at the rail, lost his balance and fell overboard" somewhere between Seguin Island and Rockland, Maine. The *Bangor Daily News* also reported it was "presumed that Mr. Vickery lost his balance while leaning over the rail" to relieve his stomach, but it was known closer to home that his eyesight had been "failing of late and it was possible that he may have made a mistake and thus gone overboard to his death."[47] Regardless, the unsettled weather with showers and thunderstorms that late evening and early morning of 8 and 9 July would have made it dangerous for anyone to be on deck.[48] A three-hundred-dollar reward was posted for the recovery of John's body, but it was never found.[49]

John Ayer Vickery I's death was no doubt "the cause of widespread sorrow and regret" that one source purported it to be.[50] He and his wife Emily Nickerson Vickery had been married for thirty-three years and had six children: sons Charles James, twenty-five, John Ayer II, twenty-three, Winslow Chambers, seventeen, and Robert Nickerson, fifteen, and daughters Emily "Josephine" and Mildred Louise who had married in a double wedding ceremony in 1919, and had given John I and Emily four grandchildren.[51] John I had been a civic and social leader who was "a valued and highly esteemed member" of his community of Brewer, Maine. He was also "one of the foremost individuals having to do with the business of the State" having helped develop the important shoe industry in Maine after the Civil War.[52] John I's sons Charles, John II, and Winslow followed their father into the shoe and boot (and later work apparel) business, helping to launch and eventually owning the W. S. Emerson Company in Bangor, Maine. John Ayer Vickery I would have been proud to know that four generations later his family continues W. S. Emerson across the Penobscot River in Brewer, an outgrowth of the industry he helped to establish, and are still as committed as he

$300 REWARD

$300 Reward will be paid per-son or persons for the recovery of the body of

JOHN A. VICKERY
of Brewer, Maine

who fell overboard from Steamer Belfast which left Boston, Tuesday P. M. July 8, at some point between Seguin Island and Rockland. Above reward will be paid by the family through O. B. Fernandez, Sheriff of Penobscot County.

BANGOR, MAINE, JULY 11, 1924

was to doing business in Maine, and like him have "a reputation for integrity and fair dealing."[53]

Seven-year-old James Berry Vickery III, who distinctly remembered his grandmother Mary Ayer Vickery's death two years earlier, would have been aware of his Uncle John Ayer Vickery I's tragic death, or at least would have sensed the sadness and interruption of routine life brought about by his death. More deaths in the complex extended Vickery family network in Waldo and Penobscot Counties marked James III's formative years throughout the 1920s and early 1930s, and the vibrancy of Unity and the surrounding regions ebbed with each passing. Mostly born in the mid nineteenth century, those who died included men and women in the Kelley, Berry, Mussey, Bartlett, Murch, Mitchell, Dodge, Stewart, Fogg, Farwell, Cornforth, Varney, Chase, and Webster families—all of whom had helped to define and give meaning to James III's life from his birth. Their photographs were on walls and tables in the parlors he visited, anecdotes and legends about them were repeated at family gatherings, and the buildings they had constructed and the landscape they had shaped formed his identity and determined his sense of place.[54]

The Berry Homestead, "Albion Road," Unity, Maine, c. 1918. More deaths in the extended Vickery family network in Waldo and Penobscot Counties marked James Berry Vickery III's formative years throughout the 1920s and early 1930s, and the vibrancy of Unity and the surrounding regions ebbed with each passing. Ruth Berry (left), unidentified woman (center), Mary Berry Cook (right).

THE TWENTIETH CENTURY

Indeed James III's very name as the third "James Berry Vickery" gave him a special connection to these disappearing ancestors. In order to keep and strengthen this connection and to discover who he was James III began at an early age to study and compile the Vickery family genealogy, which was of course the history of Unity, Maine. As a 1930 letter from James III's cousin S. Stillman Berry III (the only child of Ralph and Evie Kelley Berry) indicates, Stillman and James III's mother Annie had been much concerned with family genealogy and were instrumental in piquing his interest. "Please tell your mother that I have added quite a bit to what I had on the Vickery genealogy," wrote Stillman, "but on the Berry lines am still unable to get back of Great-grandfather."[55] James III would spend many years himself trying to solve this same genealogical "problem."

S. Stillman Berry III, who spent time during the summer at Winnecook Ranch in Montana and the rest of the year in Redlands, California, visited Maine on occasion and kept in close contact with his Unity relatives.[56] In 1930 thirteen-year-old James III and forty-three-year-old Stillman began a regular correspondence centered on their shared love of genealogy, which would last until Stillman's death in 1984. They traded data sheets, notes, research evidence, and genealogical "problems" for fifty years, but their intellectual affinity went deeper than their shared sense of family and place. S. Stillman Berry III was a biologist—among other scientific accomplishments he was a world-renowned authority on cephalopods (mollusks)—and he was a dedicated collector. Stillman's most important contribution, according to one biologist, was as a "judicious purchaser" of scientific books and journals for the collections at the Scripps Institute in California that helped to make it a premier research library.[57]

When Stillman died his private research collection numbered over forty thousand books and he owned the largest collection of snails in the world, which he left to the Smithsonian Institution, foreshadowing James Berry Vickery III's own extraordinary collection of 3,000 books, 250 pamphlets, and 300 manuscripts, as well as many photographs, prints, and maps on Maine history and literature that he would donate to the University of Maine in 1978.[58] There is no doubt that James III identified with Stillman's proclivity for preservation and consciously or unconsciously used him as a model.[59] James III would later tell Stillman, "You and I are kindred souls you see in more ways than one. Neither of us can pass up a book."[60]

Studying genealogy and documenting an inherited American lineage gave many white, Anglo-Saxon Protestants "a kind of nobility of native origins" to counter the fear of foreign immigration in the early twentieth century.[61] The 1920 census showed that for the first time in American history, there were more people in the United States living in cities than in the country. In Maine, however, three-fifths of the population still lived in rural areas, and like the Vickerys of Unity most rural Mainers were white, Anglo-Saxon, Protestants, born in Maine of parents, grandparents, and great-grandparents who had themselves been born in Maine.[62] The growing population of Franco-American, Irish, and Italian Catholic and Jewish immigrants in Maine's urban centers and mill towns threatened the identity of this homogeneous population in the countryside, creating ethnic tensions. According to historian C. Stewart Doty some 150,000 Protestant Mainers joined the Ku Klux Klan in the 1920s in an effort "to take back" what was their "own," as one minister stated at the time.[63] Most native Mainers did not join hate groups, but the perceived challenge to their American identity did affect them and many "retreated defensively" into their "exclusive WASP heritage" that genealogy helped them to document.[64]

Fear of foreign immigration was not new. New Englanders had been concerned about their special American identity and its disintegration since the seventeenth century.[65] The reaction to the arrival of immigrants who fueled American industries in the late nineteenth century helped to spur a phenomenon known as the Colonial Revival Movement. Colonial themes in architecture, literature, and art permeated American culture.[66] Historic house museums were established by organizations like the Society for the Preservation of New England Antiquities (SPNEA) to preserve the homes of WASP colonial ancestors, patriots, and their artifacts. The National Society of Colonial Dames, Daughters of the American Revolution (DAR), and the Mayflower Society (to which James III would belong) were also founded at this time, and their membership required an exclusive and certified relationship to eighteenth-century patriots or seventeenth-century Pilgrim founders. The Colonial Revival Movement also had potential for moral uplift and some hoped that it would teach American history and instill traditional "American" values and inspire patriotism in immigrants.[67]

The rise of the tourism industry at the turn of the twentieth century was especially important for promoting this nostalgic Colonial Revival, which in turn created a new economic resource for northern New England.[68] Touring in the new automobiles through the "pristine" countryside to visit regions untainted by modern ills and visiting historic homes to stand before spinning wheels, tall clocks, and recreated colonial kitchens with their huge hearths filled with cast-iron pots and fire tools entertained, comforted, and connected white Anglo-Saxon Protestants with their heritage.[69] James Berry II and Annie Stewart Vickery bought their first automobile (a "Chandler") in 1916.[70] They and their sons loved their automobile and they took many auto trips together through the "pristine" countryside during James III's childhood.[71]

According to historian Joseph A. Conforti, the Colonial Revival Movement developed further into a cultural focus on "regional thinking and feeling" during the Great Depression (1929–41), the worst economic crisis in United States history.[72] Small-town life in northern New

Left to right: unidentified man, author Elizabeth Coatsworth Beston, James Berry Vickery III, author Henry Beston, Chimney Farm, Maine, c. late 1940s. Small town life in northern New England became the guiding theme for popular authors like the Bestons. They portrayed these old Yankee towns and villages as the places where core American values of individualism, thrift, honesty, and democracy still existed.

England became the guiding theme for popular poets, writers, artists, and photographers like Robert Frost, Gladys Hasty Carroll, Robert P. Tristram Coffin, Mary Ellen Chase, Lura Beam, John Gould, Edward Arlington Robinson, Edna St. Vincent Millay, Thornton Wilder, Marsden Hartley, Rockwell Kent, and Wallace Nutting.[73] They portrayed these old Yankee towns and villages as the places where core American values of individualism, thrift, honesty, and democracy still existed. Their goal was to "enshrine the small New England town as an artifact of the real America," one of "authentic natives, place-bound lives, and unspoiled landscapes," states Conforti.[74] Though this representation of timeless Yankee towns and villages was imaginary—new technology and industries had changed much in New England—the idea of constancy made these regions seem like "islands of stability" that helped anxious Americans cope with the social and economic uncertainties of the Great Depression as they lost their jobs, homes, savings, sense of security, and belief in themselves and their government.[75]

The Colonial Revival Movement's evolution into a cultural celebration of regionalism paralleled the first twenty years of James Berry Vickery III's life, and its books, poems, photographs, and art had a great influence over him. Considering James III's sensitivity to the shrinking web of his extended family and the declining vibrancy of Unity, it is not surprising that James III would commit himself to documenting his town and his family who helped to create it.[76] Yet, to suggest that this was not surprising is to acknowledge that James III was certainly an atypical young man. Most young men of his time and indeed earlier times chose to leave a Unity in decline. While he might relocate later to other places in Maine to teach, in his heart James III never left Unity.

There is evidence that James III had decided at least by the age of sixteen to formally compile the Vickery family genealogy and write the history of Unity, Maine. In the early 1930s he also began to correspond with his third cousin, seventy-year-old Gertrude Vickery Fisher in Leominster, Massachusetts.[77] Gertrude had begun her study of genealogy when she was a teenager as well.[78] Responding to a letter from James III in 1933 in which he must have expressed some hesitation about taking on such a daunting project, Gertrude encouraged him to write Unity's history and eloquently made clear the reasons he must:

I WANT SO MUCH that you should not get discouraged with your writing on Unity's History. I know how heedless people are about these things and that is the reason that so much of value is lost. Sometime, someone will bless you for every bit you search out. There comes a time in every place when some noble soul begins a Historical society or collection of relics and it becomes a great asset to a town. Every little [bit] counts, and you may be starting a bigger interest than seems possible now. I am going to send you for you to keep always the Bible with the names in it that your great-great-grandmother Lydia Bartlett Vickery wrote. It was given to my brother Charley but he has died and left no son. You are one of the few of the name of Vickery left and we feel it ought to be in the hands of a Vickery man and that it is better to be kept in Unity—perhaps you will want it to go to a Historical collection some time—cherish it please.[79]

James III also corresponded with his seventy-six-year-old cousin James E. Kelley who was an attorney in Boston. James was helpful in validating the younger man's inclination for historic preservation:

I AM LOOKING OVER my Vickery collections and if I find anything which I think will interest you I will send them along with this letter. I assume, however, that Mrs. Fisher has supplied you with most of her data which is quite full and runs in many branches. We connect by a common ancestor in the Heald line and also in the Vickery line, my grandmother having been Sarah Vickery, daughter of David, a revolutionary Soldier whose burial place was somewhere in Unity, but it was never pointed out to me. You need not return anything I have sent you or any hereafter send you but be sure to preserve them as they may become useful. The data I sent you about the Kelley family and settlement will be useful if you decide to write a history of Unity. Of course, you realize that Mr. Taber's history is very imperfect, which although it contains some biography of former citizens, yet he has no real genealogy and the old town histories that become valuable are those that contain genealogies and if you set about preparing these genealogies you can write a history of Unity that will be of lasting value.[80]

Along with the support and encouragement of his relatives, cultural in-fluences, and his own inclinations, three important events in the early 1930s sealed James III's commitment to collecting the Vickery geneal-ogy and writing the history of Unity: his Aunt Carrie's visit to Unity; his Uncle Ted and Aunt Margaret's relocation to Unity from Montana; and his mother's death.

At last, in August 1930, sixty-one-year-old Carrie Brandenburg Vickery visited the Vickery family farm in Unity, Maine. Earlier that summer Carrie had joined a group of one hundred and four World War I widows and other Gold Star mothers (those who had lost sons in the war) on a trip to France at the expense of the "grateful" French govern-ment to visit the grave of her son Edgar Ayer Vickery who had died in World War I.[81] After docking in New York Harbor on her return to the United States, Carrie, like her daughter Carol thirteen years earlier, could not forego the opportunity while on the East Coast to visit the "old Vickery farm" in Unity on which her husband Eli Ayer had been born and about which she knew so much. Grandfather and Grandmother Vickery had died by then, but her brother-in-law James Berry Vickery II whom she had not seen for twenty years was there, as well as his wife Annie and their sons Eric and James III, her nephews. Her daughter Carol later wrote that her mother Carrie "loved their spacious beautiful old family home [in Maine]" where "she met old neighbors who would take her to their hearts with 'You are Carrie,' and proudly say 'I remem-ber Eli.'" As Carol contends, Carrie surely must have "so" missed her husband Eli Ayer, "there in the old home so filled with memories."[82]

Meeting his Aunt Carrie, the matriarch of the western Vickery family, must have been an exciting moment in James Berry Vickery III's teenage years. He would have been too young to be as affected by the earlier visits of his western cousins; he was a baby when Carol Vickery visited and only four when Ted Vickery came to work on the farm, but he would have heard all the stories about their visits. For James III his Aunt Carrie, like his cousin Stillman and Winnecook Ranch, was the embodiment of the romantic Wild West, and the family she and his Uncle Eli Ayer had created was another whole branch of uninvestigated Vickerys for his genealogical quest. These western Vickerys would num-ber more at the end of the twentieth century than his relatives would in Unity. Studying about where the western Vickerys (and Berrys) and

*Carrie Brandenburg Vickery joined a group of one hundred
and four World War I widows and other Gold Star mothers
on a trip to France at the expense of the "grateful"
French government to visit the grave of her son
Edgar Ayer Vickery in 1930.*

their Unity contemporaries settled expanded the scope of his proposed
family history.

The Wild West had its own set of poets, writers, artists, and photographers who celebrated it like those in New England as another "real
America of authentic natives, place-bound lives, and unspoiled landscapes."[83] Though James III never became the passionate collector of
western scholarship that he was of Maine books and documents, he did
collect a significant number of western books in his lifetime, most of
which are now at the Bangor (Maine) Public Library.[84] James III would

work hard to keep a connection with his Aunt Carrie until her death in 1960 at the age of ninety-one. He must have been pleased when she wrote to him while he was attending Bates College, "You seem to me more like one of my little grandsons and I will try to do better and write you some times."[85]

Three years after Aunt Carrie's visit her son William Theodore "Ted" and his wife Margaret Sandilands Vickery and their two young sons Michael Theodore and Erwin Arthur moved permanently to Unity from Montana.[86] The family's move to Maine completed a migratory circle that Ted's father Eli Ayer had begun when he left Maine to settle in Montana in the 1880s. Ted had first come to Unity in 1920 at the age of nineteen to work on the Vickery family farm. After returning to Montana where he and Margaret married, he worked at an oil refinery until he lost his job during the Great Depression. Margaret, who was expecting their second child, lived with her mother-in-law Carrie Brandenburg Vickery in Montana when Ted went back to work for the oil refinery in the winter of 1932–33. He lived in a one-room shack and stood guard against claim jumpers—dangerous work that took him away from his family, but work nonetheless. "Oh, we went through a lot, but so did everybody else," Margaret later reflected.[87] It was at this time that Ted's Uncle James II asked him to come back to Unity and help work the two-hundred-acre family farm.[88] Ted and Margaret decided to move to Maine with their family in 1933, obviously hoping it a better place than Montana to succeed in life—and succeed they did.

Ted Vickery lived the rest of his life in Unity and became, ironically, one of the "faces which mirror the face of Maine," according to the *Portland Press Herald* in 1965. Described as always wearing "a western style hat," Ted was "a one-man chamber of commerce" in Unity and was responsible for bringing a number of new businesses to his adopted town. He was a successful insurance and pulpwood broker, the director of School Administrative District Three, vice-president of the Maine Dairyman's Association, headed an office in Augusta that recruited farm labor during World War II, helped to found Unity College, and was involved in state politics.[89] The *Portland Press Herald* stated that Ted was "perhaps the only candidate to lose a Maine Primary election by drawing straws with an opponent … to break a recount tie in 1958 at the request of the Executive Council."[90]

Left: William "Ted" Theodore Vickery and unidentified child, Unity, Maine c. 1935. Born and raised in Montana, Ted lived the rest of his life in Unity and became, ironically, one of the "faces which mirror the face of Maine."

Right: Ted and Margaret Sandilands Vickery, Unity, Maine, c. 1935. Ted and Margaret decided to move to Maine with their family in 1933, obviously hoping it a better place than Montana to succeed in life—and succeed they did.

When Uncle James II asked his nephew Ted to come to Maine in 1933 he would have needed more help on the Vickery family farm.[91] At this time James II's oldest son, thirty-year-old Everett Steward Vickery, who had married Ethel Willsey of Hartford, Connecticut, in 1927, lived in Hartford and worked in sales. His second son, twenty-six-year-old Eric Arthur Vickery, who attended Shaw Business College in Waterville, Maine, had decided that like his father, grandfather, great-grandfather, and great-great-grandfather, he too was a farmer. But it must have been clear that like Everett, his youngest son, sixteen-year-old James Berry Vickery III was not going to stay on the farm. James II might also have welcomed his nephew Ted's and his wife Margaret's support at this time as well, for James II's wife Annie Stewart Vickery was terminally ill.

As a "housewife" Annie Stewart Vickery's life was dedicated to her family and the family farm. Thus she joined several community organizations for the well being of her family.[92] She was a member of the Ladies' Aid, a Christian service organization in Unity's Union Methodist church that raised money by holding baked bean suppers and yearly fairs and by producing dramas. She was a prominent member of the Order of the Eastern Star, the women's chapter of the Masons. Annie was also a member of the Farm Bureau that was established in Waldo County in the early 1920s. The Farm Bureau was part of Maine's Cooperative Extension Service and the home economics movement that sent professional women into the countryside to teach rural women how to use principles of thrift, modernity, and efficiency in the farm household. These home demonstration agents also tried to raise rural women's cul-

---

Annie May Stewart Vickery (1880–1933), c. 1930. As a "housewife" her life was dedicated to her family and the family farm. Thus she joined several community organizations for the well being of her family.

James Berry Vickery II (1872–1960), c. 1930. Letters reveal James II's struggle to balance his new role that called for tenderness as a husband and father with his image of himself forged by his heritage as a brusque, pragmatic, and unsentimental Yankee farmer.

tural awareness with music and literature appreciation classes, and attempted to set standards for personal appearance and health. While some rural women rejected these attempts by "city" women to make them "better," many enjoyed the opportunities that Farm Bureau meetings gave to socialize with other women in their communities.[93]

Annie Stewart Vickery was only fifty-two years old when she died on 11 August 1933. The cause of her death was listed as pernicious anemia. The most common cause of pernicious anemia is a lack of intrinsic factor, a substance needed to absorb vitamin B12 from the gastrointestinal tract. The onset of the disease is slow and usually does not appear before the age of thirty. It affects the gastrointestinal and cardiovascular systems, as well as the sensory and motor nerves, causing neurological problems. Shortness of breath, fatigue, pallor, rapid heart rate, loss of appetite, diarrhea, and personality changes are some of the symptoms from which Annie must have suffered for at least the final year of her life. Today, monthly injections of vitamin B12 can correct intrinsic factor deficiency and anemia.[94] Annie's husband James II's brother Eli Ayer Vickery had also died from pernicious anemia in 1914. Annie Stewart Vickery's funeral was held in the home in which she had given birth to her three sons; hers was the last generation to experience such intimacy. Home funerals and home births were going out of custom, as twentieth-century families relinquished their exclusive interaction with birth and death by moving these personal and important events into controlled environments managed by professionals.

"*J* am so sorry that you have lost your mother," wrote Gertrude Vickery Fisher to her cousin James III. "Hold on to the faith in God's goodness," she offered, "and the promise of Jesus for another home" where, according to Christian convention, James III would be reunited with his mother.[95] "I am glad you have the companionship of your western cousins," Cousin Gertrude wrote later that fall, verifying that James III was comforted somewhat during this difficult time by the presence of his western Vickery relatives in Unity.[96] His Aunt Margaret Sandilands Vickery, the mother of two young boys of her own and newly arrived in Unity, became a mother figure in James III's life after his mother's death. Aunt Margaret was a teacher who was committed to education and had great intellectual curiosity. She was an important force in cultivating these qualities in her own children as well as in her nephew.[97] Correspondence between James III and his Aunt Margaret through the years shows their fondness for each other and a mutual appreciation of music, art, theatre, literature, and the life of the mind.[98]

James Berry Vickery III was only sixteen when his mother died and her death must have precipitated the greatest yearning in his soul to preserve the history of Unity. Writing the history of his home was one way that James III could "bring back to life departed people, places, and times," and this project became the focus of his life.[99]

The Vickery family, Unity, Maine, c. 1943. "I am glad you have the companionship of your western cousins," Cousin Gertrude wrote after James III's mother died, verifying that he was comforted somewhat by the presence of his western Vickery relatives in Unity. Left to right, front row: unidentified boy, Ethel Willsey Vickery, Erwin Arthur Vickery, Eric Arthur Vickery, James Berry Vickery II. Left to right, back row: Margaret Sandilands Vickery, Cassie Hillman Hunt Vickery, William "Ted" Theodore Vickery, Michael Theodore Vickery.

11

One Hundred Percent Maine

JAMES BERRY VICKERY III

AM GLAD YOU HAVE HAD a talk with your prof. & teachers, it is worth something to understand each other and exchange views[;] it helps sometime. Try to concentrate on the main things in your work and get fixed in your mind what you want to say or write and then tell about it with some confidence. You want [to] try to put across to other people what you do know at least if possible, that comes a bit [after] meeting and mixing with people. That takes some plugging.
—James Berry Vickery II, "Home," 21 April 1938 to James Berry Vickery III, Bates College, Lewiston, Maine[1]

JAMES BERRY VICKERY III first left his family's farm in Unity to attend Maine Central Institute (MCI), a preparatory boarding school in Pittsfield, Maine, from which he graduated in 1935. James III was a shy boy who was very attached to his family and it must have been difficult for him to leave home, especially after his mother became ill. But his family recognized that he was destined for college (college was becoming more common for middle-class children), and they were willing to pay to prepare him. James III would be the first person in the ten generations of his direct ancestral line from George and Rebecca Phippen Vickery to graduate from college.

While attending Maine Central Institute a chance meeting with one of Maine's venerable figures helped to crystallize young James III's passion for Maine history. One afternoon he was getting his hair cut in a Pittsfield barbershop and socializing with a group of elderly men who were gathered there. When they all respectably stood up at once as another aged man stepped into the shop, James III was astonished. "Who was that?" he asked when the man left. It was Colonel Walter G. Morrill (1840–1935) who had "won never-to-be-forgotten laurels" at Gettysburg and was now in his nineties. It was a defining moment that made Maine history come alive for James III and it became one of his most precious memories.[2]

In 1936 James Berry Vickery III entered Bates College, a small, private liberal arts school in Lewiston, Maine, seventy miles away. Bates College was established by the Free Will Baptists as the Parsonfield Seminary in the mid nineteenth century, and was later incorporated as the Maine State Seminary in 1857. In 1864 it was renamed Bates College for Benjamin Bates, a Boston entrepreneur who started Bates Textile Manufacturing Company in Lewiston and contributed substantial financial support to the school. One of the college's goals was "making possible an education for young people of ability who needed financial aid," and from its earliest beginning as the Maine State Seminary it had included women. It remained coed when it became Bates College despite some opposition.[3] Bates College was known for preparing its students to be leaders in education—due in large part to its coeducational policy—and in the early 1930s half of its alumni were teachers or principals of New England secondary schools.[4] James III's cousins Alice Maude Vickery (Class of 1897) and Ethel Belle Vickery (Class of 1901) attended Bates College and became teachers.[5] It is not known if James III attended Bates because he desired to teach, but when he graduated from Bates he, too, became a teacher.[6]

George Colby Chase (1844–1919), who was born and grew up in Unity, had been a professor at Bates College, and was elected its second president in 1894.[7] Chase was the great-grandson of Quakers Stephen and Hannah Blethen Chase who were the first settlers of Unity in 1782. Chase, whose portrait was in the Vickery family photograph album, would have been a revered distant relative of James Berry Vickery III.[8] Another one of Unity's esteemed sons, Nelson Dingley, Jr. (1832–99), had been a member of the first Bates College Board of Overseers and a recipient of an honorary degree from the college in 1874, the governor of Maine in the 1870s, and a representative to the United States Congress, among other political positions. Bates College was a good match for James III's intellectual aspirations, sense of history, and his need for continuity of family and place.

"Your good letter received and will say we were all interested to know how you are getting along. If you were a bit home sick I guess that was a good sign," James Berry Vickery II wrote to his son his first semester at Bates in September 1936.[9]

> THE COURSE YOU ARE TAKING would not appeal very much to me, but if it suits you try and make the best of it. You are started in College now and I hope you will make good it remains to be seen whether it will be worth while for you to complete the 4 year course. We have all been very busy the past week on everything but mostly threshing Beans have got out so far 129 Bushels and there ought to be 80 or 90 Bu[shels] more.[10]

James II supported his son's ambitions and in his own way, reminiscent of the earlier letters he had written to his wife Annie when she was away, he told his son he missed him by writing, "I guess the shed has not been cleaned up since you left."[11] James II was, however, clearly skeptical of the college experience and was sure to remind James III that there was plenty of work on the farm to do if college did not prove "worth while" and he did not "make good."[12] Answering James III's next letter in which he must have written about the fun but challenging time he was having in college, his father chided him and reminded his son that sending him to college was costly.

> FROM THE TONE OF YOUR LETTER I guess you are having a pretty good time and I hope getting something that will do you some good. Any how I guess if you had put in some harder licks in your High school work here at home things would come easier to you now. I have received a Bill for the first Semester and I am sending it along to you to check up on, it just seems to me they tacked on a few extras.[13]

James Berry Vickery III, 1937. This photo of the quintessential 1930s college man standing out in a farm field is a powerful commentary on the two worlds that James III tried to span—the rural agrarian world and the scholarly academic world. "Vic" (as his classmates called him) found a way to bridge those worlds at a young age by deciding to write the history of Unity.

James Berry Vickery III, Bates College, Lewiston, Maine, c. 1938. "Try to concentrate on the main things in your work and get fixed in your mind what you want to say or write and then tell about it with some confidence. You want [to] try to put across to other people what you do know at least if possible, that comes a bit [after] meeting and mixing with people. That takes some plugging."

When James II received his son's second semester bill he turned to the barter system, the traditional form of economic exchange that farmers had used in Maine for over one hundred and fifty years. "I have your second Semester Bill due Mar[ch]," wrote James II. "Have not sent my check for the reason I have written the Busar to see if they could not use a load of potatoes. I ought to hear from him today, and then I will fix it up."[14] Bartering to pay tuition for college, as well as for many other items in the midst of the Great Depression was acceptable practice. James II wrote to his son in October 1937 that he was waiting for suitable weather "to haul the load of potatoes up there [to the college]" again that fall presumably to pay the fall semester bill, as well.[15]

"We had a letter from James last week and he enclosed a snap shot of himself," wrote James III's brother Everett to his father in 1937. "He certainly looks collegiate in that new overcoat & hat."[16] This photo of James Berry Vickery III (his classmates called him "Vic") as the quintessential college man of the mid-1930s standing out in a farm field is a powerful commentary on the two worlds that he tried to span—the rural agrarian world and the scholarly academic world. He had found a way to bridge those worlds at a young age by deciding to write the history of Unity, and he did not keep this goal a secret. As soon as he entered Bates College in the fall of 1937 the school newspaper announced that "a book dealing with the genealogical history of the old families of Unity Maine, is now being prepared by James B. Vickery III, '40, for publication at a future date."[17] Later in the fall his father wrote: "I called at Charles[?] Ware and Mrs. Ware told me she had heard come in over the Radio James Vickery 3rd was writing a history of the Town of Unity. Struck me kind of funny. What do you think. Some body locally must have wanted something to fill up. So you see you have got to make good."[18] At the age of thirteen James III proclaimed that he was going to write a book about Unity's history, but now that he was in college his family, community, and fellow students took him seriously. Throughout his four years at Bates he wrote hundreds of query letters to people who had grown up in Unity, many of whom were his relatives, asking them for genealogical data and stories about Unity to use in his book.

James Berry Vickery III's major course of study at Bates College was history and government (with a minor in economics and sociology), but he took as many English and literature classes as he did history and government classes. He joined the English, music, and arts clubs and participated in the "pioneering effort to hold a liberal arts exhibition."[19] By his junior year he had decided to become a teacher and took teaching methods and student teaching classes.[20] James III was a fair student and while he was later "ambivalent" about his Bates undergraduate education, he believed that it had prepared him adequately for his teaching

Frank M. Coffin (senior circuit judge in Maine for the United States Court of Appeals for the First Circuit), Bates College, Lewiston, Maine, c. 1938. "My own relationship with Jimmy was one based on the art of conversation. I deemed James to be one of the most civilized and interesting conversationalists on campus as well as in later life."

career.[21] What he appreciated most about Bates was its small, intimate campus life, which allowed him to make friendships that he kept for the rest of his life.[22] Frank M. Coffin (senior circuit judge in Maine for the United States Court of Appeals for the First Circuit) was in James III's class of 1940 and remembered well being friends with him at Bates:

My own relationship with Jimmy was one based on the art of conversation. I deemed James to be one of the most civilized and interesting conversationalists on campus as well as in later life. He always had something fresh to observe about books, plays, events and people…. Jimmy was a quiet person whose exploits at the college generally would not rival those of athletic heroes, but one uncharacteristic excursion in to notoriety occurred in the spring of 1939 when he ran for mayor of the campus. In those days, we ushered in spring by divesting ourselves of the late winter blahs with a mock mayoralty campaign. My roommate, Don Maggs, wrote the following in the "The Mirror" concerning Jimmy Vickery's role in that campaign: "Maharajah Vickery, assisted by make-up man Eddie Edwards, '39, introduced such well-known figures as Il Duce, Der Feuhrer, Ghandi, Frankenstein's monster and a twin Buck Howarth as supporters of his platform and promised: 'By the grace of Allah, Buddha, and sundry other jubilee, mount David revival meeting and mustard-plaster melee form the doldrums of doddering deficiency to the heights of heavenly harmony,' but to no avail."[23]

Bates College, Lewiston, Maine, 1939. "Maharajah Vickery [center], assisted by make-up man Eddie Edwards, '39, introduced such well-known figures as Il Duce, Der Feuhrer, Ghandi, Frankenstein's monster, and a twin Buck Howarth as supporters of his platform [for mayor of the campus]."

After James III graduated from college in 1940, he worked at Pratt & Whitney in Hartford, Connecticut (where his brother Everett lived), for a short while until he secured a job in 1941 teaching seventh and eighth grades in Portage Lake, Maine, and he continued his genealogical research.[24] "I have been having a delightful time working my family history, revealing all scandals & unmentioned skeletons & ghosts," he wrote to Frank M. Coffin. "To my dismay," he continued, "there are too few."[25] But before James III's teaching career had hardly begun, he was drafted in 1942 to serve in the army during World War II. Throughout the war he was stationed in northern Maine, Massachusetts, Alabama, Florida, and Virginia, and his chief duty was as a "writer of military subjects." Although he did not participate in any battles or campaigns overseas, Staff Sergeant Vickery did "Honest and Faithful Service" to his country and received the Good Conduct Medal, Victory Medal, and the American Theater Campaign Ribbon.[26]

Like so many Maine men and women who served in World War II, his time in the service broadened his worldview. His experience in the army seemed to give James III a deeper understanding and appreciation for his ancestor Private David Vickery II's extraordinary record of service in the Revolutionary War.[27] It would also be an important element in the mentoring he gave to some of his high-school students who joined the military during his career as a high-school teacher.[28] Of course, World War II did not stop James III's genealogical research. While stationed at Camp Edwards, his cousin Stillman wrote, "I'm wondering just where on the Cape Camp Edwards is located. While you are in the vicinity I hope you will not forget to try if possible to dig out the identity of Elizabeth_____, the wife of lieut. Nicholas Eldredge, whose dau. Mary married Rev. Johnathan Vickery's son Jonathan."[29]

After his honorable discharge in 1946 James III resumed his career in education by teaching English at Lee Academy, Lee, Maine.[30] In the late 1940s, however, he found himself without a job and wondered if teaching would provide him with a secure future, as he explained to his cousin Stillman, at the same time highlighting that not much had changed for women in the teaching profession in one hundred years.

UNTIL ABOUT TWO WEEKS AGO I believed that I was going to teach. The teaching positions are well filled up in Maine and the

Left: Staff Sargent James Berry Vickery III, Unity, Maine, c. 1944. Like so many Maine men and women who served in World War II, his time in the service broadened his worldview, and his experience in the army seemed to give James III a deeper understanding and appreciation for his ancestor Private David Vickery II's extraordinary record of service in the Revolutionary War.

Right: James Berry Vickery III, Newport, Maine, 1946.
"My leather flight jacket—horsehide."

competition is getting keen again. Many superintendents are hiring women teachers in English because they can contract them cheaper and then in the social science field they hire a combination athletic coach and teacher. That leaves me high and dry, so I believe now that I shall try to get into Junior-College teaching or Normal school and perhaps into college work.[31]

Embedded in this passage was James III's impression that women and those unbefitting were taking over the teaching profession. The rise of the nostalgic Colonial Revival Movement and the cultural sentimental-izing of small-town life in James III's generation was more than just a reaction by white Anglo-Saxon Protestants to ethnic and race ascendancy. The new public roles and power of women outside the home that had become particularly visible during World War I, and then later during World War II, challenged the exclusive authority of white Anglo-Saxon Protestant men in particular. This melancholy in watching the decline of patriarchy was, perhaps, an unconscious factor in James III's dedication to documenting a world and time (which he often implied was a better one) that was gone forever.

With the help of the Servicemen's Readjustment Act of 1944, or GI Bill, which among other benefits paid for tuition and living expenses of veterans of World War II who attended colleges or trade schools, James III entered the master's program in the Department of History and Government at the University of Maine in 1949.[32] It was the University of Maine and his military service that made his book on the history of the town of Unity, Maine, a reality. The structure and requirements of the graduate program impelled James III finally to put together the research he had been compiling for almost twenty years, resulting in his thesis entitled *Chapters in the History of Unity, Maine* and his Master's Degree in history in 1950. This graduate degree surely helped him to obtain his next teaching position at Dexter (Maine) High School in 1951 where he would stay until 1962.

After adding four chapters to his Master's thesis James III published *A History of the Town of Unity, Maine* in 1954 with, no doubt, much satisfaction and relief. James III's long-awaited book appeared just in time for the celebration of the 150th anniversary of Unity's incorporation.[33] James III had wanted his cousin S. Stillman Berry III to write an introduction to *A History of the Town of Unity, Maine,* but "physical disabilities" and not "enough unharried moments" kept Stillman from "getting something on paper" that he felt James III could use. "An occasional thought was jotted down, and had your book been a few months later in appearing I think perhaps that I could have been more helpful," he wrote.

NOW THE BOOK HAS finally reached me up here [in Montana] and I have been reading it at every possible opportunity, with the

James Berry Vickery III with friend and colleague Ruth Slater, Dexter (Maine) High School, c. 1960. After earning his Master's Degree in history from the University of Maine in 1950, James III taught at Dexter from 1951 until 1962.

keenest interest and enjoyment. It is very attractively printed and bound and your cuts came out remarkably well, especially the one of Great-grandmother Berry. What a <u>pretty</u> old lady she was! You did well to include so many pictures, although they are so nice one wishes the number was twice as great. In the letterpress I think the chapter on the Coming of the Settlers particularly well done, and here again I wish there were twice as much of it. And I like the ideas and the way they are set forth in the long paragraph on p. 201…. Most New England town histories err in failing to cite much of their source material. Your superb bibliography adds enormously to the value of your book. What a lot of work you put in on that![34]

Stillman drew James III's attention to "several unfortunate mistakes" in the book's notes about Montana, but on the whole sent "all good wishes and congratulations on the completion of the History." Not letting James III rest on his laurels, however, he added, "I hope you come out well enough with the sales to encourage you in the preparation of a Thorndike volume, and also a second Unity volume to contain your very rich family history material, much of which possesses quite as much permanent value and interest as the history of the town itself."[35] Stillman expressed regret that he was unable to attend Unity's celebration of its 150th anniversary, but hoped it and James III's book "resulted both in a renewal of town pride and a permanent invigoration of town spirit."[36]

James Berry Vickery III's *A History of the Town of Unity, Maine* invigorated Unity's town spirit, and represented the spirit of the times

S. Stillman Berry III and James Berry Vickery III, "Sentinel Rock,"
Winnecook Ranch, Montana, c. 1960s. James III identified with
Stillman's proclivity for preservation and consciously or unconsciously
used him as a model.

James Berry Vickery III and his long-awaited book, The History of
the Town of Unity, Maine, *c. 1954. After years of facing his father's
challenge that he "had to make good," it must have been fulfilling for
thirty-seven-year-old James III to have his eighty-two-year-old father
write, "I guess you are making good."*

as well. John M. Cates, Jr. (who apparently traced his heritage to Waldo
County) was stationed with the military in Germany in 1955 when he
read the book and thought that while its regional appeal was important,
it had civic and patriotic relevance in a Cold War world as well.

> I HAVE READ GREAT parts of it [*A History of the Town of Unity,
> Maine*] and enjoyed it greatly. It is indeed the raw material of so
> many of the Sarah Orme Jewett stories. Have you read her "Coun-
> try of the Pointed Firs"? … Here in Germany, so far from our
> roots and with the ever present prospect of an even further
> removal, it is good to have books like yours with us and to keep
> in mind the accomplishments of those hardy early settlers in
> Maine and what they stood for…. I meant to ask this before, but
> how did you happen to pick Unity? Also, have you even thought

of a small booklet on the wonderful names of Maine towns? It would read like a lesson in patriotism of the better sort and a lesson in brotherhood![37]

The 1950s were an era of "conservatism, boosterism, and unabashed patriotic celebration" and many Americans believed that historians should laud the special values that had united Americans and made the United States great.[38] This mood is reflected in James III's Preface. "It is in our local towns that many of our distinctive American qualities have developed, especially those places long associated with the frontier," he stated. "It is from the sturdy spirit of the settlers that we partially received our traits of resourcefulness, independence, self-reliance, adaptability, inquisitiveness, and other outstanding characteristics which have become a part of our American heritage."[39] *A History of the Town of Unity, Maine* was just the right book for the political climate.[40]

In the March 1955 issue of the *New England Quarterly* James III's friend Maine historian Elizabeth Ring reviewed *A History of the Town of Unity, Maine*. First Ring described "the function of local history."

IN ITS FULLEST EXPRESSION, town history is more than a compilation of facts. In its own right it may tell a readable and inspiring story of the everyday life of people who through successive generations have lived together. To accomplish this result, the story itself must have unity and integration, and at its best be chronologically told and fitted into the national and state scene of which it is a part. For in its relation to national history, town history is both cause and result. It is *cause* because the pattern of history has been established by the collective behavior of all the people living in the cities and hamlets through the nation at any one time. It is *result* because what people did in a town in generations past has made its impress on its own life course—in time present and time future.... The local historian [must] ... point up the national trend ... and ... interpret in terms of an integrated narrative story which for the town will interlock all generations.[41]

"At his best," Elizabeth Ring wrote, James Berry Vickery III had "caught the spirit just described" and "gave his townsmen an understanding of what they were celebrating in 1954 on the occasion of the 150th anniversary of the town's incorporation."[42] Ring's review implies that the essence of local history, indeed all history, is people and their networks of relationships—connections—to other people, which is the foundation of genealogy. Today many historians use genealogical information, as historian Samuel P. Hays points out, to understand "migration and vertical mobility, changes in family size and life cycle, and the impact of modernization on traditional values and practices in religion, family, and recreation."[43] Academic scholars, however, have not always appreciated the wealth of information that genealogists have doggedly unearthed. *A History of the Town of Unity, Maine* was an early example of how genealogy and political, economic, military, and social history might come together in "an integrated narrative story" to tell a more complete history of Maine and the United States.[44]

James III's father had offered moral and financial support, as well as sound economic advice for the publication of *A History of the Town of Unity, Maine.* The following letter that James III received from his

James Berry Vickery III (center) with four-year-old Kathleen Ellen Vickery and Margaret Sandilands Vickery (in bonnet fourth from left, back row) gather with others in period costume to celebrate the one hundred and fiftieth anniversary of Unity's incorporation, August 1954. Everyone hoped the celebration and the release of James III's book on Unity's history would renew "town pride and a permanent invigoration of town spirit." COURTESY OF UNITY HISTORICAL SOCIETY.

father in the fall of 1953 reveals not only the hard-nosed relationship that James III's father had with him, but it captures the essence of why James Berry Vickery II had been a very successful Maine farmer.

YOUR GOOD LETTER RECEIVED. I note all you say or the most of it in regard to the publishing of your book[.] You did not say who you had chosen or are in touch with in regard to getting it out. As far as the cost of getting the book published I would say as good a way as any would be to shop around to some extent and have a chance to examine & look over books that publishers have brought out similar to what yours will be like and compare them with the cost. As for setting a price of $7.50 to $10. Bucks a copy I know you have done a good job or may feel it is worth it but that is only one side of it. You might sell a few copies or 100 at that price, but the others would go so slow you would hardly notice. I would say it would be much better to set a price that the general public would feel like paying in order to practically sell all of them. What you would not sell would not be much benefit to you financially. I do not know what the job may cost you but I am just guessing that if you are able to sell 300 copies at $5.00 each you will do well. There is another matter of sending copies out of State of postage & packing. I note you say the book is all done and already in the Publishers hands [Falmouth Publishing House, Manchester, Maine], what about the contract if you have one and how it reads. Sure, I will back you to the extent of a thousand bucks and you may pay me back as you are able to sell your book. I note all about how busy you are: every body for his truck[.] I suppose that is what you are getting paid for. Well, anyhow hope every thing school and book turns out all right.[45]

School and his book did turn "out all right" for James Berry Vickery III.[46] In the spring of 1954 after years of facing his father's challenge that he "had to make good," it must have been fulfilling for thirty-seven-year-old James III to have his eighty-two-year-old father write, "I guess you are making good."[47]

In 1954 eighty-two-year-old James Berry Vickery II no longer lived on the "old family farm" on Quaker Hill. His sister Josephine (for whom he would have felt responsible) had died in 1946, and his own health had begun to decline in the late 1940s.[48] In April 1948 he retired and sold the farm that his grandfather, Eli Vickery, had built in the 1830s to Harry M. Brown. Brown was from neighboring Brooks, Maine, and after buying the "old Vickery place" he kept a herd of milk cows and continued to grow the potatoes, sweet and field corn, shell beans, and oats that supplied the Portland Packing Company in Unity that he had managed since 1915.[49] But mid-sized family farms in Maine like the Vickery farm that Brown hoped to continue had been steadily decreasing since 1910 and after 1940 the total number of Maine farms dropped by 80 percent. "A mechanical-biological-chemical revolution" had changed farming, making it too expensive for many family farms to compete with the growing presence of giant agribusinesses, and they shut down. The large-scale specialized producers of potatoes, dairy products, and poultry replaced the family farms that had defined Maine for 150 years.[50]

In 1940 at the age of sixty-eight James Berry Vickery II and thirty-seven-year-old Cassie Hillman Hunt had married, and after they sold the farm in 1948 they, Eric, and Cassie's cats moved to another historic family home. James II explained their new living circumstances in a letter to S. Stillman Berry III:

> HERE WE ARE ABOUT 3 miles above the Village at what is called the Bither Brook property[,] a large 2 story white house in from the road about 10 or 12 feet. This place was built in 1812 & the land cleared by Isaac Mitchell who James says had 11 children[,] his wife was a Vickery [Hannah] a sister to my great grandfather David [III]. Anyhow it is very pleasant here & has a shore front on Winnecook lake of nearly half a mile.[51]

Surely the sale of the family farm must have immersed James Berry Vickery III in nostalgic feelings, which were mitigated somewhat by the fact that at the time he was living in Orono while attending the University of Maine. "I don't blame you for missing the old farm, and I too feel badly to have it leave the Vickery name, but I can understand your father's point of view too," wrote Stillman sympathizing with his cousin James III in August 1949.

James Berry II and Cassie Hillman Hunt Vickery, Unity, c. 1940.
Cassie felt very much a part of the Vickery family. Her fondness for
S. Stillman Berry III is prevalent in letters to him, and in September
1964 she went west to visit Winnecook Ranch and Vickery relatives.

While no mention was made what James III's father's "point of view" was, an astute businessman like James II surely understood that family farms were no longer a good investment, especially without sons and grandchildren to take over.[52] James II was right, as historian Richard H. Condon affirms because "by 1945, in most areas of Maine, the end was in sight for rural communities centering economically and socially on farms."[53] In the same August 1949 letter, perhaps to help James III embrace the move, Stillman (ever the preservationist) added, "I know the old Mitchell-Bither place, at least from the road, but I've never been inside it. Did you ever explore the attic on the chance of something being left there?"[54]

In 1957 James Berry Vickery III wrote to his cousin Stillman that while his father was "quite well," his memory had been failing. "Day to day he retains very little," he said, "but continues daily conversation well enough if he doesn't have to recall who anyone is."[55] In an October 1959 letter to Stillman James III mentions in a brief postscript that his father was "not too well."[56] On 2 June 1960 James Berry Vickery II died at his

Bither Brook house, Untiy, Maine, c. 1950. "This place was built in 1812 & the land cleared by Isaac Mitchell who James [III] says had 11 children[,] his wife was a Vickery [Hannah] a sister to my great grandfather David [III]. Anyhow it is very pleasant here & has a shore front on Winnecook lake of nearly half a mile."

home at Bither Brook at the age of eighty-eight. The three-page type-written letter to Stillman that James III wrote shortly after his father's death reveals the life he had made for himself—quite independent from his father and the rural agrarian world. Opening with talk of spring flowers in bloom and his "frantic times at school with so much prepa-ration for making out exams and rehearsing for graduation," at Dexter (Maine) High School where he was still teaching, James III inserted,

> PROBABLY BY THIS TIME you have heard that my father passed away. When I saw him at Easter time, he seemed much like he was last Thanksgiving when you saw him. Then he took sick about four days after Easter, and the doctor pronounced his illness as cancer of the liver; it was also aggravated by prostate gland trou-ble and a hernia, and some growth in his intestine. He lived much longer than I expected he would, because I saw him about May 12th, when I didn't think that he would live through the night. He just lost weight until he was skin and bones, but Cassie took very good care of him and he didn't have to go to the hospital which he dreaded.[57]

James III typed a few lines about the funeral and the rest of the letter is full of his research on Civil War Colonel Walter G. Morrill of the Twen-tieth Maine, trips he had taken to Montreal, Ottawa, and the Shelburne Museum [Vermont] that spring, and plans for an auto trip to Montana that he hoped to make with his brother Eric.[58] While James III mourned his father's death, he clearly had a full life to assuage his loss.

James Berry Vickery II's funeral service with organ music of old hymns that he had requested was held at the Unity Union Church. By 1960 it was rare even in rural areas for funerals to be held at home. "There was a profusion of flowers, and despite the fact there [were] so few contemporaries," James III told his cousin Stillman, "the church was nearly filled."[59] James II was buried next to his first wife Annie Stewart Vickery in Unity Pond Cemetery. The Bither Brook house and property was left to his sons. Any financial arrangements James II may have made for his fifty-seven-year-old widow Cassie Hillman Hunt Vickery seem sketchy as she went out to work soon after his death, nursing an elderly couple, then moving to Skowhegan, Maine, to keep house in the Meth-

James Berry Vickery II (1872–1960), age eighty-eight. An astute businessman like James II surely understood that family farms were no longer a good investment, especially without sons and grandchildren to take over.

odist parsonage for the minister.[60] Cassie did feel very much a part of the Vickery family, though. Her fondness for S. Stillman Berry III is prevalent in letters to him, and in September 1964 she went West to visit Vickery relatives in Montana, planning to visit Winnecook Ranch as well.[61] She eventually moved back to her hometown of Hartland, Maine, dying there in 1997.

S. Stillman Berry III died in California in 1984 at the age of ninety-seven. Stillman had never married and had no children, so he conceived of the Goodly Heritage Foundation, a charitable trust that would distribute income from his Winnecook Ranch Corporation stock and his other investments after his death. The Internal Revenue Service, however, dismantled the trust and Stillman's $900,000 estate was distributed among Stanford University, the Redlands (California) Community Hospital, and the A. K. Smiley Library in Redlands. In 1992 Winnecook Ranch, which had gone out of the sheep business and had converted to cattle in 1947, was sold to the Farm Management Company, a subsidiary of the Mormon church.[62] At least one of Stillman's planned legacies does endure, however. In 1982 Stillman purchased the 1813 brick home of his and James Berry Vickery III's ancestors Lemuel and Hannah Chase Bartlett in Unity as the permanent location of the Unity Historical Society.[63] The Unity Historical Society today is a thriving and vibrant organization. Not far away, S. Stillman Berry III is buried, next to his father and mother Ralph and Evie Kelley Berry and surrounded by centuries of his Unity relatives in Unity Pond Cemetery on the shores of Winnecook Lake.

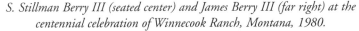

S. Stillman Berry III (seated center) and James Berry III (far right) at the centennial celebration of Winnecook Ranch, Montana, 1980.

Unlike previous generations, deaths in the ninth generation of the Unity, Maine, branch of the Vickery family were not offset by the births of new Vickery children in the tenth. An "avid outdoorsman and fisherman" Everett Stewart Vickery had returned with his wife to Unity from Connecticut to live after he retired in 1970.[64] Everett and his wife Ethel never had children, and he died at the age of eighty-four on 27 March 1986. Ethel Willsey Vickery died on 21 June 1991.

Eric Vickery continued to live in the Bither Brook house, and James III moved back to Unity to live with him each summer when his teaching responsibilities in Dexter, and later Brewer, Maine, ended for the year. Eric Arthur Vickery, like his cousin Stillman and his brother James III, never married. By all accounts Eric was a good-humored, humble man who was content to live his life farming in Unity, involving himself in town government and service organizations, and playing baseball, contract bridge, and cribbage. "His great love was his car" and he and his brother James III, who had never learned to drive, often took auto trips together.[65] After their father's death in the summer of 1960 Eric and James III drove to Montana to visit their cousin Stillman at Winnecook Ranch. They took pleasure from their times together, and Eric was unflappable as James III's growing collection of books turned their home into a library.[66] Eric shared James III's passion for American history, and they enjoyed shooting small firearms together for sport. Without fail, year in and year out, Eric drove every Sunday to have breakfast with his brother James III who lived in Brewer during the school year and in Bangor after 1981.[67]

William H. Bunting, who spent a great deal of time with Eric and James III while working on his two-volume book of historic Maine photographs *A Day's Work*, said although Eric and James III were "very different in many ways, no two brothers were ever more devoted." Bunting's dedication to the memory of James III and Eric in *A Day's Work* captured the rhythm of the Vickery brothers' last years together in the Bither Brook house:

DURING THE SUMMER the Vickery brothers, in some ways the oddest of couples, were renowned for the unique style with which they maintained bachelors' hall at Eric's Unity house. This house was stacked from floor to ceiling with Jim's books, and during the

Eric Arthur Vickery, Unity, Maine, 1962. Although Eric and James III were "very different in many ways, no two brothers were ever more devoted."

winter Eric doubtless was the best read farmhand in the state of Maine. Eric, like Jim, was a man of great intelligence and curiosity, and observed the human comedy and tragedy with a sharp eye tempered by a large heart.[68]

When managing the Bither Brook house became too much for Eric, he and James III sold the house in 1980. Eric moved into a new elderly housing unit in Unity that was close to the favorite breakfast place where he and his Unity friends liked to meet. After a long illness eighty-four-year-old Eric died on 28 March 1991, almost five years to the day after his older brother Everett.[69]

James Berry Vickery III had taught English at Brewer (Maine) High School since 1962. He was the type of teacher, as one of his students remembered, "who was warm, funny, and made the kids see the big picture" and was "a dynamo" who "knew everything."[70] During the school year he lived in a tiny apartment in Cox's Lodge on North Main Street in Brewer and walked to his teaching job at Brewer High. The former tourist home was like a "1920s time warp" and felt comfortable to James III.[71] In 1981, a year before his sixty-fifth birthday, he retired from teaching after thirty-four years and moved into an apartment in a historic brick townhouse on Broadway in Bangor. James III likened his retirement to a "snake" shedding its skin, and said he had decided to "enjoy writing and traveling" before he grew "too old."[72] In his retirement James III indulged his lifelong passion for historical research, spending countless hours at the Bangor (Maine) Public Library. Scholars working on Maine history often started or ended their projects consulting with James III as he loved to share his research discoveries and knowledge. Maine historian James H. Mundy, who became a close friend of James III, believed that "no one could 'work' the Bangor Public Library" and its wealth of Maine history sources like "Jim Vickery."[73]

James Berry Vickery III became a notable figure in Bangor and central Maine, giving public talks and acting as "official" custodian of the region's history, and he was appreciated for his dedication. Acknowledging his extraordinary collection of rare Maine books and documents, James III was given the Historic Preservation Award from the Maine

James Berry Vickery III's seventy-five birthday party at the Cole Land Transportation Museum, Bangor, Maine, 1992. Left to right: Galen L. Cole, James Berry Vickery III, John Arthur Vickery, Jr., John Arthur Vickery, Sr., Betsy Jones Vickery.

*In 1993 the University of Maine bestowed James Berry Vickery III
with an honorary doctorate, describing him as "a highly respected
scholar of Maine history who has devoted more than 50 years of his
life to researching this important subject."*

Historic Preservation Commission in 1973. For his "lifelong commitment to promoting the understanding and appreciation of Maine History" he received the prestigious Award of Merit from the American
Association for State and Local History, as well as a Distinguished Service Award from the University of Maine in 1983.[74] He was honored
with the key to the City of Bangor, and he was feted at the Cole Land
Transportation Museum on his seventy-fifth birthday in 1992. In 1993
the University of Maine bestowed James Berry Vickery III with an honorary doctorate, describing him as "a highly respected scholar of Maine
history who has devoted more than 50 years of his life to researching
this important subject."[75]

Eventually moving into the Schoolhouse apartments right next
door to his beloved Bangor Public Library—an establishment some
thought he "owned"—James III found his nirvana in the last years of
his life.[76] "I've never married," he said, "so I've lived as I've wanted. I go
downtown to eat when I don't want to cook. I read three to four books
a week. I get calls from people [for information]; it's more fun researching than writing. Every day I do just what I want to do."[77]

While James III was doing just what he wanted to do, he was often doing it alone after his brother Eric died in 1991. Eric's death signaled James III's own mortality. He was the last of the three brothers, and in a "matter-of-fact business approach to life" he began to make major decisions about his own death, determined that no one else would be burdened with the responsibility.[78] Earlier in his life James III's cousin Stillman advised him to "place all the priceless mass of genealogical and historical materials" that he had been working on all his life "in safe hands so that whatever befalls it will be cared for and preserved."[79] This was an admonition that he never forgot, and he now made provisions in his will for his "mass of genealogical and historical materials" to be transformed into this book. Each Sunday James III walked to Miller's restaurant on Main Street (Bangor) at noon for dinner, and took a taxi home to await the call that he received every Sunday afternoon from his longtime friend Earle G. Shettleworth, Jr.[80]

James Berry Vickery III sensed that time was running out, and he wanted to pass on to someone with his "name and blood" the "pride" in his family history that he and his cousin Stillman had felt.[81] Thus it was the journey that he made with his twenty-five-year-old third cousin

---

A "generous, private, quirky and dedicated man of many dimensions," James Berry Vickery III's essence is captured by Pete Stapler, 1972.

James Berry Vickery III (1917–1997), 1989. "In each generation, it is given to a few to have vision to preserve our cultural heritage."
©BANGOR DAILY NEWS, USED WITH PERMISSION.

John "Johnny" Arthur Vickery II in 1993 to Montana that surely must have meant the most to him at the end of his life.[82] He had made a number of trips there through the years, but he had never written the history of his western relatives that he hoped to, and his obligation to pass on this history before he died compelled him to make this journey with his young cousin. After this trip, his familial duty fulfilled, seventy-six-year-old James III began to fail.

James Berry Vickery III was described by his friends, relatives, and colleagues as a "generous, private, quirky, and dedicated man of many dimensions" and while respecting his freedom, they kept watch over him as he became more and more disengaged from life.[83] In the spring of 1997 close friends, concerned because they could not contact James III, entered his Bangor apartment and found that he had suffered a stroke. The next six weeks that he spent in the hospital was a time of "incredible grace," as Earle G. Shettleworth, Jr., recalled, because James III (who remained cognizant) was "showered with visits from people" and he "knew he was appreciated."[84] When there was no more that could be done to bring him back to health, James III moved to the Maine Veteran's Home in Bangor on Memorial Day weekend. He liked it there (his first Jacuzzi bath was a thrill) and thought the nurses were "wonderful."[85] James Berry Vickery III died at the Maine Veteran's Home on 13 June 1997. Speaking at his funeral, Earle G. Shettleworth, Jr., eloquently confirmed the meaning of James III's life:

> IN EACH GENERATION, it is given to a few to have vision to preserve our cultural heritage. Jim was one of those keepers of the light. We who knew him will deeply miss him, but are consoled that his spirit will live on through his life's work to illuminate the minds of future generations.[86]

James III was buried with the many generations and branches of the Vickery family in Unity Pond Cemetery "back home" in Unity, Maine.

NOTES

INTRODUCTION

1. S. Stillman Berry III (hereafter cited as SSB III) to James Berry Vickery III (hereafter cited as JBV III), 25 June 1942. JBV III Papers, Special Collections, Raymond H. Fogler Library, University of Maine, Orono (hereafter cited as JBV III Papers).

2. See William C. Cronon, "Revisiting Turner's Vanishing Frontier," in Clyde A. Milner II, editor, *Major Problems in the History of the American West* (Lexington, MA: D. C. Heath and Company, 1989), 668–81. For an initial call to use and a fine analysis on the use of genealogy and local histories as important sources for understanding state and national history, see Elizabeth Ring, a review of *A History of the Town of Unity, Maine*, by James Vickery III, *The New England Quarterly* 36 (March 1955), 124–26.

3. See Linda Gordon, "History Matters Forum on Family History," 11 March 2002. familiesforum@ashp.listserv.cuny.edu,

4. Consummate definition of JBV III as "teacher, historian, and antiquarian" in the dedication of W. H. Bunting's *A Day's Work: A Sampler of Historic Maine Photographs, 1860–1920*, Part I (Gardiner, Maine: Tilbury House, Publishers, 1997).

5. See Sarah P. Twiss to JBV III, 6 August 1936. JBV III Papers. Twiss wrote in response to a genealogical inquiry from JBV III: "Now Mr. Vickery I hope you will have the best success in your good work[;] altho I do not know you, I know you are one of the 'Unity Vickerys.'"

6. Geneviere B. McAlary to JBV III, 5 October 1949. JBV III Papers.

7. See Elizabeth Ring, *Maine in the Making of the Nation, 1783–1870* (Camden, Maine: Picton Press, 1996).

8. For the connection between identity formation and genealogy see Thomas S. Rue, "Genealogy as a Tool for Self-Knowledge and Family Therapy," 1998, http://free pages.genealogy.rootsweb.com/~tomrue/systems.htm: "Beginning to learn about one's heritage, even by speaking with available older relatives about their pasts, can help facilitate self-awareness as a member of a group and provide a bridge to a forgotten cultural base, empowering individuals and family systems to confirm or reweave their values, identity patterns, and make changes in personal, family and cultural activities; all of which in turn may give hope for curing present social ills."

9. See Harry Macy, Jr., "Recognizing Scholarly Genealogy and Its Importance to Genealogists and Historians," *The New England Historical and Genealogical Register* 150, no. 597 (January 1996), 7–28. Historian Perry Miller argued that "ancestor worship" as a "literary formulation" that was to become "a staple of the New England mind" started as early as 1676, after the first generation of colonists died. See Perry Miller, *The New England Mind: From Colony to Province* (Cambridge: The Belknap Press of Harvard University, 1953), 135. For a good overview of the history of genealogy see Ralph S. Crandall and Robert M. Taylor, "Historians and Genealogists: An Emerging Community of Interest," in Ralph Crandall and Robert M. Taylor, editors, *Generations and Change: Genealogical Perspectives in Social History* (Macon, GA: Mercer University Press, 1986), 3–26.

10. See Alan Axelrod, editor, *The Colonial Revival in America* (New York: W. W. Norton & Company, 1985), 266–67. There were 26 men known to have been on the MAYFLOWER, and according to a former governor general of the General Society of MAYFLOWER Descendants, there were approximately 35 million MAYFLOWER

descendants worldwide in the year 2000—the largest single group in Massachusetts, and the second largest in California. See "Ancestors on the MAYFLOWER? Welcome to the Club," *Boston Globe*, 18 November 2000.

11. Crandall and Taylor, *Generations and Change*, 10.
12. See Macy, "Recognizing Scholarly Genealogy and Its Importance to Genealogists and Historians," 7–28.
13. See JBV III to SSB III, 24 March 1975: "I spoke … last Saturday to the MAYFLOWER Society, to which I have applied for membership. I have three MAYFLOWER ancestors: Richard Warren, Edward Doty & Francis, of another Henry Sampson. I joined the Portland chapter of S.A.R. [Sons of the American Revolution] three years ago." S. Stillman Berry Papers, Smithsonian Institution Archives (hereafter cited as SSB III Papers).
14. Elizabeth Crockett to "Cousin" JBV III, 28 November 1947. JBV III Papers.
15. Olive A. Gould to JBV III, 2 August 1933. JBV III Papers.
16. Edith A. Gilman to JBV III, 3 September 1934. JBV III Papers.
17. See SSB III to JBV III, 9 July 1930. JBV III Papers. The following is how JBV III and SSB III were related "in two ways": First, JBV III's great-great-great-grandfather and grandmother David II and Sarah Stone Vickery's daughter Sarah Vickery married Samuel Kelley. Samuel and Sarah Vickery Kelley were the grandparents of Evelyn Crie Kelley Berry, SSB III's mother. Second, JBV III's great-grandmother Clarissa Berry Vickery was the sister of SSB III's grandfather Samuel Stillman Berry I.
18. Gertrude Vickery Fisher to JBV III, c. 1933. JBV III Papers.
19. James E. Kelly to JBV III, 7 February 1934. JBV III Papers. Kelley was also related to JBV III "in two different ways" as he tells JBV III: "We connect by a common ancestor in the Heald line and also in the Vickery line, my grandmother having been Sarah Vickery[Kelley], daughter of David, a Revolutionary Soldier." James E. Kelley to JBV III, 16 January 1934. JBV III Papers. Full citation: Rufus King Sewall, *Ancient Dominions of Maine* (Bath, Maine: Elisha Clark and Company, 1859).
20. Robert H. Newall, "In retirement, Vickery plans to write, travel," *Bangor Daily News*, 21 May 1981.
21. Description of JBV III from Tom Weber, "Mining a Historical Treasure: James Vickery Collection Chronicles Maine's Past," *Bangor Daily News*, 15 August 1997.
22. JBV III to Earle G. Shettleworth, Jr., (hereafter cited as EGS, Jr.), 3 January 1972. Earle G. Shettleworth, Jr., Private Papers (hereafter cited as EGS, Jr. Papers).
23. JBV III donated 3,500 books, 250 pamphlets, and 300 manuscripts relating to Maine to Special Collections, Raymond H. Fogler Library at the University of Maine, Orono, in 1978. At the time it was acknowledged as "the most extensive private (noninstitutional) collection of Maine history and Maine literature extant." JBV III also helped organize and catalog this collection. See Project Grant Application, Maine State Commission on the Arts and Humanities, "Arrangement, Cataloging and Preservation of the Vickery Collection, Part 1, 1977–1978." JBV III Papers. When JBV III died in 1997 he left the rest of his collection to the University of Maine and the Bangor Public Library. According to librarian Muriel Sanford at Special Collections, "Not a day goes by without someone using an item from Jim's collection." From "James B. Vickery III Eulogy" by EGS, Jr., 17 June 1997. EGS, Jr., Papers. Quote on duplication of collection by EGS, Jr., conversation with author, 11 January 2002.
24. After reading award-winning author William Maxwell's book, *Ancestors: A Family History* (New York: Knopf, 1971), Jim allowed that while he told "an interesting

story," Maxwell's family did not have "half the romance" of "the Berry, Vickery, Bartlett, Jackson, Files, Kelley, etc. background" of his family. See JBV III to SSB III, 17 January 1972. SSB III Papers.

25. JBV III to Mrs. Howe, 15 October 1951. JBV III Papers.

26. Tom Weber, "Bangor's greatest natural resource," *Bangor Daily News*, 20 June 1992.

27. Ibid.

28. For a fine tribute to JBV III and his relationship to the Bangor Public Library, see Marc Berlin, "James B. Vickery III," in *Seven Books in a Footlocker: A Commemorative History of the Bangor Public Library* (Bangor, Maine: The Bangor Public Library, 1998), 66–67.

29. JBV III to EGS, Jr., 25 September 1972. EGS, Jr., Papers.

30. Gertrude Vickery Fisher (hereafter cited as GVF) to JBV III, ca. 1933. As written in a note from Lt. Chas. Edwin Vickery to GVF. JBV III Papers.

31. Kate Banning, *Genealogical and Biographical Records of the Banning and Allied Families* (n.p.: The American Historical Society, Inc., 1924), 46.

32. See Steven Mintz and Susan Kellogg, *Domestic Revolutions: A Social History of American Family Life* (New York: The Free Press, 1988), 39. While this idea is studied here within the context of the colonial South, I believe it is relevant for colonial through twentieth-century New England, as well.

33. David Hackett Fisher, "Forenames and the Family in New England: An Exercise in Historical Onomastics," in Crandall and Taylor, *Generations and Change*, 217.

34. GVF to JBV III, c. 1933. JBV III Papers. Elizabeth Ring makes a similar pronouncement about "the juggling of family names" in her work with the town of Limington, Maine: "This tangle of names, combined with the frequent appearance of the same name in the person of two, and sometimes three different persons whose life span often overlapped is an adjustment which the local historian must patiently solve." See Ring, *Maine in the Making of a Nation*, 62–63.

35. William Lynwood Montell, in the preface to *The Saga of Coe Ridge: A Study in Oral History*, in David K. Dunaway and Willa K. Baum, editors, *Oral History: An Interdisciplinary Anthology* (Nashville, Tennessee: American Association for State and Local History in cooperation with the Oral History Association, 1984), 165–76.

36. "Montana Pioneer and Poet—Carol Townsend Myers," interview by Ester Johansson Murray, Winter 1970–71, 9. JBV III Papers.

37. Susan Sontag, *On Photography* (New York: Anchor Books, 1989), 8–9.

38. JBV III to EGS, Jr., 27 September 1967. EGS, Jr., Papers. See JBV III to SSB III, 1 November 1964: "Can you guess what person from Unity or Thorndike went to Montana in the eighties whose picture I have; I got it from Bill Farwell's house and the picture was taken by the famous frontier—Huffman. The Farwells themselves never went West, but Bill's mother was a Ware and related to Cornforths, Riches, and Stevens. He has a goatee much like the one your father wore. I wish that I might identify it." SSB III Papers.

39. See Joan Severa, *Dressed for the Photographer: Ordinary Americans & Fashion, 1840–1900* (Kent, OH: The Kent State University Press, 1995) for best source in visual analysis of nineteenth-century images.

40. See note 34 above.

PART ONE

CHAPTER 1

1. JBV III Papers.
2. For description of journey see John T. Horton, "Two Bishops and the Holy Brood: A Fresh Look at the Familiar Fact," *New England Quarterly* 40, 342; and Benjamin W. Labaree, William M. Fowler, Jr., Edward W. Sloan, John B. Hattendorf, Jeffrey J. Safford, and Andrew W. German, in the introduction to *America and the Sea* (Mystic, CT: Mystic Seaport Museum, 1988).
3. For the best account of the motivations behind the Great Migration see Virginia DeJohn Anderson, *New England's Generation: The Great Migration and the Formation of Society and Culture in the Seventeenth Century* (New York: Cambridge University Press, 1991). See also Bernard Bailyn, *The Peopling of British North America: An Introduction* (New York: Alfred A. Knopf, 1986).
4. See N. Grier Parke II, *The Ancestry of Lorenzo Ackley & His wife Emma Arabella Bosworth*, edited by Donald Lines Jacobus (Woodstock, VT: The Elm Press, 1960), 198–200. The name Phippen was spelled alternately as Fitzpen, Fippen, Fippenny, or Phippenney. According to Parke: "The name Phippen is a patronymic, being originally Fitzpen or FitzPayn. In the twelfth century, the baronial family of Fitz-Payn held the manor of Oaksey, Wiltshire, and held lands in Dorsetshire. When Rev. George Fitzpen, brother of David Phippen of New England, entered his pedigree and arms in the Visition of Cornwell, 1620, the pedigree was headed 'Fitzpen al's Phippen'.... As late as 1663, David's son appears in Boston deeds as Joseph 'Phippen al's Fitzpen." Parke, *The Ancestry of Lorenzo Ackley*, 198.
5. For the family in early New England see Edmund S. Morgan, *The Puritan Family: Religion and Domestic Relations in Seventeenth-Century New England*, new ed. (New York: Harper & Row, 1966); John Demos, *A Little Commonwealth: Family Life in Plymouth Colony* (New York: Oxford University Press, 1970); Steven Mintz and Susan Kellogg, "The Godly Family in New England and Its Transformation," *Domestic Revolutions: A Social History of American Family Life* (New York: The Free Press, 1988), 1–23.
6. For the system of land distribution in Massachusetts Bay Colony see Anderson, *New England's Generation*, 89–100.
7. For more on Phippen family see George Lincoln, *History of the Town of Hingham, Mass.*, vol. III, the genealogies, reprint (Somersworth, NH: New England History Press, 1982), 112; and Donald Lines Jacobus, "The Phippen Family and the Wife of Nathan Gold of Fairfield, Connecticut," *The American Genealogist*, vol. XVII, no. 1 (July 1940), 1–9.
8. In a 2 April 1977 letter from Oliver Vickery of San Pedro, California, to SSB III, Oliver wrote: "The Vickery name is not too common and no doubt we are long lost cousins along the line someplace.... When you read Admiral Howard Vickery's historical account of the Vickery clan you will see where King Henry VIII had a Vickery Doctor who administered to him, and later to his daughter Elizabeth I. Yep, the Vickery may not be royal, but they are loyal." SSB III Papers.
9. See Mark Kurlansky, *Cod: A Biography of the Fish That Changed the World* (New York: Walker and Company, 1997).
10. For the best account of fishing colonies in Massachusetts Bay Colony and attitudes about fishermen see Daniel Vickers, "Work and Life on the Fishing Periphery of Essex County, Massachusetts, 1630–1675," in *Seventeenth-Century New England* (Boston: The Colonial Society of Massachusetts, 1984), 83–117; and

Daniel Vickers, *Farmers & Fishermen: Two Centuries of Work in Essex County, Massachusetts, 1630–1850* (Williamsburg, VA: Institute of Early American History and Culture, 1994).

11. Rebecca Phippen Vickery's father David (born about 1588–90) died before 31 October 1650, when his will was proved, and her mother Sarah, who had married George Hull of Fairfield sometime after 11 July 1654, died in August 1659. See Parke, *The Ancestry of Lorenzo Ackley*, 199.

12. For architecture at this time see James Deetz, *In Small Things Forgotten: The Archaeology of Early American Life* (New York: Doubleday, 1977), 92–108.

13. For the history of George Vickery, Rebecca Phippen Vickery, their children, and their community in Hull see Ethel Farrington Smith, "Seventeenth Century Hull, Massachusetts, and Her People," *The New England Historical and Genealogical Register* 142 (April 1988), 107–25 and 143 (October 1989), 338–460. See also, Solomon Lincoln, *Sketch of Nantasket: (Now called Hull,) in The County of Plymouth* (Higham: Gazette Press, 1830).

14. Son Jonathan Vickery I (c. 1648–1702) and grandson George Vickery III (1688–1716) were drowned, and grandson David Vickery (c.1685—unknown after 1714) and great-grandsons David Vickery I (1707–44) and Jonathan Vickery III (1709–44), who were brothers, were lost at sea.

15. See Vickers, *Farmers & Fishermen*, 116–29.

16. Smith, "Seventeenth Century Hull," 338.

17. From records of Suffolk County Court. JBV III Papers.

18. See Vickers, "Work and Life on the Fishing Periphery," 99–101.

19. Vickers, *Farmers & Fishermen*, 135–36.

20. See "A true Inventory of the Estate of George Vickery of Hull who dyed suddenly the 12 July [16]79" in Anna C. Kingsbury, "Vickery," 7–8, unpublished manuscript in "Vickery Family in Notes and Compilations, Genealogical Lines of William E. Nickerson." New England Historic Genealogical Society.

21. See Laurel Thatcher Ulrich, *Good Wives: Image and Reality in the Lives of Women in Northern New England, 1650–1750* (New York: Oxford University Press, 1983).

22. Dorcas Paine Vickery (c.1669–1707) who was the wife of Benjamin Vickery (c.1664–1718) was the daughter of Thomas and Mary Snow Paine; the granddaughter of Nichols and Constance Hopkins Snow; and the great-granddaughter of Stephen Hopkins of the MAYFLOWER. See Robert L. Massard's genealogical notes, "MAYFLOWER Lines of Descent." JBV III Papers. See also Smith, "Seventeenth Century Hull," 344–45.

23. See Cotton Mather, *A Family Well-Ordered*, edited by Dr. Don Kistler (Morgan, PA: Soli Deo Gloria Publications, 2001), 1.

24. Demos, *A Little Commonwealth*, 182–84.

25. For a good history of the development of the structure and function of patriarchy through time see Gerda Lerner, *The Creation of Patriarchy* (New York: Oxford University Press, 1986).

26. For family life and political responsibilities see Demos, *A Little Commonwealth*.

27. For authority of Puritan parents see Morgan, *The Puritan Family*, 65–86.

28. Smith, "Seventeenth Century Hull," 339.

29. Demos, *A Little Commonwealth*.

30. Kingsbury, "Vickery," 7.

31. See Ulrich, *Good Wives*, 7, 38. This discussion of Rebecca Phippen Vickery's life relies heavily on the model of analysis that Laurel Thatcher Ulrich introduced in *A Midwife's Tale: The Life of Martha Ballard, Based on Her Diary, 1785–1812* (New York: Vintage Books, 1991). See also Abbott Lowell Cummings, *Rural Household Inventories: Establishing the Names, Uses and Furnishings of Rooms in the*

Colonial New England Home, 1675–1775 (Boston: The Society for the Preservation of New England Antiquities, 1964); and Robert Blair St. George, "'Set Thine House in Order': The Domestication of the Yeomanry in Seventeenth-Century New England," *New England Begins: The Seventeenth Century* (Boston: Museum of Fine Arts, 1982), 159–88.

32. For the place of grandparents and widows households see Demos, *A Little Commonwealth*, 75–76.

33. See Anderson, *New England's Generation*, 179–82.

34. Bailyn, *The Peopling of British North America*, 18, 92–93.

35. For example of "kinship networks of astonishing complexity" in Massachusetts Bay Colony see Mintz and Kellogg, *Domestic Revolutions*, 5.

CHAPTER 2

1. JBV III Papers.

2. See Francis Jennings, *The Invasion of America: Indians, Colonialism, and the Cant of Conquest* (New York: W.W. Norton & Company, 1976); and Alden T. Vaughan, editor, *New England Encounters: Indians and Euroamericans, ca. 1600–1850* (Boston: Northeastern Press, 1999).

3. See William Cronon, *Changes in the Land: Indians, Colonists, and the Ecology of New England* (New York: Hill and Wang, 1983).

4. See Sara M. Evans, *Born for Liberty: A History of Women in America* (New York: Free Press, 1997), 8, 18–19.

5. Jill Lepore, *The Name of War: King Philip's War and the Origins of American Identity* (New York: Alfred A Knopf, 1998), xi.

6. Smith, "Seventeenth Century Hull," 343.

7. Smith, "Seventeenth Century Hull," 120.

8. "Material Towards the History of Hull: Hull Petition Presented 3 March, 1675," *New England Historical Genealogical Register* 6 (October 1852), 338.

9. Sydney E. Ahlstrom, *A Religious History of the American People* (New Haven, CT: Yale University Press, 1974), 114, 157; Demos, *A Little Commonwealth*, 15–16.

10. Lapore, *The Name of War*, xiii.

11. *New England Historic Genealogical Register* III (1849), 245.

12. Kingsbury, "Vickery," 9.

13. William C. Smith, *A History of Chatham, MA: Formerly the Constablewich or Village of Monomoit* (Harwich, MA: Chatham Historical Society, 1947 Reprint), 145, note 39.

14. See Anderson, *New England's Generation*, 184–85.

15. Mintz and Kellogg, *Domestic Revolutions*, 6–7.

16. Ahlstrom, *A Religious History*, 158–64.

17. From Records of the Suffolk County Court, Session of 29 July 1679. JBV III Papers.

18. See Perry Miller, *Errand Into the Wilderness* (Cambridge, MA: The Belknap Press of Harvard University Press, Eleventh Printing, 1993), 2–6; and Anderson, *New England's Generation*, 194–201.

19. Ahlstrom, *A Religious History*, 118.

20. Smith, *A History of Chatham*, 144.

21. William E. Nickerson, "Notes on line of Vickery, Sketch compiled April 1923," 34, unpublished manuscript in "Vickery Family in Notes and Compilations, Genealogical Lines of William E. Nickerson." New England Historic Genealogical Society.

22. Ibid., 34–35.

23. See Gary B. Nash, *The Urban Crucible: The Northern Seaports and the Origins of the American Revolution,* abr. ed. (Cambridge, MA: Harvard University Press, 1986), 33–35.

24. Nickerson, "Notes on line of Vickery," 34.

25. Frederic Lewis Weis, *The Colonial Clergy and the Colonial Churches of New England* (Baltimore: Genealogical Publishing Co., Inc., 1977), 211.

26. Smith, *A History of Chatham*, 145.

27. See Nash, *The Urban Crucible*, 34–39; Labaree, et al., *America and the Sea*, 39; Richard W. Judd, Edwin A Churchill, Joel W. Eastman, editors, *Maine: The Pine Tree State from Prehistory to the Present* (Orono, Maine: University of Maine Press, 1995), 124–30.

28. Shebnah Rich, *Truro, Cape Cod or Land Marks and Sea Marks* (Boston: D. Lothrop and Co., 1884), 268.

29. Ibid. Elizabeth Vickery and Jonathan Collins married in 1704/05. While some sources claim she and Jonathan had ten children, they only had two children together before she died c. 1714. Any other children Jonathan Collins had were with his second wife. Shebnah Rich did not cite the origins of this story, but he could trace his lineage to the Collins family (and of course the MAYFLOWER), so perhaps this was a family legend, as JBV III suggests in his papers: "How often in her (Elizabeth Vickery Collins') years as a woman must she have recalled her unusual experience and told them of her life that winter on a bleak island in the stormy Atlantic."

30. Mary Rowlandson, "A True History of the Captivity and Restoration of Mrs. Mary Rowlandson," in William L. Andrews, editor, *Journeys in New Worlds* (Madison: The University of Wisconsin Press, 1990), 27–65.

31. Rich, *Truro, Cape Cod or Land Marks and Sea Marks*, 81.

32. See Smith, *A History of Chatham*, 148.

33. Undocumented description in JBV III Papers.

34. See Smith, *A History of Chatham*, 146–49.

35. Smith, *A History of Chatham*, 149.

CHAPTER 3

1. JBV III Papers.

2. Smith, *A History of Chatham*, 149–50.

3. Ibid., 214.

4. Rich, *Truro, Cape Cod or Land Marks and Sea Marks*, 566.

5. Henry David Thoreau, *Cape Cod* (New York: W.W. Norton & Company, 1951), 14.

6. Thoreau, *Cape Cod*, 47.

7. See Jamie H. Eves, "'The Valley White with Mist': A Cape Cod Colony in Maine, 1770–1820," *Maine Historical Society Quarterly* 32, no. 2 (Fall 1992), 74–107.

8. JBV III Papers.

9. For women in churches at this time see Ulrich, *Good Wives*, 215–16.

10. Anderson, *New England's Generation*, 193.

11. Demos, *A Little Commonwealth*, 58.

12. See "Religion: The Sources of American Denominationalism," in Bernard Bailyn, Robert Dalleck, David Brion Davis, David Herbert Donald, John L. Thomas, Gordon S. Wood, editors, vol. 1 of *The Great Republic: A History of the American People*, 4th ed. (Lexington, MA: D.C. Heath and Company, 1992), 166–74.

13. Anderson, *New England's Generation*, 214–15.
14. Ibid., 128–29.
15. For a study that illustrates the continued importance of religion at this time see Christine Leigh Heyrman, *Commerce and Culture: The Maritime Communities of Colonial Massachusetts, 1690–1750* (New York: W.W. Norton & Company, 1984).
16. Genesis 1:28.

CHAPTER 4

1. JBV III Papers.
2. See Labaree, et al., *America and the Sea*, 86; Vickers, *Farmers & Fishermen*, 145–53.
3. Nash, *The Urban Crucible*, 39, 72.
4. See Boston "Selectmen's Minutes, 1742," 365. JBV III Papers.
5. See Stuart Bruchey, *Enterprise: The Dynamic Economy of a Free People* (Cambridge, MA: Harvard University Press, 1990), 63–64, 94–96.
6. Bruchey, *Enterprise*, 85–86; Kurlansky, *Cod*, 82–83, 89.
7. Hannah Parker Vickery's link to the MAYFLOWER comes from her grandmother Patience Cobb Parker who was the second wife of Robert Parker of Barnstable. For Robert Parker's connection to the MAYFLOWER see Gary Boyd Roberts, vol. 1 of *Genealogies of Mayflower Families from the New England Historical and Genealogical Registers* (Baltimore: Genealogical Publishing Co., Inc., 1985), xii–xiii.
8. From unattributed poem "The Sailor's Wife" in Labaree, et al., *America and the Sea*, 298.
9. Nash, *The Urban Crucible*, 71.
10. On moving within New England at this time see Ralph J. Crandall, "New England's Second Great Migration: The First Three Generations of settlement, 1630–1700," *New England Historical and Genealogical Register* 129 (1975), 347–60. For "warning out" in Boston at this time see Nash, *The Urban Crucible*, 115.
11. See Boston "Selectmen's Minutes, 1742." JBV III Papers.
12. Ibid.
13. See Nash, *The Urban Crucible*, 101–06.
14. Ibid., xi, 106–07, 139.
15. Ibid., 101–03.
16. See Vee N. Toner to JBV III, 4 April 1975. JBV III Papers.
17. See Theoda Mears Morse to JBV III, 18 June 1951. JBV III Papers. See also Nickerson, "Notes in the line of Vickery," 24. Captain Jonathan Vickery III's widow Susannah Thomas Vickery executed his will on 21 October 1745. He left Susannah, who was pregnant, with a six-year-old daughter, a four-year-old son, and a sixteen-month-old daughter. Another son was born posthumously.
18. Some family notes claim that David I and Hannah Parker Vickery and their children moved to the District of Maine and then David I was lost at sea. The evidence strongly suggests that Hannah and her children moved to Maine (after she married Joseph Weston or in order to marry him) after David I was lost at sea.

PART TWO

CHAPTER 5

1. JBV III Papers.
2. Charles E. Clark, *Maine: A History* (Hanover: University Press of New England, 1990), 42–48.
3. Alan Taylor, "Center and Peripheries: Locating Maine's History," *Maine History* 39, no. 1 (Spring 2000), 3–15. See also Francis Jennings, *Empire of Fortune: Crowns, Colonies, and Tribes in the Seven Years' War in America* (New York: W.W. Norton & Company, 1988), 481: "Like myself, many scholars now see 'frontiers' as regions of mingling peoples rather than a line between myths of *savagery* and *civilization*."
4. It is recorded in the records of the First Church of Falmouth Church that Hannah Parker Vickery and Joseph Weston were married at Falmouth, Maine, 18 May 1746. JBV III Papers.
5. Charles E. Clark, *The Eastern Frontier: The Settlement of Northern New England, 1610–1763* (Hanover: University Press of New England, 1970, Reprint 1983), 145.
6. Judd, et al., *Maine: The Pine Tree State*, 218.
7. Clark, *The Eastern Frontier*, 145–46.
8. Ibid., 177, 199.
9. JBV III Papers.
10. See GVF to JBV III, ca. 1933. JBV III Papers. GVF wrote: "Their [David I and Hannah Parker Vickery's] son David born in Truro 1734/5 is found with one Joseph Atwood on boats between Provincetown & Cape Elizabeth."
11. See Jennings, *Empire of Fortune*; Judd, et al., *Maine: The Pine Tree State*, 139–41.
12. See Bailyn, et al., *The Great Republic*, 188–93.
13. The best account of the experiences of men from Maine and Massachusetts in the French and Indian War is Fred Anderson, *A People's Army: Massachusetts Soldiers and Society in the Seven Years' War* (The Institute of Early American History and Culture, Williamsburg, VA: University of North Carolina Press, 1984). See also John Tebbel, editor of the Works of Francis Parkman, *Battle for North America* (Garden City, NY: Doubleday & Company, Inc., 1984). In family genealogical notes it is stated that David Vickery II fought in the French and Indian War as a private in "Capt. Loring Cushman's Cape Elizabeth Company." This is inaccurate. The leader of this militia was Colonel Ezekeil Cushing, who had a son Loring Cushing and a grandson Loring Cushing, Jr. who both fought in the Revolutionary War. These erroneous notes were passed on to JBV III, who in turn preserved this mistake, a general problem in genealogical research. See William B. Jordan, Jr., *A History of Cape Elizabeth, Maine* (Portland, Maine: House of Falmouth, Inc., 1965), 168–69, 258–59.
14. See Robert E. MacKay, editor, *Massachusetts Soldiers in the French and Indian War, 1744–1755* (The Society of Colonial Wars in the Commonwealth of Massachusetts: New England Historic Genealogical Society, 1985), viii.
15. All statistics and analysis from Anderson, *A People's Army*. Quote, 135.
16. See Anderson, *A People's Army*, 222–23. For the best analysis of the development of American identity at this time see Gordon S. Wood, *The Radicalism of the American Revolution* (New York: Vintage Books, 1993).
17. See Judd, et al., *Maine: The Pine Tree State*, 149–52; and Nash, *The Urban Crucible*, 147–247.
18. For events leading to the Revolution see Bailyn, et al., *The Great Republic*, 235–40;

and Robert A. Gross, *The Minutemen and Their World* (New York: Hill and Wang, 1984).

19. For war in Maine see Judd, et al., *Maine: The Pine Tree State*, 152–56; James S. Leamon, *Revolution Downeast: The War for American Independence in Maine* (Amherst: University of Massachusetts Press, 1993). While the evidence is conflicting John Mitchell (1738–1830) was the second husband of David Vickery II's sister Mary Vickery Weston Mitchell (1739–1822). Mary's first husband was Edmund Weston (the son of her stepfather Joseph Weston). According to family lore Edmond was "Killed by Indians" in 1760. Mary married John Mitchell shortly after Edmond's death and they moved from Falmouth to Machias. Family notes state that John Mitchell "was a chief leader of those men at Machias who took a Privateer schooner of the British, which was sent in 1775 to enable Ichabod Jones, the tory, to load a vessel with lumber for Boston." After the war John, Mary, and their nine children were the second family to settle in Unity. See JBV III Papers and James B. Vickery III's *A History of the Town of Unity, Maine* (Manchester, Maine: Falmouth Publishing House, 1954), 18–19.

20. "Commonwealth of Massachusetts. Office of the Secretary. Revolutionary War Service of David Vickery." JBV III Papers.

21. Information about soldiers during the Revolutionary War from Charles Patrick Neimeyer, *America Goes to War: A Social History of the Continental Army* (New York: New York University Press, 1996); Charles Royster, *A Revolutionary People at War: The Continental Army and American Character, 1775–1783* (The Institute of Early American History and Culture, Williamsburg, VA: University of North Carolina Press, 1979); and Jack P. Greene and J. R. Pole, editors, *A Companion to the American Revolution* (Malden, MA: Blackwell Publishers, 2000).

22. By this time David II's sister Hannah Vickery Paine Whitney also lived in Gorham. She had married Barnabas Paine, Jr., of Truro in 1755, but according to the Vital Records of Truro, MA, he "dyed in Portsmouth Harbor in old England on the 10th day of December 1757 in the thirtieth year of his age being carried there by John Stott commander of a Man-of-War schooner called the Gibralter prize." JBV III Papers. Hannah Vickery Paine was left with a five-month-old baby daughter when her husband died. She probably came to live with her family in Maine as she and her second husband Isaac Whitney of Gorham, Maine, were married there in 1765.

23. For women during the Revolutionary War see Linda K. Kerber, *Women of the Republic: Intellect & Ideology in Revolutionary America* (New York: W.W. Norton & Company, 1986); Evans, *Born for Liberty*, 45–59; Ronald Hoffman and Peter J. Albert, editors, *Women in the Age of the American Revolution* (Charlottesville, VA: United States Capitol Historical Society by the University Press of Virginia, 1990); Joan Hoff Wilson, "The Illusion of Change: Women and the American Revolution," in Alfred F. Young, editor, *The American Revolution: Explorations in the History of American Radicalism* (DeKalb: Northern Illinois University Press, 1976), 383–445; and Mary Beth Norton, *Liberty's Daughters: The Revolutionary Experience of American Women, 1750–1800* (Boston: Little, Brown and Company, 1980).

24. JBV III Papers.

25. See Neimeyer, *America Goes to War*; Royster, *A Revolutionary People at War*; Greene and Pole, *A Companion to the American Revolution*.

26. Quote from JBV III Papers. One of these canes was later found in the Unity house in which David Vickery II once lived and it became a cherished family memento. See 1951 photo of JBV III, SSB III, and Eric Arthur Vickery with this cane.

27. The now classic study of the clash between the Liberty Men and the Great Pro-

prietors in Maine is Alan Taylor, *Liberty Men and Great Proprietors: The Revolutionary Settlement on the Maine Frontier, 1760–1820* (Williamsburg, Virginia: The Institute of Early American History and Culture, 1990).

28. See Taylor, *Liberty Men*, 17. See also "Sketches of Waldo County No. 8," *Republican Journal*, 26 September 1851: "'Unison in Political Settlement' we are told was what suggested the name of the town [of Unity]."

CHAPTER 6

1. JBV III Papers. This description of "Black David" originally came from "Grandmother Isabella Vickery." See "Miscellaneous Stories." JBV III Papers.

2. Descriptions of coming to Unity from JBV III, *A History of the Town of Unity, Maine*, Chapter II. See also Edmund Murch, *A Brief History of the Town of Unity* (Belfast, Maine: G. W. Burgess, Printers, 1893). For more on Maine at this time see Charles E. Clark, James S. Leamon, and Karen Bowden, editors, *Maine in the Early Republic: From Revolution to Statehood* (Hanover, NH: University Press of New England, 1988).

3. See JBV III Papers.

4. Description of early homes and agriculture from Judd, et al., *Maine: The Pine Tree State*, 245–47; Taylor, *Liberty Men*, 61–87; Clarence Albert Day, *A History of Maine Agriculture, 1604–1860* (Orono, Maine: University Press, 1954), 74–80; and Ring, *Maine and the Making of a Nation*, 75–99. "America's first generation" from Joyce Appleby, *Inheriting the Revolution: The First Generation of Americans* (Cambridge: Belknap/Harvard University Press, 2000).

5. See Day, *A History of Maine Agriculture*, 108–14. See also David C. Smith, William R. Baron, Anne E. Bridges, Janet TeBrake, and Harold W. Borns, Jr., "Climate Fluctuation and Agricultural Change in Southern and Central New England, 1765–1880," *Maine Historical Society Quarterly* 21, no. 4 (Spring 1982), 179–218.

6. On wedding and romance at this time see Ulrich, *A Midwife's Tale*, 134–61; Ellen K. Rothman, *Hands and Hearts: A History of Courtship in America* (Cambridge: Harvard University Press, 1984), 56–84; For setting up a household see Jane C. Nylnader, *Images of the New England Home, 1760–1860* (New Haven: Yale University Press, 1993), 54–73.

7. For an insightful discussion about the importance of using family stories concerning mental health in writing history see Joseph A. Amato, *Rethinking Home: A Case for Writing Local History* (Berkeley: University of California Press, 2002), "Anger: Mapping the Emotional Landscape," 77–96 and "Madness," 113–27.

8. All descriptions of David Vickery, Lydia Bartlett Vickery, and their stormy marriage from JBV III Papers; Mental health from Ulrich, *A Midwife's Tale*, 258–60; Maine rum drinking in Judd, et al., *Maine: The Pine Tree State*, 253; Final quote "all that she had" from Ring, *Maine and the Making of a Nation*, 87. Ring also forwards this speculation on women's lives: "Perhaps the fact that all she had in life lay with the man she had married accounts for the constancy of marriage in the early days [of Maine history]. Women seemed able to put up with an ill-tempered husband, often suffering physical abuse."

9. Genesis 3:16.

10. Wealthy fathers who wanted to protect the property they left to daughters from their husbands could do so, offering some women the potential for economic autonomy, but this option was in effect only available to the wealthy—and even then only rarely used. See Mary R. Beard, *Woman as Force in History: A Study in Traditions and Realities* (New York: Persea Books, 1946), 158–66.

11. For current legal reference to "rule of thumb" see: Mather, *The Skeleton in the Closet: The Battered Woman Syndrome, Self-Defense, and Expert Testimony,* 39 Mercer L. Rev. 545 (1988); State of South Dakota v. Burtzlaff, 493 N.W.2d 1n, *12 (1992); Hannel, *Missouri Takes a Step Forward: The Status of "Battered Spouse Syndrome" in Missouri,* 56 Mo. L. Rev. 465, *467 (1991). My thanks to Nancy Torresen for helping me locate these sources. On domestic violence at this time see Elizabeth Pleck, *Domestic Tyranny: The Making of American Social Policy against Family Violence from Colonial Times to the Present* (New York: Oxford University Press, 1987), 17–66. Descriptions of "family quarrels" from JBV III Papers.

12. Ring, *Maine in the Making of a Nation,* 86.

13. Ellen Skinner, *Primary Sources in American History: Women and the National Experience* (Addison-Wesley Educational Publishers Inc., 1996), 28.

14. Evans, *Born for Liberty,* 59–66; Skinner, *Primary Sources,* 21–22.

15. See Article I, Section 2, *The Constitution of the United States.* Howard Zinn, *A People's History, 1492–Present* (New York: HarperPerennial, 1995), 76–101, 102–23; Young, *The American Revolution,* 317–445; Judd, et al., *Maine: The Pine Tree State,* 164–67.

16. See Brooks Atkinson, *The Complete Essays and Other Writings of Ralph Waldo Emerson* (New York: The Modern Library, 1950), 749.

17. This land is located on what is now Routes 202 and 9.

18. Both Bowdoin women were wealthy widows and thus were able to own land in their own right. See JBV III Papers for these land transactions. David Vickery III continued to purchase land adjoining the family farm from the Bowdoin heirs throughout the years.

19. Hal S. Barron, "Staying Down on the Farm," in Steven Hahn and Jonathan Prude, editors, *The Countryside in the Age of Capitalist Transformation* (Chapel Hill: The University of North Carolina Press, 1985), 334. For more evidence of ultimogeniture in New England see James A. Henretta, "Families and Farms: Mentalite in Pre-Industrial America," *William and Mary Quarterly* 35 (1978), 26–27; Judd, et al., *Maine: The Pine Tree State,* 256.

20. Appleby, *Inheriting the Revolution.*

21. Petition from William King Papers, as presented in JBV III, *A History of the Town of Unity, Maine,* 42–43.

22. Taylor, *Liberty Men.*

23. Family legend from JBV III Papers.

24. See John Resch, *Suffering Soldiers: Revolutionary War Veterans, Moral Sentiment, and Political Culture in the Early Republic* (Amherst: University of Massachusetts Press, 1999).

25. Judd, et al., *Maine: The Pine Tree State,* 246–49.

26. See Bailyn, *The Great Republic,* 362–68.

27. See, Judd, et al., *Maine: The Pine Tree State,* 7, 181–83.

28. JBV III, *A History of the Town of Unity, Maine,* 102.

29. For a comprehensive history of the English invasion of Central Maine see *History of Penobscot County, Maine, with Illustrations and Biographical Sketches* (Cleveland: Williams, Chase & Co., 1882), 558–69; For other stories of fearless Maine women during the War of 1812 see Helen Coffin Beedy, *Mothers of Maine* (Portland, Maine: The Thurston Print, 1895), 121–25.

30. Judd, et al., *Maine: The Pine Tree State,* 178–91.

31. Revolutionary War veterans' files, JBV III Papers.

32. The last mention of Sarah Stone Vickery in family lore contends that Sarah's brother Jonathan Stone and his wife Damaris (who "were strong Congregationalists and stood up by the bedside when they prayed") visted her in Unity about

1827, and that "the date of her death is unknown," however, "Charles A. Vickery, her grandson asserted that she died in 1830." JBV III Papers.

33. See, Ulrich, *A Midwife's Tale*, 281–82.
34. JBV III Papers.
35. Judd, et al., *Maine: The Pine Tree State*, 250–55.
36. See JBV III to SSB III, 7 August 1972. SSB III Papers: "My cousin Earl [Nelson] Vickery now 86 [born 1886] has the old Vickery tall clock which David and Lydia had. His son Charles [Nelson Vickery] was killed in Mexico City this last March [1972 at age 43]. It is supposed to be kept in the Vickery male line. He was an only son, so I wonder what will become of this. It is a handsome piece, & still runs, has a ship at top which moves back & forth." Earl Nelson Vickery was the son of Charles Edwin Vickery; Charles Edwin Vickery was the son of Nelson Vickery (1819–95); Nelson Vickery was the son of David III and Lydia Bartlett Vickery. Earl Nelson Vickery lived in Pittsfield, Maine, and died in 1978. Earl's wife was Nellie Maude Hillman Vickery, and his only other child was Ruth Hillman Vickery who never married and died in Portsmouth, New Hampshire, 1999.
37. For the cultural desires of farmers after 1820 see Richard L. Bushman, "Opening the American Countryside" in James A. Henretta, Michael Kammen, and Stanley N. Katz, editors, *The Transformation of Early American History: Society, Authority, and Ideology* (New York: Alfred A. Knopf, 1991), 239–56; For responsibilities of school agent see JBV III, *A History of the Town of Unity, Maine,* 81, note 6.

CHAPTER 7

1. JBV III Papers.
2. Classic term from Paul W. Gates, *The Farmer's Age: Agriculture, 1815–1860* (New York: Holt, Rinehart and Winston, 1960).
3. Figures from USDA Economic Research Service, www.usda.gov.
4. Thomas Jefferson, *Notes on the State of Virginia,* edited by William Peden (The Institute of Early American History and Culture at Williamsburg, Virginia: University of North Carolina Press, 1955), 164–65. For the importance of the family farm in the history of western civilization see Victor Davis Hanson, *The Other Greeks: The Family Farm and the Agrarian Roots of Western Civilization,* 2nd ed. (Berkeley: University of California Press, 1999). The idea of the "noble farmer" was still prevalent in the twentieth century as evidenced by a letter from GVF to young JBV III, 25 May 1933: "I think Farming one of the noblest things one can do and if done with a hearty desire to do well, most satisfying. I often listen at the radio to the "Farm & Home hour" and am impressed with what is accomplished by the youth of America." JBV III Papers.
5. See Joseph Ellis, *American Sphinx: The Character of Thomas Jefferson* (New York: Alfred A. Knopf, 1997), 137: "Indeed the entire history of farming in nineteenth-century and twentieth-century America can be written as a clash between the mythical status of the Jefferson tiller of the soil and the harsh realities of capricious weather and equally capricious markets."
6. The classic study is Barbara Welter, "The Cult of True Womanhood:1820–1860," *American Quarterly* 16 (Summer 1966), 151–74. This was not just an American phenomena, see Erna Olafson Hellerstein, Leslie Parker Hume, and Karen M. Offen, editors, *Victorian Women: A Documentary Account of Women's Lives in Nineteenth-Century England, France, and the United States* (Stanford: Stanford University Press, 1981), 8–21.
7. "Woman," *Bangor Register,* 14 December 1830.

8. See Mintz and Kellogg, *Domestic Revolutions*, 90–91.

9. For lives of farm children see: David B. Danbom, *Born in the Country: A History of Rural America* (Baltimore: The Johns Hopkins University Press, 1995), 87–93; Jack Larkin, *The Shaping of Everyday Life, 1790–1840* (New York: Harper & Row, Publishers,1989), 1–61; Joseph F. Kett, "Growing Up in Rural New England, 1800–1840" in Tamara K. Harven, editor, *Anonymous Americans: Explorations in Nineteenth-Century Social History* (Englewood Cliffs, NJ: Prentice-Hall, Inc., 1971), 1–15; Nancy Grey Osterud, *Bonds of Community: The Lives of Farm Women in Nineteenth-Century New York* (Ithaca: Cornell University Press, 1991); and Day, *A History of Maine Agriculture*, 130–31.

10. Mintz and Kellogg, *Domestic Revolutions*, 101.

11. See Judd, et al., *Maine: The Pine Tree State*, 252; Thomas C. Hubka, "Farm Family Mutuality: The Mid-Nineteenth-Century Maine Farm Neighborhood," in Peter Benes, editor, *The Farm* (The Dublin Seminar for New England Folklife: Annual Proceedings 1986: Boston University, 1988), 13–23; Danbom, *Born in the Country*, 91–94. For an earlier history see Ulrich, *Good Wives*.

12. Carl F. Kaestle, *Pillars of the Republic: Common Schools and American Society, 1780–1860* (New York: Hill and Wang, 1983), 13–29; For Unity schools specifically see JBV III, *A History of the Town of Unity, Maine,* Chapter VI, 80–100.

13. See Thomas Dublin, *Women at Work: The Transformation of Work and Community in Lowell, Massachusetts, 1820–1860* (New York: Columbia University Press, 1979); For how this new opportunity for women "evaporated" see Gerda Lerner, "The Lady and the Mill Girl: Changes in the Status of Women in the Age of Jackson" in *The Majority Finds Its Past: Placing Women in History* (New York: Oxford University Press, 1981), 15–30.

14. All information about Eli Vickery from JBV III Papers.

15. Eli Vickery account book in Vickery Papers at Unity Historical Society, Unity, Maine.

16. For social activities at this time see Larkin, *The Reshaping of Everyday Life*, 258–303; and Karen V. Hansen, *A Very Social Time: Crafting Community in Antebellum New England* (Berkeley: University of California Press, 1994).

17. Clarissa Berry sold her quarter share of the Berry estate to her mother Olive Jackson Berry for $50.00 on 24 May 1831. See Vickery Papers at Unity Historical Society, Unity, Maine.

18. See JBV III, *A History of the Town of Unity, Maine,* 118.

19. Rothman, *Hands and Hearts*, 45.

20. See John D'Emilio and Estelle B. Freedman, *Intimate Matters: A History of Sexuality in America* (New York: Harper & Row, Publishers, 1989), 46–47, 73; Larkin, *The Reshaping of Everyday Life*, 191–95; Rothman, *Hands and Hearts*, 44–55.

21. See Joyce K. Bibber, *A Home for Everyman: The Greek Revival and Maine Domestic Architecture,* 2nd ed. (Portland, Maine: Greater Portland Landmarks, 2000), 93–110.

22. Quote describing the Vickery farm as "one of the finest situations in town" from childhood memory of James E. Kelley to JBV III, 16 January 1934. JBV III Papers.

23. Thomas C. Hubka, *Big House, Little House, Back House, Barn: The Connected Farm Buildings of New England* (Hanover, NH: University Press of New England, 1984).

24. D'Emilio and Freedman, *Intimate Matters*, 57–58.

25. Judith Walzer Leavitt, *Brought to Bed: Childbearing in America, 1750–1950* (New York: Oxford University Press, 1986), 18.

26. See JBV III to SSB, 17 July 1979. SSB III Papers. For potato crops in Waldo

County at this time see Clarence Day, *Farming in Maine, 1860–1940* (Orono, Maine: University of Maine Press, 1963), "The Humble Potato," 117–39.

27. Reuel Mussey was the brother of Olive Mussey who had married Samuel Stillman Berry I (the brother of Hannah Berry and Clarissa Berry Vickery) in 1837.

28. Christopher Clark, *The Roots of Rural Capitalism: Western Massachusetts, 1780–1860* (Ithaca: Cornell University Press, 1990), 55.

29. For intergenerational conflict see Ulrich, *A Midwife's Tale,* 264–85; and Nylander, *Images of the New England Home,* 35–36. Descriptions of Eli and Clarissa from JBV III Papers; "A Waldo County Farmer" in *Republican Journal,* 6 May 1876.

30. For politics at this time see the classic Arthur M. Schlesinger, Jr., *The Age of Jackson* (Boston: Little, Brown, and Company, 1953); and Edward Pessen, *Jacksonian America: Society, Personality, and Politics,* rev. ed. (Urbana: University of Illinois Press, 1985).

31. Quotes describing Selectman Vickery's jobs from 1845 account, "Town of Unity to Eli Vickery." JBV III Papers.

32. See Edward O. Schriver, "Antislavery: Maine and the Nation" in Ronald Banks, editor, *A History of Maine,* 4th ed. (Dubuque, Iowa: Kendall/Hunt Publishing Company, 1976,), 236–45.

33. See Eric Foner, *Free Soil, Free Labor, Free Men: The Ideology of the Republican Party Before the Civil War* (New York: Oxford University Press, 1995).

34. See Henry Chase, editor, *Representative Men of Maine: The Portraits and Sketches of All the Governors Since the Formation of the State,* "Gov. John Hubbard," (Portland, ME: The Lakeside Press, Publishers, 1893), 29.

35. From JBV III Papers.

36. For politics in Maine at this time see: Judd, et al., *Maine: The Pine Tree State,* 193–215; Frank L. Byrne, "The Napoleon of Temperance" in Banks, *A History of Maine,* 229–35; Ring, *Maine in the Making of the Nation,* Part Two and Three.

37. See Edward O. Schriver, "'Deferred Victory': Woman Suffrage in Maine, 1873–1920," in David C. Smith and Edward O. Schriver, editors, *Maine: A History through Selected Readings* (Dubuque, Iowa: Kendall/Hunt Publishing Company, 1985), 410. For suffrage in Maine see also the Maine Memory Network, http://www.mainememory.net.

38. Evans, *Born for Liberty,* 94–95; For complete story of Women's Rights Movement leading to the Nineteenth Amendment see Eleanor Flexner, *Century of Struggle: The Woman's Rights Movement in the United States* (New York: Atheneum, 1974). All information about Maine women's rights legislation from Phyllis Vonherrlich scholarship in electronic message to author from Dr. Mazie Hough, 28 February 2001.

39. JBV III Papers.

40. Quote from "Burial of the Dead" in *The Book of Common Prayer,* 333; For death at this time see Larkin, *The Shaping of Everyday Life,* 98–104; Nylander, *Our Own Snug Fireplace,* 39–41.

41. See Ruth Schwartz Cohen, *More Work for Mother: The Ironies of Household Technology from the Open Hearth to the Microwave* (London: Free Association Books, 1989), 16–68.

42. Bruchey, *Enterprise,* 221–53; Clark, *The Roots of Rural Capitalism;* Judd, et al., *Maine: The Pine Tree State,* 256–59. See "Sketches of Waldo County, No. 8," *Republican Journal,* 26 September 1851: "A good part of the goods consumed came from Waterville … and a good part of the produce goes there."

43. JBV III, *A History of the Town of Unity, Maine,* 34.

44. "Sketches of Waldo County, No. 8," *Republican Journal,* 26 September 1851.

PART THREE

CHAPTER 8

1. JBV III Papers.
2. All descriptions and information about the Ayer family from "My Grandmother" by Lucy Ayer in JBV III Papers. For a fine study of Mary True Ayer Vickery's grandmother Hannah Chase Bartlett see Jennifer Wixson, "'All My Sencear Friends': An Intimate Portrait of Maine Quaker Minister Hannah Chase Bartlett (1769–1835)." Senior Thesis, Goddard College, 2001.
3. See "Inventory Peter Ayer by Wm. Chase, Daniel Tripp, & Lorenzo McGray," 11 July 1854. JBV III Papers.
4. All family notes in JBV III Papers. See Richard L. Bushman, *The Refinement of America: Persons, Houses, Cities* (New York: Vintage Books, 1993), 280–312 and Mary Ryan, *Cradle of the Middle Class: The Family in Oneida County, New York, 1790–1865* (Cambridge, England: Cambridge University Press, 1981.)
5. JBV III, *A History of the Town of Unity, Maine*, 92.
6. JBV III Papers.
7. Women's right to hold offices not mentioned in Maine Constitution in Dr. Mazie Hough's electronic message to author, 28 February 2001.
8. See Skinner, *Women and the National Experience*, 73–75 for the "Declaration of Sentiments" that listed women's demands and was presented at the first women's rights convention at Seneca Falls, New York, in 1848.
9. Best book to read to get an overall sense of the antebellum reform era is Ronald G. Walters, *American Reformers, 1815–1860*, rev. ed. (New York: Hill and Wang, 1997).
10. See Day, *Farming in Maine*, "Abandoned Farms," 171–79.
11. See Bushman, "Opening the American Countryside" in Henretta, et al., *The Transformation of Early American History*, 239–56.
12. See for example: "The Rush to California," *Maine Farmer*, 12 February 1852; "Farming Life in New England," *Atlantic Monthly* (August 1858), 334–41; "What shall we do with Maine," *Maine Farmer*, 26 August 1876; "Making the Boys Like It," *Republican Journal*, 24 January 1878.
13. See Judd, et al., *Maine: The Pine Tree State*, 256–59 and Clark, *The Roots of Rural Capitalism*.
14. See JBV III, *A History of the Town of Unity, Maine,* 146–57 and 228–29.
15. Ibid.
16. For more on the agricultural press at this time see: Brenda Bullion, "The Agricultural Press: 'To Improve the Soil and the Mind,'" in Benes, *The Farm*, 74–94; For establishment of University of Maine see Judd, et al., *Maine: The Pine Tree State*, 406; and Day, *A History of Maine Agriculture*, 272–80.
17. J.P.C. of Morrill, "A Waldo County Farmer," *Maine Farmer*, 6 May 1876.
18. While Newman was to take over the Quaker Hill farm from his mother and father, it still legally belonged to them and thus Eli's name appears on all the legal transactions. James I also paid his father Eli an added $2,000 for the farm, about $26,000 in 2001 dollars per www.westegg.com/inflation. See 3 May 1869 "Mortgage Deed," from James B. Vickery to Eli Vickery, 3 May 1869 "Bill of Received Estate Eli Vickery to James B. Vickery," and 3 May 1869 "Quit-Claim Deed" from Eli Vickery to James B. Vickery. Vickery Papers, Unity Historical Society, Unity, Maine.
19. 3 May 1869 "Mortgage Deed," from James B. Vickery to Eli Vickery. Vickery Papers, Unity Historical Society, Unity, Maine. Eli also included two other impor-

tant conditions in this deed: "Said James B is to keep a red white faced horse now on the premises in good condition as good hay & grain pasturing care keep him for use of said Eli & he 'E' to have the full control of the use of said horse during the life of said Eli if said horse lives so long and also the wagon Eli has used for the years past is to be kept for his use & control by the Said James B...."

20. Fred Vickery (1876–1950) was Newman and Sarah's only child. He lived in Bangor, was a salesman for Snow and Neally, Co., and was a "drummer." JBV III said that Fred Vickery "was a sort of black sheep" in the family. JBV III to SSB III, 1 November 1964. SSB III Papers.

21. See Vickery, *A History of the Town of Unity, Maine*, 105–17.

22. For evidence that Newman Whipple Vickery was drafted, see James Edwin Berry correspondence 24 August 1863 in JBV III Papers. The best study of the Civil War is James M. McPherson's, *Ordeal by Fire: The Civil War and Reconstruction*, 2nd ed. (New York: McGraw-Hill, Inc., 1992). For information on conscription in the north see McPherson, *Ordeal by Fire*, 353–55. For Maine during the Civil War see Judd, et al., *Maine: The Pine Tree State*, 358–69. For the rural north during the Civil War see Danbom, *Born in the Country*, 110–14. For occupational statistics of soldiers, see McPherson, *Ordeal by Fire*, 355–57.

23. John F. Berry was the son of Alfred and Hannah Hatch Berry.

24. James E. Berry transcibed correspondence, 5 March 1863. JBV III Papers.

25. James E. Kelley to JBV III, 7 February 1934. JBV III Papers. For blacks in Civil War see McPherson, *Ordeal by Fire*, 346–53.

26. See for example Steve Whalen, "'Everything Is the Same': The Civil War Home Front in Rural Vermont." Ph.D. Dissertation, University of Maine, 1999.

27. *Republican Journal*, 31 March 1870.

28. After her husband's death Abigail Murch Vickery moved to Pittsfield, Maine, where her daughters Claribel, Ella, and Luna attended Maine Central Institute.

29. See GVF to JBV III, 25 May 1933. JBV III Papers.

30. For Mainers going West see: Day, *History of Maine Agriculture*, "A Cold Year and Westward Ho," 108–14; Ring, *Maine in the Making of the Nation*, "Maine and Manifest Destiny," 209–376. See also, Henry Nash Smith, *Virgin Land: The American West As Symbol and Myth* (Cambridge, MA: Harvard University Press, 1978); Annette Kolodny, *The Land Before Her: Fantasy and Experience of the American Frontiers, 1630–1860* (Chapel Hill: University of North Carolina Press, 1984); Julie Roy Jeffrey, "Glimpses of Western Life," *Frontier Women: The Trans-Mississippi West, 1840–1880* (New York: Hill and Wang, 1979), 3–23.

31. Hannibal Kelley to William Kelley, 30 September 1864. JBV III Papers.

32. James E. Berry transcribed correspondence, 21 March 1864. JBV III Papers.

33. James E. Berry to Ralph Berry, 21 August 1892. JBV III Papers.

34. James E. Berry to Olive Mussey Berry, 30 November 1888. JBV III Papers.

35. For Charles W. Cook's story see Josephine Cook Mueller to JBV III, 25 July 1946. JBV III Papers. SSB III claims that Charles Cook, as a Quaker, was a conscientious objector to the Civil War and went West where he would be "more comfortable" because he was not "respected" in Unity for his decision to refuse the draft. See S. Stillman Berry, "The Founding and Early History of the Winnecook Ranch" in Harold M. Hill, Marcel A. Callant, and Mary Dole Smith, *Winnecook Ranch on the Musselshell* (Harlowton, Montana: Lynn & Dunn, 1999), 1–5. While Cook's parents Daniel and Elizabeth Hussey Cook were practicing Quakers, and he had a heritage of Quaker relatives in the Hussey and Chase families, I have found no evidence to support Berry's claim that Quakers were made to feel uncomfortable or disrespected in Unity during the Civil War. Indeed Cook's daughter Josephine Cook Mueller said that her father was not living in Unity at this time, but was in

his third year of college at Providence, Rhode Island, when he read Captain Fisk's account about Montana in a Maine paper. See James McClellan Hamilton, *From Wilderness to Statehood: A History of Montana, 1805–1900* (Portland, Oregon: Binfords & Mort, Publishers, 1957), 148–76. Some students of the Civil War posit the theory that Congress paid for the expeditions by Fisk to the Montana Territory even in the midst of fighting the war because they wanted new settlers loyal to the Union to populate an area they feared was controlled by Confederate sympathizers. The U.S. Government hoped to secure gold from the territory that would help fund and win the war. See Tom Sargent, "The Civil War in Montana," 28 March 1999, 2nd rev., http://www.virginiacity.com.

36. See www.westegg.com/inflation.
37. See "An inventory of the Estate of Eli Vickery late of Unity deceased 22nd day of May AD 1877" and "The second and final account of Clarissa Vickery administratrix of the Estate of Eli Vickery late of Unity deceased." JBV III Papers. In JBV III's notes he states that "Eli Vickery had [a] very sore throat" and that "Lois Varney states that Eli Sr. died of [the] same sickness as Eli Jr.," though JBV III counters, "My father [JBV II] believes differently."

CHAPTER 9

1. See SSB III, Redlands, CA, to JBV III 29 March 1950. JBV III Papers. SSB III's genealogy was mixed up. Charles Cook led "Unity's Montana hegira." His father and mother were Daniel and Elizabeth Hussey Cook. His maternal grandparents were James and Bethia Chase Hussey. Thomas Cook, who apparently stayed in Unity, was Charles and Benjamin Cook's older brother.
2. Judd, et al., *Maine: The Pine Tree State*, 404–10.
3. Hubka, "Farm Family Mutuality," 13–23.
4. See Howard S. Russell, *A Long, Deep Furrow: Three Centuries of Farming in New England* (Hanover and London: University Press of New England, 1982).
5. "The Montanians," *Atlantic Monthly* 81, no. 488 (June 1898), 738.
6. Waldo County description from 1873 reports as quoted in Judd, et al., *Maine: The Pine Tree State*, 405.
7. "The Montanians," *Atlantic Monthly*, 81, no. 488 (June 1898), 738.
8. "The Call of the West" is in reference to the title JBV III used in describing this western migration in Chapter XV of his book *A History of the Town of Unity, Maine*. For discussion of cultural notions about the American West see *The Same Great Struggle*, 115–18.
9. Quoted in Clyde A. Milner II, "The Shared Memory of Pioneers," in Milner, *Major Problems in the History of the American West*, 463.
10. See Edward B. Nealley, "A Year in Montana," *Atlantic Monthly* 18 (August 1866), 246, for description of a new emmigrant as a "pilgrim," or "tenderfoot" in Montana at this time. For a fine study on the relationship through time between the Pilgrims and New England identity see Joseph A. Conforti, *Imagining New England: Explorations of Regional Identity from the Pilgrims to the Mid-Twentieth Century* (Chapel Hill: The University of North Carolina Press, 2001).
11. Hebrews 11:13–16.
12. Hebrews 11:16.
13. For a good narrative on Lewis and Clark see Stephen E. Ambrose, *Undaunted Courage: Meriwether Lewis, Thomas Jefferson, and the Opening of the American West* (New York: Simon & Schuster, 1996), 396–411. For fur trade in this area see Paul C. Phillips, "The Fur Trade in Montana," in Michael P. Malone and Richard B.

Roeder, editors, *The Montana Past: An Anthology* (Missoula: University of Montana Press, 1969), 35–60; and Michael P. Malone, Richard B. Roeder, and William Lang, "The Era of the Fur Trade,"*Montana: A History of Two Centuries,* rev. ed. (Seattle: University of Washington Press, 1991), Chapter Three. Quote from ethnologist John C. Ewers as presented in Malone, et al., *Montana,* 114. The best comprehensive history of Montana is Malone, et al., *Montana.*

14. For racial dimensions of western migrations see Glenda Riley, *The Female Frontier: A Comparative View of Women on the Prairie and the Plains* (Lawrence, Kansas: University of Kansas, 1988); and Richard White, "Race Relationships in the American West," *American Quarterly* 38, no. 3 (1986), 390–416.

15. Neally, "A Year in Montana," 236–50.

CHAPTER 9 / WESTERN BERRYS

1. JBV III Papers.
2. Josephine Cook Mueller to JBV III, 25 July 1946. JBV III Papers.
3. Benjamin B. Cook obituary, *DailyTribune* [Great Falls, MT], 22 February 1920.
4. Charles W. Cook would later become the mayor of White Silver Springs, MT.
5. The published account of the Cook Brothers' success in Hamilton. *From Wilderness to Statehood,* 407. Nowhere in Charles Cook's daughter Josephine Cook Mueller's account in her letter of 25 July 1946 to JBV III does she mention her Uncle Benjamin Cook's partnership with her father. The Hamilton account seems to be substantiated by Benjamin Cook's wife Mary Berry Cook. In a letter to her sister she sets the record straight: "People at home [in Unity] have the idea that Cha[rle]s C. is worth considerable and that Ben has only a share. They both started together without a dollar of capital C[harles]. having lost everything in mines. They took sheep of a Mr. McGreagor six years ago on shares. The first year was almost a failure as the sheep was not climated and they lost a great many through their inexperience. But from that time until the present they have prospered. They own equally in everything (or did before Ben sold) and why people should think C.W.C <u>rich</u>, or any better than anybody else is more than I can understand. To be sure he has enough to support <u>him</u>self in ease and comfort and need not labor. So has Ben but neither of them can be termed rich. Ben does not intend to settle down into a life of idleness and we shall make Montana our home for some two or three years perhaps, although he is anxious to live East." Mary Berry Cook (hereafter cited as MBC), White Sulphur Spring, Montana, to Ruth Berry, Unity, Maine, 24 April 1879. JBV III Papers.
6. Hubka, "Farm Family Mutuality," 13–23.
7. JBV III to SSB III, 15 June 1959. SSB III Papers.
8. From Sam Berry II's letters as presented by Harold M. Hill, "The Berry Family Correspondence," Hill, et al., *Winnecook Ranch,* 8–9.
9. Ibid.
10. Lottie Berry born 21 September 1876 and died suddenly 11 May 1877. See Mary Jane Adler Berry, Forest City, California, to Evie Kelley Berry, Unity, Maine, 13 May 1877 for discussion about Lottie whom her Aunt Mary Jane believed was still alive. JBV III Papers.
11. SSB III, Winnecook, Montana, to JBV III, Unity, Maine, 9 July 1930. JBV III Papers.
12. Hill, "Ralph and Evie Berry: Founders of the Winnecook Ranch," Hill, et al., *Winnecook Ranch,* 7.

13. See Hill, "S. Stillman Berry, Ph.D.: A Biographical Sketch," Hill, et al., *Winnecook Ranch*, 35, 8.

14. See Malone, et al., *Montana*, 245–46; and Jeffrey, *Frontier Women*, 25–36. For opposing evidence in the South see Joan E. Cashin, *A Family Venture: Men and Women on the Southern Frontier* (New York: Oxford University Press, 1991).

15. MBC to Evelyn Kelley Berry (hereafter cited as EKB), 7 April 1879. JBV III Papers.

16. See Carroll Smith-Rosenberg, "The Female World of Love and Ritual: Relations Between Women in Nineteenth-Century America," in *Disorderly Conduct: Visions of Gender in Victorian America* (New York: Oxford University Press, 1985), 53–76.

17. MBC to Olive Mussey Berry (hereafter cited as OMB), 17 April 1879. JBV III Papers.

18. There is some discrepancy concerning Mary Berry Cook's name. Clearly in letters she signs with and is referred to by the nickname "Maym." However, SSB III calls her "Aunt May." Both nicknames were probably used, but to simplify the issue I will use her given name Mary.

19. See MBC opening quote. Apparently going West to marry a fiancé was not an unusual occurrence. When Flora I. Black journeyed from Belfast, Maine, to Montana in 1881 she said: "There was a young lady in our party, Miss Clara Wing, from Searsmont, going to Montana to meet her future husband." See "Letter from Montana Territory, May 29, 1881," *Republican Journal*, n.d. JBV III Papers. For another view on the subject of marriage and young women going West see Gen. James S. Brisbin, U.S.A., *The Beef Bonanza; or, How to Get Rich on the Plains* (Philadelphia: J.B. Lippincott & Co., 1881), 194: "It [the West] is not a good place for ladies to come who wish to keep single. There are so many bachelors a young lady finds herself surrounded at once with suitors, and some of the applicants will not be put off."

20. JBV III Papers.

21. Hill, "The Berry Family Correspondence," Hill, et al., *Winnecook Ranch*, 9.

22. All quotes from MBC to Samuel Stillman Berry I (hereafter cited as SSB I) and OMB, 9 June 1878. JBV III Papers.

23. MBC to Ruth Berry, 20 May 1879. JBV III Papers.

24. See Kolodny, *The Land Before Her*; and John Mack Faragher, *Sugar Creek: Life on the Illinois Prairie* (New Haven: Yale University Press, 1986).

25. Throughout Mary Berry Cook's correspondence reference is made to making pets of these animals, for example see MBC to Ruth Berry, 23 June 1878. See also Donna M. Lucey, *Photographing Montana, 1894–1928: The Life and Work of Evelyn Cameron* (Missoula, MT: Mountain Press Publishing Company, 2001), 128–31, and 237.

26. MBC to OMB, 28 January 1879. JBV III Papers.

27. See Kathryn Kish Sklar, *Catherine Beecher: A Study in American Domesticity* (New York: W.W. Norton & Company, 1976), 179; and Jeffrey, *Frontier Women*, 12–13.

28. See Jeffrey, *Frontier Women*, Chapter Four, "Am Beginning to Feel Quite Civilized," 79–106; and Geraldine Jonich Clifford, "Women's Liberation and Women's Professions: Reconsidering the Past, Present, and Future," in John Mack Faragher and Florence Howe, editors, *Women and Higher Education in American History* (New York: W.W. Norton & Company, 1988), 165–82.

29. See Jeffrey, *Frontier Women*, 190–94. Rather than being progressive, Jeffrey maintains that it was a "conservative impulse" that granted women suffrage in Utah and Wyoming 1869–70. In Utah women voted as they were told so as to "maintain Mormon society and plural marriage" and in Wyoming women were granted suffrage because legislators hoped to "attract stable and responsible settlers to the ter-

ritory." For women's suffrage in Montana see also, Paula Petrik, *No Step Backward: Women and Family on the Rocky Mountain Mining Frontier, Helena, Montana, 1865–1900* (Helena: Montana Historical Society Press, 1987), 115–33.

30. MBC to Ruth Berry, 20 March 1880. JBV III Papers.
31. MBC to Ruth Berry, 23 June 1878. JBV III Papers,
32. MBC to OMB, 24 July 1878. JBV III Papers.
33. Ibid.
34. MBC to Ruth Berry, 23 June 1878. JBV III Papers.
35. Milton Shatraw, *Thrashin' Time: Memories of a Montana Boyhood* (Palo Alto, CA: American West Publishing Company, 1970), 161.
36. MBC to OMB, 24 July 1878. JBV III Papers.
37. For a fine discussion of the gendering of work out West see Dee Garceau, *The Important Things of Life: Women, Work, and Family in Sweetwater County, Wyoming, 1880–1929* (Lincoln: University of Nebraska Press, 1997), 89–111. See also, Jeffrey, *Frontier Women*, 22–23; and Ruth B. Moynihan, Susan Armitage, and Christiane Fischer Dichamp, editors, *So Much to Be Done: Women Settlers on the Mining and Ranching Frontiers*, 2nd ed. (Lincoln: University of Nebraska Press, 1998).
38. MBC to SSB I and OMB, 9 June 1878; MBC to Ruth Berry, 23 June 1878; MBC to OMB, 24 July 1878; MBC to OMB 28 January 1879. JBV III Papers.
39. MBC to Ruth Berry, 26 March 1879. JBV III Papers.
40. Sadie Lord Webster to EKB, 4 September 1890. JBV III Papers.
41. MBC to OMB, 24 July 1878. JBV III Papers.
42. MBC to SSBI and OMB, 9 June 1878. JBV III Papers.
43. Hill, "The Berry Family Correspondence," Hill, et al., *Winnecook Ranch*, 16.
44. "Letter from Montana Territory, Scammon's Ranch, Musselshell River, May 29 1881," *Republican Journal*, n.d. JBV III Papers.
45. Theodore Roosevelt, *An Autobiography* (New York: Charles Scribner's Sons, 1926), 96–97.
46. Sam Berry II to OMB, July 1878. Hill, "The Berry Family Correspondence," Hill, et al., *Winnecook Ranch*, 9.
47. Sam Berry II to SSB I, Summer 1878. Hill, "The Berry Family Correspondence," Hill, et al., *Winnecook Ranch*, 9.
48. See Harold F. Wilson, "The Rise and Decline of the Sheep Industry in Northern New England," *Agricultural History* 9, no. 1 (January 1935), 12–40.
49. See Day, *A History of Maine Agriculture*, "Changes in Sheep Husbandry: 1820–1860," 186–94; and Judd, et al., *Maine: The Pine Tree State*, 407.
50. Bruchey, *Enterprise*, 288.
51. MBC and OMB, 24 October 1878. JBV III Papers.
52. Hamilton, *From Wilderness to Statehood*, 408.
53. Ralph Berry to SSB I, August 1878. Hill, "The Berry Family Correspondence," Hill, et al., *Winnecook Ranch*, 9.
54. Sam Berry II to SSB I, Summer 1878. Hill, "The Berry Family Correspondence," Hill, et al., *Winnecook Ranch*, 9–10.
55. Ralph Berry to SSB I, December 1878. Hill, "The Berry Family Correspondence," Hill, et al., *Winnecook Ranch*, 10.
56. Ralph Berry to SSBI and OMB, July 1879. Hill, "The Berry Family Correspondence," Hill, et al., *Winnecook Ranch*, 11.
57. MBC to Ruth Berry, 20 May 1879. JBV III Papers.
58. Glenda Riley, *The Female Frontier: A Comparative View of Women on the Prairie and the Plains* (Lawrence, Kansas: University Press of Kansas, 1988), 98.
59. EKB to Charlotte Files Kelley, 20 July 1879. JBV III Papers.
60. MBC to OMB, 5 January 1880. JBV III Papers. See MBC to OMB, 24 October

1878: "Evie writes that the woods are looking their best this Fall. I would like to see them and gather some Autumn leaves, but Evie said she would gather some and bring to me. Tell her not to forget the ferns." JBV III Papers.

61. MBC to Ruth Berry, 20 March 1880. JBV Papers.
62. MBC to EKB, 7 April 1879. JBV III Papers.
63. See Edward Norris Wentworth, *America's Sheep Trails: History and Personalities* (Ames: The Iowa State College Press, 1948), 409–13.
64. MBC to Ruth Berry, 20 May 1879. JBV III Papers.
65. Hill, "The Berry Family Correspondence," Hill, et al., *Winnecook Ranch*, 12.
66. MBC to SSB I and OMB, 9 June 1878. JBV III Papers.
67. EKB to Ruth Berry, 8 June 1879. JBV III Papers.
68. Sam Berry II to OMB, August 1879. Hill, "The Berry Family Correspondence," Hill, et al., *Winnecook Ranch*, 12.
69. Wentworth, *America's Sheep Trails*, 419–22.
70. Malone, et al., *Montana*, 158.
71. MBC to Ruth Berry, 23 June 1878. JBV III Papers.
72. Ibid.
73. Hamilton, *From Wilderness to Statehood*, 356, 408–09.
74. *Republican Journal*, 16 October 1884.
75. JBV III, *A History of the Town of Unity, Maine*, 155.
76. Hill, et al., *Winnecook Ranch*, 125. See also "Letter From Montana, July 1885," *Republican Journal*, n.d.: "Quite a delegation of Waldo County people think of visiting Maine in season to attend Campmeeting at Northport." JBV III Papers. For description of other visits see "Matters in Montana," *Republican Journal*, 28 October 1886.
77. "Our Home Folks in the South and West," *Republican Journal*, 24 February 1887.
78. Malone, et al., *Montana*, 153–54.
79. Peter Nabokov, editor, *Native American Testimony: A Chronicle of Indian-White Relations from Prophecy to the Present, 1492–1992* (New York: Penguin Books, 1992), 171.
80. Nealley, "A Year in Montana," 237.
81. MBC to OMB, 24 October 1878. JBV III Papers.
82. For a concise overview of Native American history in Montana see Malone, et al., *Montana*, 8–21.
83. MBC to Ruth Berry, 24 April 1879. JBV III Papers.
84. See Milner, "The Shared Memory of Pioneers" in *Major Problems*.
85. "The Hostile Indians," *Maine Farmer*, 15 August 1876. For a good overview of the "Indian Wars" see Malone, et al., *Montana*, "Indian Removal, 1851–1890," 114–44.
86. MBC to Ruth Berry, 20 May 1879. JBV III Papers.
87. MBC to OMB, 24 October 1878. JBV III Papers.
88. MCB to OMB, 17 April 1879. In a letter to Stuart W. Conner of the Billings, Montana Archaeological Society, 29 August 1962, SSB III wrote when his family established the Winnecook Ranch in 1880, "It was then Indian country…. And Indians there were plenty. Many tribes were represented…. I note your statement that this was Blackfoot country. I do not think it was so considered then. Rather it was thought, with its rich buffalo, antelope, and elk herds, to be treaty ground over which no one tribe had complete jurisdiction, but in which all had hunting rights. No Indians were then or recently had been permanently settled here, but were constantly coming with their horses, non-combatants, and travois to camp and hunt, then leave again. The last large herd of bison in this part of Montana was surrounded by the Flathead Indians just as it was attempting to ford the River

perhaps half a mile below the old [ranch] buildings and slaughtered to the last animal. This was in the early 1880s (I have no record of the exact year, but know that my mother [Evelyn Kelley Berry] watched part of it from the old cabin, so I know that it was prior to 1885 when the second house was built). My people never had any real trouble with the Indians—mother used even to bake bread for them,—but of the friendliness of two tribes, the Sioux and Blackfeet, I understood that they never felt sure. The only fighting on the place after my people came was amongst the Indians themselves, more especially the Crows and Piegans." SSB III Papers.

89. L. E. Munson, "Montana as it was, and it is," *New Englander and Yale Review* 51, no. 233 (August 1889), 102.

90. Ralph Berry to EKB, 20 July 1880. Hill, "The Berry Family Correspondence," Hill, et al., *Winnecook Ranch*, 14.

91. See Wentworth, *America's Sheep Trails*, 499–500. The Utes were part of the Shoshones and were called the "Sheep-Eaters" because wild mountain sheep had been their principal food long before Spanish soldiers introduced domestic sheep in the West. See Wentworth, *America's Sheep Trails*, 20.

92. Malone, et al., *Montana*, 151.

93. Harold Joseph Stearns, *A History of the Upper Musselshell Valley of Montana to 1920* (Harlowton, Montana: Times-Clarion Publishers, 1966), 38.

94. Hamilton, *From Wilderness to Statehood*, 407.

95. MBC to Ruth Berry, 20 May 1879. JBV III Papers. See also Wentworth, *America's Sheep Trails*, 487–90 and 406–08.

96. EKB to "Mother" [Charlotte Files Kelley], 20 July 1879. JBV III Papers.

97. MBC to OMB, 17 April 1879. JBV III Papers.

98. In the 1870s the Chinese were 10 percent of Montana's population. They had come during the gold rush and while many worked mines, nearly half of the Chinese made their living as servants, cooks, and laundry operators in mining towns. They were particular targets of violent racism and discrimination by whites, and few Chinese remained in Montana at the turn of the century. See Malone, et al., *Montana*, 85.

99. MBC to Ruth Berry, 24 April 1879. JBV III Papers.

100. "Miscellaneous Stories." JBV III Papers.

101. Ibid.

102. Ibid.

103. See EKB to Ruth Berry, 2 October 1880. JBV III Papers.

104. Benjamin B. Cook obituary, *Daily Tribune* [Great Falls, MT], 22 February 1920.

105. "Miscellaneous Stories." JBV III Papers. Ruth Berry died 6 June 1947 and was buried next to her sister Mary and their parents in Unity Pond Cemetery.

106. Writing from Montana to his mother Mary Berry Cook in 1905 twenty-four-year-old Hal stated: "The Fall is awful quiet and hardly anything going on. If I had known it was to be so quiet I should have come east this winter…. It will soon be spring and then I shall go back on the ranch. I should like to see you very much and get awful home sick sometimes. I want to pick up a few more dollars and then I think I shall come East for good. If I can land in Unity with $600.00 [?] I think we can make a prety nice little home. Oh! Mother you don't know [how] often I wish we were together. (You, Aunt Ruth and myself) But we soon shall be." See Hal [Cook], Great Falls, Montana, to Mrs. B. B., Cook, Belfast, Maine, 29 January 1905. SSB III Papers.

107. Harold M. Hill, M.D. believes that Sam Berry II, as well as his brother Ralph and his sister Mary Berry Cook had adult-onset diabetes, and that while in Montana Sam II contracted pneumonia, which precipitated a diabetic coma leading to his

untimely death. See Hill, et al., *Winnecook Ranch*, 19. Sam II and Florence Bartlett Berry's daughter Sybil Samuel Berry (the "other SSB" as she was called by her cousin SSB III) graduated from Wellesley College, married John B. Myrick, and settled in West Newton, Massachusetts. SSB III spent time with Sybil and her family at their summer home in Prince Edward Island, Canada. Florence Bartlett Berry married again to Harold H. Grant and she died 18 May 1899.

108. Hill, "The Berry Family Correspondence," Hill, et al., *Winnecook Ranch*, 19.

109. Sadie Lord Webster, Winnecook Ranch, to EKB, White Sulpher Springs, 4 September 1890. JBV III Papers.

110. Hill, "The Berry Family Correspondence," Hill, et al., *Winnecook Ranch*, 23.

111. Malone, et al., *Montana*, 167. After the Panic of 1893 sheepmen started to invest more in mutton breeds of sheep, however, as there was an increase in demand for meat as urban populations rose, and new refrigerated railroad cars made it possible to deliver meat to more distant cities.

112. See Hill, "A Biographical Sketch," Hill, et al., *Winnecook Ranch*, 35.

113. Ibid.

114. Hill, "The Berry Family Correspondence," Hill, et al., *Winnecook Ranch*, 25.

115. For evidence that Ralph sent money to his brother James Edwin (who suffered from depression) and to his sister Ruth Berry and mother Olive Mussey Berry in Maine see Hill, "The Berry Family Correspondence," Hill, et al., *Winnecook Ranch*, 22, 23. It is not clear, however, whether the money Ralph sent to his mother in Maine was a gift or income from investments in the sheep business that she and Ralph's father SSB I (who died in 1890) had made. Evie's brother Samuel Kelley had also come to Montana in the 1880s and invested in sheep ranching. When he died suddenly in 1907 while in Montana, Ralph also took over looking after the business interests for Sam Kelley's widowed wife Sarah Harmon Kelley, who lived in Unity. Sam and Sarah Harmon Kelley had two daughters named Charlotte May and Leta Evelyn who lived with their Aunt Evie in Redlands for a while. See Hill, "The Berry Family Correspondence," Hill, et al., *Winnecook Ranch*, 26, and 29–30.

116. See Hill, "A Biographical Sketch," Hill, et al., *Winnecook Ranch*, 43.

117. See Hill, "The Berry Family Correspondence," Hill, et al., *Winnecook Ranch*, 29–30.

118. Quote from Ralph Berry monument in Unity, Maine, cemetery.

119. See Hill, "A Biographical Sketch," Hill, et al., *Winnecook Ranch*, 44–46, 51–52.

120. Stearns, *A History of the Upper Musselshell Valley*, 46. For a listing of more Waldo County people who started sheep ranches in this area see "Letters from Montana Territory, Scammon's Ranch, Musselshell River, May 29 1881," *Republican Journal*, n.d. JBV III Papers. "Waldo County People in Montana," *Republican Journal*, 19 March 1885.

121. *Republican Journal*, 16 October 1884.

122. See Michael Zuckerman, *Peaceable Kingdoms: New England Towns in the Eighteenth Century* (New York: Knopf, 1970). Zuckerman quote from Hubka, "Farm Family Mutuality," 22.

123. See Linda Gordon, "History Matters Forum on Family History," 7 March 2002. familiesforum@ashp.listserv.cuny.edu. See also Stephanie Coonty, *The Way We Never Were: American Families and the Nostalgia Trap* (New York: Basic Books, 1992).

1. James E. Kelley to JBV III, 4 December 1933. JBV III Papers.
2. See Eli Ayer Vickery obituary, "Eli A. Vickery Is Dead After Years of Illness," n.p., May 1914. JBV III Papers. See also teaching certificates for E. A. Vickery dated Unity, Maine, 28 November 1878 and 26 November 1879 by James R. Taber, Supervisor. Copies in JBV III Papers.
3. Ultimogeniture seemed to be the Vickery family's arrangement for the past few generations. David Vickery III, who inherited the original Vickery farm in Unity, was twenty-five when his father David II turned seventy. When David III turned sixty-five his son David IV was twenty-five and the farm eventually went to him. Although Eli Ayer's parents James Berry I and Mary Ayer Vickery now owned the family farm on Quaker Hill, James I's younger brother Newman Whipple Vickery had been set to own it until he traded farms with them in the 1860s. When James I turned sixty-five, his youngest son James II would be twenty-five and the farm did indeed go to him.
4. See JBV III, *A History of the Town of Unity, Maine,* 185; and Myers, "Montana Pioneer," 3. Elisha Mosher Clark, his brothers Frank Leslie Clark and Lindley Clark, and their sister Carrie Clark Wellington, the children of Alfred and Judith Mosher Clark of Unity, all went to Montana in the late nineteenth-century and lived the rest of their lives in the Red Lodge area. Other members of the extended Clark family in Unity like Agnes, Etta, Marjorie, and Theresa Clark went to Montana as well and several married there.
5. Apparently Ralph Berry also owned another ranch called Lowell Ranch near Hunter Hot Springs in the Big Timber area on the Yellowstone River. However, there is no evidence that Eli Ayer Vickery was involved at all with his cousins in Montana. See Hill, "The Berry Family Correspondence," Hill, et al., *Winnecook Ranch,* 24.
6. *Belfast City Press,* 7 December 1886.
7. Ibid.
8. MBC to OMB, 2 July 1878. JBV III Papers. In reference to the fashions in Helena at this time see Petrik, *No Step Backward,* 15: "Helena's rapid growth meant money, and chief among the townspeople who joyously displayed their wealth were the wives of the city's elite…. In imitation of their Eastern sisters, Helena's wives dressed in the latest fashion, decked themselves with jewelry, and gave costly dinners, dances, and teas."
9. The "large leather bound ledger that Eli Ayer Vickery used in his store keeping days" is still in the family. In a letter from Rosalie Swain Reimers to JBV III, 5 January 1989, she wrote: "My Mother, Elizabeth [Vickery Swain], used it for her scrap book and pasted her treasures over the pages. I remember being shown this book on a couple of very special occasions…. David Vickery, son of [Uncle] Fred and Louise Sparhawk Vickery, ended up with this book." JBV III Papers.
10. Quoted material from "The Brandenburg Family," n.d. JBV III Papers. In an 1898 letter that Carrie Brandenburg Vickery (hereafter cited as CBV) wrote to her mother-in-law Mary True Ayer Vickery who had asked Carrie to tell her about her father's family, she stated: "The little newspaper clipping that I sent was printed in 1888. I was in Kentucky that Fall and visited with Mr. Bell who is a cousin of my father. At that time Mr. Bell and others of the family had great hopes of obtaining the fortune that rightfully belongs to the Brandenburgs in America. Lawyers were employed and sent to Berlin but were never heard from and the supposition was that they were paid more there to drop the case than the American heirs could pay

them. I have never heard, and I do not suppose that anything more has been done in regard to it." Transcribed letter from CBV to Mary True Ayer Vickery, 10 January 1898, sent to author from Carrie and Eli's grandaughter Mary O'Shea Dell.

11. CBV to JBV III, 6 January 1936. JBV III Papers.

12. There seem to be some discrepancies in the sources about who went to Montana when, and where in Montana the Brandenburg children went. In 1961 Carrie's ninety-nine-year-old brother Jackson "Jay" Brandenburg (1863–1964) was interviewed by the *Great Falls Tribune* and he remembered that after his parents' death, at the age of seventeen he was diagnosed with consumption and went to Montana for his health bringing only two of his younger sisters Mary and Emma with him. He said he found a family to care for his sisters and then found work at Hunter Hot Springs. However, family notes say that the children went to live with their Aunt Sue Murray Hunter and her husband Dr. Hunter. It seems logical to think that young Jay had a destination in mind and some plans when he went to Montana with his sisters, perhaps first bringing two sisters and going back for the other three later. The 1961 article mentions all five of his sisters (in birth order: Mary Susan Brandenburg Yule, Nancy Jane Brandenburg Osbourne, Carrie Brandenburg Vickery, Algia Mason Brandenburg, and Emma Brandenburg Reese), though there is no mention of the youngest Brandenburg child Samuel Edward. Carrie told JBV III that "we children [were] brot to Montana," with no mention of splitting up the family, so perhaps Samuel died at the same time as his mother, or shortly after. According to Frederick Brandenburg Vickery, Eli and Carrie's son, "An epidemic took both the father and mother of the [Carrie's] family, and my mother's aunt, Susan Hunter, took the children to Hunter's Hot Springs, Montana." See Fred B. Vickery to Mrs. Cliff Williams, 20 February 1984. JBV III Papers. Original with David F. Vickery.

13. Dr. Andrew Jackson Hunter (1816–94), so the family history maintains, was a "lineal descendant of Pocohantas." Hunter had been a surgeon in the Confederate army before he and Susannah C. Murray Hunter moved to Montana, hoping to find gold. They moved to Bozeman first, then Virginia City, Helena, Confederate Gulch, and New York Gulch before settling and building a house at the hot springs. Hunter continued to practice medicine in each place they moved. The Hunters had seven children of their own. See "Mary L. Hunter Doane" obituary, *Bozeman Chronicle*, 1952. White Silver Springs, where the Berry community settled, was just north of Hunter's Hot Springs and Mary Berry Cook, like many nineteenth-century women took baths there for her health. "I am here [at the Springs] for my health, and am going to stay until I feel better if it is a month. The fact is I am billious, as is usual with me in the Spring, and a little run down. The Sulphur Springs are very good for people troubled with that complaint. Am going to take baths everyday and drink of the Sulphur water. How much better this medicine is, than drugs & pills! The baths are delicious. They make one feel like a new being after taking them." MBC to EKB, 7 April 1879. JBV III Papers.

14. See Carrie Brandenburg Vickery obituary, "Aged Bridger Matron Dies," n.p., n.d. JBV III Papers.

15. See Jeffrey, *Frontier Women*, 195.

16. David F. Vickery to author, December 2002. JBV III claims another of Carrie Jerusha Brandenburg's uncles was Captain Gustavus Doane "who was with [General] Custer's party, but he came the day after the massacre." JBV III to SSB III, 3 July 1961. SSB III Papers.

17. Bustle story from handwritten notes by JBV III. JBV Papers. See Myers, "Montana Pioneer," 3, who claims Eli Ayer and Carrie first met at Carrie's sister and brother-in-law Alec and Mamie Brandenburg Yule's home.

18. Lillian Schlissel, *Women's Diaries of the Westward Journey* (New York: Schocken Books, 1982), 45. Eli Ayer Vickery's mother Mary True Ayer Vickery was anxious that he marry, and when he went back East she encouraged him to take a Maine woman as his wife, but "Eli told his mother that he was going back to Montana, find an orphan schoolteacher, and marry her." David F. Vickery to author, December 2002. That Eli Ayer described his future wife Carrie with such clarity suggests that he and Carrie might have known each other before he went back East.

19. JBV III, "Eli and Carrie's Story," 2. JBV III Papers. Dr. James Craig (1850–1922) was born in Dixmont, Maine, and graduated from Bowdoin Medical College in 1876. He practiced in Unity, Maine, until the early 1890s when he moved to White Silver Springs, Montana, then settled in Columbus, Montana. See JBV III, *A History of the Town of Unity, Maine*, 246–47. Dr. Craig also attended Unity native Frank Harmon's death in White Silver Springs on 15 January 1894. See Grace Olive Berry to "Grandma" [Olive Mussey Berry], 29 January 1894. JBV III Papers.

20. Quoted words of banker from "The Brandenburg Family," n.d., 2. JBV III Papers.

21. Evelyn Cameron who came from England in 1889 and settled in east central Montana to ranch with her husband wrote her mother in 1893 perfectly describing the situation in Montana at this time: "Most of the people that we know around here are ruined or in great financial difficulties through a panic in the money market.... In some of the Western towns all of the banks failed in one day." Lucey, *Photographing Montana*, 24.

22. In "The Brandenburg Family," 2, is the official family account of losing the farm in a bank foreclosure. JBV III's account of losing the farm in a card game is from JBV III, "Eli and Carrie's Story," 2. There is however a problem with chronology if indeed JBV III's story is true because his father JBV II did not arrive in Montana until April 1893 and by that time Allie had been born in Columbus, apparently where the Vickery family already lived.

23. See Leavitt, *Brought to Bed*, 79; and Schlissel, *Women's Diaries*, 106–11.

24. Description of weather from "Allie Remembers," interview of Mary Alverda "Allie" Vickery O'Shea, ca. 1972. JBV III Papers. Original with Mary A. Dell.

25. See Malone, et al., *Montana*, "The Mining Frontier," 64–91.

26. "The Brandenburg Family," 2.

27. JBV III, "Eli and Carrie's Story," 2.

28. Myers, "Montana Pioneer," 4.

29. There is no information about the other people who went to Clark's Fork with the Vickerys except JBV III's cryptic note stating that, "Abbie Sawyer was a lady which Mary Vickery helped in Unity. She evidently married [Tom] Trail in Columbus, but know nothing further of them." JBV III, "Eli and Carrie's Story," 2.

30. Myers, "Montana Pioneer," 4.

31. See Malone, et al., *Montana*, "The Mining Frontier," 64–91.

32. Gun story from collection of nine handwritten notes by JBV III. JBV III Papers. David F. Vickery, Eli Ayer and Carrie's grandson (son of Frederick Brandenburg and Louise Sparhawk Vickery) contends that the road agent was one of the many cowboys employed by large cattle ranchers to intimidate homesteaders and keep them from settling and breaking up the open range in northern Wyoming. David F. Vickery to author, December 2002. Indeed, this incident occurred shortly after the Johnson County Cattle or Range War of 1892 that was made famous by Jack Warner Schaefer's novel *Shane* (1949) and the United Artists movie *Heaven's Gate* (1980).

33. Floor of cabins described by Carol Vickery Myers in Fay Kulman, "Facts of Carbon," *Carbon County News* [Montana], 19 January 1967.

278

34. JBV III, "Eli and Carrie's Story," 2.
35. A number of people aside from Tom and Abbie Sawyer Trail are mentioned either working with Eli and Carrie or establishing their own mining claims around the Vickerys, though nothing is known about them. They include Don Rosner, Charlie Chouning, John Bush, "a boy named Darrah," and George Berry who does not appear to have any connection with the Vickerys' Berry cousins ranching in the Upper Musselshell Valley, Montana. JBV III, "Eli and Carrie's Story."
36. Mary A. Dell, "Memories of Clark, Wyoming," *Montana Free Press: The Journal of Rural Montana* 6, no. 4 (June 1995), 36.
37. JBV III, "Eli and Carrie's Story," 5. Eli and Carrie's grandson, David F. Vickery, owns "Eli's old gold pan."
38. For a good description of gold value and use in Montana at this time see Munson, "Montana as it was and it is," 116.
39. O'Shea, "Allie Remembers," 2. JBV III Papers.
40. Hamilton, *From Wilderness to Statehood*, 411.
41. In Carrie Brandenburg Vickery's obituary the Vickery homestead is called a farm, although in "Dorothy's Story" it is referred to as the "V/V Ranch," which was the brand used for livestock. David F. Vickery to author, December 2002. Unlike their previous venture of raising primarily cows and sheep which was a ranch, the Wyoming venture of growing oats, alfalfa, and market vegetables was the main industry and was clearly a farm. In Western vernacular both ventures might be called ranching, but to differentiate between the two time periods in the Vickery story I will call their homestead a farm.
42. Dell, "Memories," 36.
43. Dell, "Memories," 36. For more about "Ma" Sirrine, see "Generations," *Montana Free Press: The Journal of Rural Montana* 6, no. 4 (June 1995), 30–35.
44. [Dorothy Brandenburg Vickery Buck Brumpton?], "Dorothy's Story," n.d., 1. JBV III Papers. Again, chronology here seems off. The timing of a birth when Eli was "building sluice boxes preparatory for the 'gold rush days'" suggests that Carrie might have meshed some memories from Emma's birth the previous April with Dorothy's birth. Allie Vickery O'Shea says that her father fed Dorothy catnip tea until Carrie's milk came in. See "Allie Remembers," 2. Catnip or catmint tea is a folk remedy for babies, used especially to cure thrush, a disease caused by a fungus and marked by white patches in an infant's mouth. I want to thank Dr. Marli F. Weiner for sharing references about the uses of catnip tea from her research on nineteenth-century medicine.
45. Dorothy Vickery Buck to Elizabeth Vickery Swain, April 1932. JBV III Papers.
46. Dell, "Memories," 38.
47. Description of the Vickery log cabin from Dell, "Memories," 38.
48. "Dorothy's Story," 4.
49. Riley, *The Female Frontier*, 83: "Doctors were scarce in most areas of the Plains" even into the opening decade of the twentieth century.
50. Dell, "Memories," 38; "Allie Remembers," 4.
51. Mintz and Kellogg, *Domestic Revolutions*, 51–52. See also Riley, *The Female* Frontier, 82–83. Riley says that "on the Great Plains women avidly discussed the issue of birth control, offered advice to each other, and purchased the various devices that were still advertised and marketed in defiance of the Comstock Law," 82. The federal Comstock Act of 1873 defined all birth-control information as obscene and barred it from interstate commerce and mail.
52. JBV III Papers.
53. Myers, "Montana Pioneer," 13.
54. "Dorothy's Story," 4–5.

55. "Dorothy's Story," 7.
56. Food descriptions from "Dorothy's Story" and Myers, "Montana Pioneer."
57. "Memories" from "Grama Carol" [Vickery Myers] to Shawn [Townsend], 14 May 1964. JBV III Papers.
58. O'Shea, "Allie Remembers," 10.
59. Myers, "Montana Pioneer," 10.
60. Ibid., 7 and "Dorothy's Story," 5.
61. "Dorothy's Story," 7.
62. O'Shea, "Allie Remembers," 6.
63. "Dorothy's Story," 6.
64. Myers, "Montana Pioneer," 10.
65. O'Shea, "Allie Remembers," 5.
66. Ibid.
67. For another discussion on "chores" on a Montana ranch at the turn of the twentieth century see Shatraw, "*Thrashin' Time*, 53–75.
68. O'Shea, "Allie Remembers," 3.
69. "Dorothy's Story," 10.
70. Myers, "Montana Pioneer," 5. Eli and Carrie's grandaughter Eileen O'Shea Hyem (daughter of Mary "Allie" Alverda Vickery O'Shea) had a different account of shooting rattlesnakes around the Vickery farm: "It was Allie that killed rattle snakes by shooting them, along with Edgar who taught her to shoot firearms, as she worked by his side helping with the outside chores. She even skinned the snakes and made a hat band & a belt covering—I shudder to think of it. Grandmother Carrie did have her time of killing a rattle snake, and it was a most frightening experience for her. She never used firearms, as she was not a "wild-west Annie Oakley" type of a lady…. One very warm afternoon Carrie was going out to do an errand—check on children or drying clothes, and as she opened the cabin door there on the doorstep was a large rattle snake, coiled & soaking up the Wyoming sun. Grandmother said she nearly died of fright, but grabbing the sharp shovel Grandfather kept by the door, she began chopping & chopping until she was sure the snake was dead—then disposed of it with the shovel. She said she was just limp afterwards from the fright & the frantic work, but realized she had to do this nasty job." See Eileen O'Shea Hyem to author, 7 May 2002.
71. Riley, *The Female Frontier*, 84. From David F. Vickery to author, December 2002: "Buffalo Bill Cody was one of the most famous residents of the area. One day as Fred (my father) and other Vickery children were in school, a man rode up to the school on his horse and came inside. It was Buffalo Bill … who entertained the class for a time with some wonderful tales of the early West."
72. Myers, "Montana Pioneer," 8.
73. O'Shea, "Allie Remenbers," 5.
74. Jeffrey, *Frontier Women*, 95.
75. O'Shea, "Allie Remembers," 5.
76. Eileen O'Shea Hyem to author, 9 October 2001.
77. Myers, "Montana Pioneer," 9.
78. "JBV III handwritten notes," 9.
79. Myers, "Montana Pioneer," 12.
80. Allie Vickery O'Shea and Elsie Vickery Liston also visited with their brother Ted and other Vickerys in Unity in June 1976. See Nora O'Shea Robertson to author, 31 August 2001. Mary Ann O'Shea Dell, Allie's daughter, visited her relatives in Unity, Maine, in 1975 and JBV III later visited Mary in California in 1985. See Mary Ann O'Shea Dell to author, 24 July 2001.

81. "Grama Carol" [Vickery Myers] to Shawn [Townsend], 14 May 1964. JBV III Papers.

82. O'Shea, "Allie Remembers," 8.

83. Mary Ayer Vickery to "Dear Children," 19 May 1903. JBV III Papers. Other evidence that there was regular communication between the Vickery families in the East and West in "Dorothy's Story," 7. Dorothy mentions that the "news of the world" reached the Vickery family out West "via the few good magazines allowed [into the home] and letters from the far-away relatives."

84. O'Shea, "Allie Remembers," 7.

85. From "Sister Carrie" to "Sister Mamie," 5 June 1902, Clark, Wyoming. JBV III Papers. Original with Eileen O'Shea Hyem. Carrie's quote "take no thought of the morrow" from Matthew 6:34: "Take therefore no thought for the morrow; for the morrow shall take thought for the things of itself." Carrie's reaction to her sister's faith in "our happiness in the future" (probably a reference to heaven and a tenet of nineteenth-century Christianity), seems to hint at Carrie's acceptance of a less sentimental, non-evangelical theology of the early twentieth century.

86. JBV III Papers.

87. Carol also left high school at this time and in fact never graduated even though she later attended Billings Polytechnic (now Rocky Mountain College). See Carol Vickery to Mr. E. T. Krueger, Dean of Billings Polytechnic, 13 August 1917. JBV III Papers. Apparently after Eli Ayer suffered a heart attack and was taken in a wagon to the hospital in Bridger, Montana, his brother James Berry Vickery II ("Uncle Jim") in Maine went west in February 1911 to be with Eli and his family for an unspecified time. See "Thy loving Mother [Mary Ayer Vickery]" to "My Dear Children, & grand-dears," 28 February 1911; and Fred B. Vickery to Mrs. Cliff Williams, 20 February 1984. JBV III Papers.

88. Myers, "Montana Pioneer," 13. For a discussion of "pernicious anemia" in the early twentieth century see *The Same Great Struggle*, 222. Because Eli Ayer Vickery always worked so hard, his son Frederick "Fred," who was eleven years old when his father died, believed he "worked himself to death." David F. Vickery to author, December 2002.

89. Ibid.

90. Dell, "Memories," 38.

91. "Eli A. Vickery Is Dead After Years of Illness," n.p., n.d. JBV III Papers.

92. Fred B. Vickery to Mrs. Cliff Williams, 20 February 1984. JBV III Papers.

93. Myers, "Montana Pioneer," 14.

94. CBV, "The Home Ranch," to Carol Vickery, 17 June 1917. JBV III Papers.

95. CBV to Carol Vickery, 6 January 1918. JBV III Papers. The lines Carrie was thinking about were from Shakespeare's *Julius Caesar*, IV, iii, 217:
There is a tide in the affairs of men,
Which taken at the flood, leads on to fortune;
Omitted, all the voyage of their life
Is bound in shallows and in miseries.

96. Evans, *Born for Liberty*, 171–72.

97. CBV, "Home," to Carol Vickery, 8 September 1918. JBV III Papers.

98. See for example Private Edgar A. Vickery to CBV, 20 September 1918. JBV III Papers. Original with Mary A. Dell.

99. Private Edgar A. Vickery to CBV, 15 September 1918. JBV III Papers. Original with Mary A. Dell.

100. Eileen O'Shea Hyem to author, 7 August 2001. See also "Will Visit Son's Grave 'Over There,'" n.p., 1930. JBV III Papers.

101. See Gina Kolata, *Flu: The Story of the Great Influenza Pandemic of 1918 and the Search for the Virus That Caused It* (New York: Farrar, Straus and Giroux, 1999), Prologue, 7. Victims died from the influenza epidemic when their lungs filled with fluid and they literally drowned. Thus many death certificates listed pneumonia (which was caused by the flu) as the cause of death. See Kolata, *Flu*, 4, 22.

102. The French cemetery was officially called "Oise-Aisne American, Seringes-et-Nesles, Aisne, France."

103. Myers, "Montana Pioneer," 15–16.

104. Dell, "Memories," 38. Carrie eventually sold the homestead to Ted Paddock, but she retained the mineral rights on the land, which included oil, gas, and gold rights. According to Lyn Vickery (grandson of Eli Ayer and Carrie Brandenburg Vickery, and son of Frederick Brandenburg and Louise Sparhawk Vickery), "the original ranch house and authentic log cabin is still standing," and "over the years sundry oil companies have, at one time or another, paid for the lease rights to those mineral properties," but "none of these companies ever did anything to develop them." Acting as the family representative with any potential "deep-pocket purchaser of these rights," he stated that, "Seeking for the sale of the 'valuable' stuff has been an on-going activity, in an on-again off-again manner for decades." See Lyn Vickery to Carol Oberweiser, 7 May 2001, and Fred B. Vickery to Mrs. Cliff Williams, 20 February 1984. JBV III Papers.

105. Rosalie Swain Reimers [daughter of Elizabeth Vickery Swain] to JBV III, 5 January 1989. JBV III Papers. Mary A. Dell [daughter of Mary "Allie" Vickery O'Shea] also commented on the legacy of her grandparents: "When my Grandmother died at age 91 she had 30 Grandchildren and 65 Great-grandchildren. Many more have been added since. Her descendants are as the stars in the sky!" Mary A. Dell to author, 29 April 2002.

106. Anthony F. C. Wallace, "Extended Family and the Role of Women in Early Industrial Societies," in Glenn Porter and William H. Mulligan, Jr., editors, *Working Papers from the Regional Economic History Research Center* (Wilmington, Delaware: Eleutherian Mills-Hagley Foundation, 1982), 3. Joan E. Cashin saw women as connectors in her study of men and women on the southern frontiers in the years between 1810 and 1860: "Migration was a family venture in the sense that men and women both took part in it, but they went to the frontier with competing agendas: many men tried to escape the intricate kinship networks of the seaboard while women tried to preserve them if they could." *A Family Venture*, 4. For women as "preservers" of family see also, Evans, *Born for Liberty*, 68–70.

107. Schlissel, *Women's Diaries of the Westward Journey*, 31, 148. See also Jeffrey, *Frontier Women*, 73–75.

108. A well-known saying was coined in the nineteenth century by English novelist, poet, and essayist Dinah Maria Mulock Craik (1826–87) in her book *Young and Old* to express how mothers and daughters were connected in families: "Oh, my son's my son till he gets him a wife, But my daughter's my daughter all her life." For more on mother and daughter relationships in the nineteenth century see Ryan, *Cradle of the Middle Class*, 191–98; and Nancy M. Theriot, *Mothers and Daughters in Nineteenth-Century America: The Biosocial Construction of Femininity* (Lexington: The University Press of Kentucky), 1996.

109. Nora O'Shea Robertson to author, 31 August 2001.

282

PART FOUR

CHAPTER 10

1. JBV III Papers. Claribel S. Vickery (1854–?) was the daughter of John and Abigail Murch Vickery, and the granddaughter of David and Lydia Bartlett Vickery.

2. Weber, "Bangor's greatest natural resource."

3. See Richard H. Condon, "Living in Two Worlds: Rural Maine in 1930," *Maine Historical Quarterly* 25, no. 2 (Fall 1985), 59.

4. See JBV III, *A History of the Town of Unity, Maine,* 126–45, 172–76.

5. Ibid., 195. In the midst of the Great Depression JBV II revealed how important the ready cash from his timber stand was for the family farm: "Well we have finished our woods work and trucked 27 or 28 cord of Birch to Oakland[.] We are planning to use the proceeds for a refrigerator, enamel sink and remodel the pantry some what." See JBV II, "Home," to JBV III, Bates College, 2 March 1938. JBV III Papers.

6. See Margene Stewart Johns to JBV III, 3 April 1960. JBV III Papers.

7. Lafayette Edmund Stewart's mother was Elizabeth Dunham Stewart (1820-1879) from Carmel, Maine, who could trace her lineage to Pilgrim John Dunham who came to Plymouth, Massachusetts, during the MAYFLOWER years. Lafayette's great-grandmother Mary Robbins Stewart's mother, as the family lore maintains, "was a Newbury who was carried off when a child by Indians and was with them until she was 14 years old [ca. 1760s] and finally ransomed." See " Dear Dr. Stephenson" photocopy of unsigned typed letter in Stewart File, JBV III Papers. In a 7 December 1952 letter to JBV III his cousin Shirley Stewart Harris [daughter of Arthur Gilman Stewart who was Lafayette and Abigail Douglas Stewart's son and brother of JBV III's mother Annie May Stewart] tells another significant family story: "Did you know that when your Grandfather [Lafayette] Stewart was born his mother had a very bad time—they thought he wouldn't live so they put him in a pan and slid him under the stove, later after tending to his mother they looked and found him kicking and squirming as lively as you please. And that's how close you & I came to not being either!!!" JBV III Papers.

8. Leavitt, *Brought to Bed,* 171–95.

9. See Harvey Green, *The Light of the Home: An Intimate View of the Lives of Women in Victorian America, 1870–1910* (New York: Pantheon Books, 1983), 109.

10. Description of the value of baby photographs in middle-class culture at the turn of the century from Shawn Michelle Smith, *American Archives: Gender, Race, and Class in Visual Culture* (Princeton: Princeton University Press, 1999), 125.

11. JBV II, Unity, to Annie Stewart Vickery (hereafter cited as ASV), Brooks, 13 March 1904. JBV III Papers. JBV II's reference is to the large magnifying, or refracting telescope with a 36-inch aperture at the Lick Observatory, Mt. Hamilton, California.

12. JBV II, Unity, to ASV, Brooks, 8 September 1907. JBV III Papers. While James II apparently wanted to use his mother's family name of Ayer as Eric's middle name, Eric's middle name became Arthur, seemingly after Annie's brother Arthur Gilman Stewart (1884–1933). Neither Everett's or Eric's first name appear to be used in either James II or Annie's family genealogies.

13. JBV II to ASV, 17 September 1907. JBV III Papers.

14. Elements of this temperament are often attributed to the stereotypical "Yankee farmer," pragmatic, stubborn, independent, and self-reliant—not particularly the qualities that enhance marriages.

15. See Mintz and Kellogg, *Domestic Revolutions,* "The Rise of the Companionate Family, 1900–1930," 107–31; and Evans, *Born for Liberty,* 176–81.
16. See Clark, *The Roots of Rural Capitalism,* 55; Ulrich, *A Midwife's Tale,* 264–85; Nylander, *Images of the New England Home,* 35–36.
17. JBV II to ASV, 17 September 1907. JBV III Papers.
18. Judd, et al., *Maine: The Pine Tree State,* 407–08.
19. See Day, *Farming in Maine,* 176-179.
20. For another source poignantly describing grandparents holding down the farm in late nineteenth-century Maine as the next generation disperses, see C. A. Stephens, *Stories from the Old Squire's Farm,* compiled and edited by Charles G. Waugh and Eric-Jon Waugh (Nashville, Tennessee: Rutledge Hill Press, 1995).
21. Although the family name of Lura Beam's grandparents was Berry, there is no evidence that the Marshfield Berry family and the Unity Berry and Vickery families were related, but I have no doubt that a link between these pioneer Maine families could be found.
22. Lura Beam, *A Maine Hamlet* (Gardiner, Maine: The Maine Humanities Council/Maine Historical Society/Tilbury House, Publishers, 1999), 5.
23. Ibid., 210.
24. Ibid., 3, 5, 14, 20.
25. James Berry Vickery I obituary, *Republican Journal,* 16 November 1911.
26. From "Death of David E. Vickery," n.p., n.d. JBV III Papers.
27. From "Mama" [Abigail Nancy Douglas Stewart?], Montville, Maine, to ASV, Unity Maine, 20 March 1911. JBV III Papers.
28. From "Eli A. Vickery is Dead after Years of Illness," n.p., n.d. JBV III Papers.
29. Mintz and Kellogg, *Domestic Revolutions,* 114.
30. Weber, "Bangor's greatest natural resource."
31. Robert H. Newall, *Bangor Daily News,* 21 May 1981.
32. Ibid.
33. From "He gave his Life for his Country," n.p., n.d. JBV III Papers.
34. CBV to Carol L. Vickery, 26 June 1918. JBV III Papers.
35. Myers, "Montana Pioneer and Poet," 15.
36. Ibid.
37. Through the years other western cousins visited Unity and the Vickery family farm. See Carrie Brandenburg Vickery to JBV III, 18 January 1944: "Seems a long time since my visit to the old Farm in Maine, and you were a little lad.... I do not know if you were home when my grandson Ted Townsend [son of Ted and Carol Vickery Townsend] visited at the farm." In 1975 Mary O'Shea Dell, daughter of Allie Vickery O'Shea visited her Uncle and Aunt Ted and Margaret Vickery in Unity and as she said, "saw the old Vickery farm and other historical places." From Mary O'Shea Dell, "Gram's Father, Eli Vickery, of Unity, Maine," 1985. In 1994 David Frederick Vickery, son of Frederick Brandenburg Vickery, and his family visited JBV III. Aileen Swain Silbernagel, the daughter of Elizabeth Chase Vickery Swain visited JBV III in 1996. See Aileen Swain Silbernagle to JBV III, 21 July 1996. All JBV III Papers.
38. Mary True Ayer Vickery obituary, *Republican Journal,* 9 November 1922.
39. Ibid.
40. JBV III Papers.
41. See Hal S. Barron, *Mixed Harvest: The Second Great Transformation in the Rural North, 1870–1930* (Chapel Hill: The University of North Carolina Press, 1997), 197–98.
42. See Virginia Scharff, *Taking the Wheel: Women and the Coming of the Motor Age* (New York: The Free Press, 1991), 142–45.

43. All about Grandmother Vickery from "Miscellaneous Stories." JBV III Papers.
44. *Republican Journal*, 9 November 1922.
45. Judd, et al., *Maine: The Pine Tree State*, 307. Unfortunately, steamers were usually built in England and their ascendancy weakened the important wooden sailing ship building industry in Maine.
46. "Vickery Falls from Boston-Bangor Boat," *Boston Globe*, n.d. JBV III Papers.
47. "John A. Vickery Lost Overboard," *Bangor Daily News*, 10 July 1924. See also "Falls Overboard On Trip From Boston," *Bangor Daily Commercial*, 9 July 1924.
48. See "The Weather" in *Bangor Daily News*, 9 July 1924, and *Bangor Daily Commercial*, 8 July 1924.
49. See reward poster in JBV Papers. One family story posits that John Ayer Vickery I was mugged when he went on deck that night and then thrown overboard.
50. Harrie B. Coe, ed., *Maine Resources, Attractions, and Its People: A History*, vol. v (New York: The Lewis Historical Publishing Company, Inc., 1931), 52.
51. **1. Emily Josephine Vickery (1892–1987)** and Harvey Prescott Sleeper married in 1919, and they had three children: Harvey Prescott Sleeper II (b. 1920), June Emily Sleeper Sasso Myers (b. 1922), and David Page Sleeper (b. 1937). **2. Mildred Louise Vickery (1895–1949)** and Waldemar Littlefield married in 1919 and they had three children: Waldemar Vickery Littlefield (b. 1920), Emily Louise Littlefield Danforth (b. 1923), and Mary Betty McKenney (b. 1927). **3. Charles James Vickery (1899–1944)** and Marjorie O'Connell married in 1925. Charles worked for Arnold Shoes, and later for the W. S. Emerson Company, Brewer, Maine. He died in the Northwest Territory, Canada, while working for a construction company doing engineering work for the U.S. government. Charles and Marjorie had no children.
    4. John Ayer Vickery II (1901–85) and Eva Stanley Brown married in 1940. John worked in the W. S. Emerson Company for more than sixty-five years, serving as president and chairman of the board. John II and Eva had no children. **5. Winslow Chambers Vickery (1907–82)** and Claire Bradley married in 1934. Winslow graduated from the Carnegie Institute of Technology, and worked in Massachusetts and New Jersey before he joined his family at the W. S. Emerson Company, where he became president and treasurer. Winslow and Claire had three children: Kathleen Clarie Vickery Nisco (1936–79), husband Joseph V. Nisco, and children Steven Joseph Nisco (b. 1962), Laura Kathleen Nisco (b. 1963), Emily Marie Nisco Frank (b. 1965), and Nancy Claire Nisco Clark (b. 1970); John Arthur Vickery, Sr. (b. 1938), the current president and treasurer of W. S. Emerson, wife Elizabeth Sandowsky Vickery, and children Lynn Marie Ibarra Walsh (b. 1966) and John Arthur Vickery, Jr. (b. 1968), who with his wife Betsy Jones Vickery are the third generation of Vickerys at W. S. Emerson; and Russell Michael Vickery (b. 1948), the current vice president of W. S. Emerson, wife Jane Dexter Vickery, and children Amy Vickery (b. 1980) and Chad Vickery (b. 1982). **6. Robert Nickerson Vickery (1909–49)**, John Ayer I and Emily Nickerson Vickery's last child never married.
52. Coe, *Maine,* 52.
53 . "John A. Vickery Lost Overboard," *Bangor Daily News*, 10 July 1924. For history of W. S. Emerson see "W. S. Emerson Company 75th Anniversary, 1921–1996," Advertising Supplement, *Bangor Daily News*, 12 December 1996. JBV III wrote an article about the growth of the shoe industry in the Bangor area after the Civil War in which his cousins played such an important role. See James B. Vickery, "E. A. Buck Mail Order Boots" from *Maine in Bangor: Economic Emergence and Adaptation, 1834–1911* (Bangor, Maine: 1984) in William David Barry, ed., *L. L. Bean, Inc., Outdoor Sporting Specialties: A Company Scrapbook* (Portland, Maine:

The Anthoensen Press, 1987), 10.

54. For JBV III's childhood reminiscences and family stories see Weber, "Bangor's greatest natural resource."

55. SSB III to JBV III, 9 July 1930. JBV III Papers.

56. It is interesting to note that one of Eli Ayer and Carrie Brandenburg Vickery's granddaughters Shirley Swain Kaiser (daughter of Elizabeth Vickery Swain) also lived for a while in Redlands. Shirley told JBV III that she and her family "spent quite a few days with Mr. Berry while we lived in Redlands and I was so enchanted by the many stories and all the historical background of our relatives." Shirley Swain Kaiser to JBV III, 16 January 1986. In 1980 Ted and Margaret Sandilands Vickery visited SSB III in California. See Margaret S. Vickery to SSB III, 14 August 1982. All JBV III Papers.

57. Larry T. Spencer, "S. Stillman Berry, Biologist Extraordinaire," http://oz.plymouth.edu/~biology/dizie/ssberry.html

58. JBV III told SSB III that his *alma mater* Bates College had "hinted that they would like to have my collection of Maine books, manuscripts, maps, etc. but I have not taken the bait." JBV III to SSB III, 3 July 1971. SSB III Papers. Indeed, after it became public in 1974 that JBV III's "valuable collection of Maine historical books" was willed to the University of Maine, one source at Bates College still hoped "maybe someone can change his mind." See "Memo," December 1974 in JBV III Bates College Alumni Files. Edmond S. Muskie Archives and Special Collections Library, Bates College. It was JBV III's intent to give his collection to the University of Maine in memory of his mother Annie Stewart Vickery. EGS, Jr., to author, August 2002. JBV III did establish a scholarship fund at Thorndike High School in his mother's memory.

59. See also "Brewer historian donates 3,000 books on Maine to UMO," *Bangor Daily News*, 8 August 1978.

60. JBV III to SSB III, 18 November 1962. SSB III Papers.

61. Celia Betsky, "Inside the Past: The Interior and the Colonial Revival in American Art and Literature, 1860–1914" in Alan Axelrod, editor, *The Colonial Revival in America* (New York: W. W. Norton & Company, 1985), 266.

62. Judd, et al., *Maine: The Pine Tree State*, 507.

63. C. Stewart Doty, "The KKK in Maine was not OK," *Bangor Daily News*, 11–12 June 1994.

64. David Lowenthal, *The Past Is a Foreign Country* (New York: Cambridge University Press, 1985), 121.

65. See Joseph A Conforti, *Imagining New England: Explorations of Regional Identity from the Pilgrims to the Mid Twentieth Century* (Chapel Hill: The University of North Carolina Press, 2001).

66. One of the finest examinations of this period in one region of New England is Sarah L. Griffen and Kevin D. Murphy, editors, *"A Nobile and Dignified Stream": The Piscataqua Region in the Colonial Revival, 1860–1930* (York, Maine: Old York Historical Society, 1992.) For an in-depth examination of historic house museums created at this time see Warren Leon and Roy Rosenzweig, editors, *History Museums in the United States: A Critical Assessment* (Urbana: University of Illinois Press, 1989); and Susan Porter Benson, Stephen Brier, and Roy Rosenzweig, editors, *Presenting the Past: Essays on History and the Public* (Philadelphia: Temple University Press, 1986).

67. William B. Rhoads, "The Colonial Revival and the Americanization of Immigrants," in Axelrod, *The Colonial Revival in America*, 341–61.

68. See Dona Brown, *Inventing New England: Regional Tourism in the Nineteenth Century* (Washington: Smithsonian Institution Press, 1995).

69. See Melinda Young Frye, "The Beginnings of the Period Room in American Museums: Charles P. Wilcomb's Colonial Kitchens, 1899, 1906, 1910," in Axelrod, *The Colonial Revival in America*, 217–40.

70. See JBV III, *A History of the Town of Unity, Maine*, 200. While JBV II owned an automobile "ever since 1916," JBV III stated that his father continued to farm "with at least two pairs of heavy draft horses." As the automobile replaced the horse and carriage as the main form of transportation, and more and more farmers turned to tractors, the need for hay to feed horses diminished. Hay had once been "the crop of greatest value" in Unity. See George J. Varney, *A Gazetteer of the State of Maine* (Boston: B. B. Russell, 1886), 548.

71. One extant postcard Annie wrote to her young son James III in 1928 from an auto trip to Quebec announced that "Here we are safe in Quebec…. We are having a lovely time." See "Mother" to "Junior," 17 August 1928. JBV III Papers. Throughout the years in their correspondence Everett, Eric, and their father often mention their new automobiles or ones they were thinking of buying. See for example Everett to JBV II, 18 February 1937. JBV III Papers. While JBV III never drove or had a license, he too loved "to go." Eric usually had a new automobile every year and he and JBV III took numerous trips together and they were the highlights of both their lives. See also note 65, Chapter 11.

72. Conforti, *Imagining New England*, 285.

73. Both JBV III and his cousin SSB III had personal interactions with Henry Beston, a popular regionalist author who wrote *Northern Farm: A Chronicle of Maine* (New York: Rinehart & Company, Inc., 1948). See photo of JBV III with Beston and his wife Elizabeth Coatsworth Beston, ca. late 1940s in JBV III Papers. See also SSB III to JBV III, 17 August 1949: "I had a nice letter from Mr. Beston in the late winter. He wanted more prints of my picture of the fireplace at Chimney Farm, which I have since sent him. Have you read his recent book, Northern Farm, and Elizabeth Coatsworth's book on Hingham?" JBV III Papers.

74. Conforti, *Imagining New England*, 286–87, 308.

75. Ibid., 286–87. For a good overview of Maine at this time see: *Modern Times in Maine & America, 1890-1930*. "The Century Project," Maine Humanities Council, VHS, 30 min., 1995.

76. Throughout the 1950s and 1960s in JBV III's correspondence with SSB III, he painfully detailed the declining vibrancy of Unity by recounting the deaths and deteriorating houses in the village. See for example JBV III to SSB III, 11 May 1964: "Unity is certainly changing. There are ten houses in the village now up for sale. The Conner place, the Dr. Whitney place, the Taber place, the Whitaker house, the Ruel Berry house…. Also the old hotel has been torn down, and someone wants to erect a super-market there. The pretty village is fast changing into the sad aspect of modern materialism." SSB III Papers.

77. Gertrude Vickery Fisher (1863–1942) was the daughter of Charles Augustus and Mary Heald Vickery, and the granddaughter of David III and Lydia Bartlett Vickery.

78. GVF to JBV III, ca.1933: "I was 17 [in 1880] when my father had letters from Vickerys in Indiana and in New York asking for family history, he gave them to me and I went to the Worcester Antiquarian society and began my search." JBV III Papers.

79. GVF to JBV III, 23 August 1933. JBV III Papers. In this same letter GVF told JBV III: "The Charles Vickerys of Pittsfield [Maine] have the old tall clock [belonging to David III and Lydia Bartlett Vickery] & we have this Bible which we want you to have."

80. James E. Kelley to JBV III, 16 January 1934. JBV III Papers. The opening para-

graph of this letter contains an interesting WASP chastisement by James E. Kelley (1858–1936): "I see you get my name spelled wrong, for it contains two E*s*—'Kelley.' I am obliged to be particular about this because it draws the line of distinction between two different breeds, our line having been English originally and the other kind came from Ireland." JBV III later wrote to SSB III, JBV III, 14 July 1976: "Isn't it curious I do not think that I have a single Irish ancestor." SSB III Papers.

81. See *Bits and Pieces: Your Own Western History Magazine* 4. no. 10 (1968), 10–11; and Myers, "Montana Pioneer," 15–16.

82. From Myers, "Montana Pioneer," 16.

83. Conforti, *Imagining New England*, 6, 11. See also Chapter Nine in *The Same Great Struggle* for a longer discussion on the hold that the American West has had on the imaginations of Americans and Europeans.

84. JBV III stated in an interview that his "Western-history collection now stands at nearly 700 volumes." See Weber, "Bangor's greatest natural resource." JBV III also collected and appreciated material culture of the Wild West: "I had a chance to visit some of the scores of antique shops [in Bristol, Maine] looking for books and pictures for my Maine collection. Among the items I spotted an old leather bag made of buffalo hide and stamped with the Wells-Fargo stamp. How did it get to Maine? The man said it had been stolen from a train; oh well, such are the vicissitudes of Americana. I should liked to have had it —it sort of spelled out romance and those lusty days of the frontier." JBV III to SSB III, 15 June 1959. SSB III Papers.

85. Incomplete letter from CBV to JBV III, ca. January 1937–January 1940. JBV III Papers. In 1961 JBV III wrote to SSB III: "My aunt Carrie died in Billings last fall. She was 91 years old; I wish that I had gleaned more stories of her life in the West for she moved to Montana about 1881." JBV III to SSB III, 3 July 1961. SSB III Papers.

86. Margaret Sandilands Vickery (1905–99), the daughter of David and Alice (Dore) Sandilands, was born in Sumpter, Oregon, grew up in Salmon, Idaho, and was a teacher in Washington State when she married Ted Vickery in 1930. After they moved to Unity in 1933 Margaret taught in Unity and was active for many years in Unity government and other civic, school, and church organizations. See Margaret S. Vickery obituary, *Bangor Daily News*, 1 April 1999.

87. Mark Greenleaf Schlotterbeck, "Well-traveled woman shares treasures," *Sun-Journal* [Auburn, Maine], n.d. JBV III Papers.

88. See "Face of Maine," *Portland Press Herald*, June 1965. JBV III Papers.

89. See William T. Vickery obituary, *Bangor Daily News*, 24 September 1984; and JBV III, *A History of the Town of Unity, Maine*, 204.

90. See "Face of Maine."

91. It appears, for a while at least, just before or after Annie Stewart Vickery's death, Ted, Margaret, and their two young sons moved into the Vickery family farm on Quaker Hill with JBV II, Eric, JBV III, and probably JBV II's seventy-two-year-old sister Josie—a crowded home indeed. See Claribel S. Vickery to JBV II, 2 January 1934. JBV III Papers.

92. For ASV's occupation of "housewife" see her "Record of Death," Certificate of Vital Records, State of Maine. JBV III Papers.

93. See Abbe L. Karmen, "Putting the House in Order: Women's Cooperative Extension Work in the Early Twentieth Century," *Maine Historical Quarterly* 32, no. 1 (Summer 1992), 30–50.

94. I want to thank Lori Edwards, medical technologist in microbiology at Affiliated Laboratory, Bangor, Maine, for her help in understanding and explaining pernicious anemia.

95. GVF to JBV III, 30 August 1933. JBV III Papers.

96. GVF to JBV III, 12 November 1933. JBV III Papers.
97. Ted and Margaret Sandilands Vickery's oldest child Michael (b. 1931) was a Fulbright Scholar, received his doctorate from Yale, is an authority on Cambodia, and is a professor at the University of Malaysia in Penang. Their second child Erwin Arthur (b. 1932), graduated from Colby College, Maine, taught math at Dexter High School for a while and now lives in Burnsville, Minnesota. Their last child Kathleen Ellen (b. 1950) married Igor Iturriaga from Chile and they and their son Yvan (b. 1980) lived in Santiago, Chile, until their son was ready for high school. Kathleen now lives in Berkeley, California, where she teaches Spanish in the same high school that Yvan attended. See Margaret Sandilands Vickery to JBV III letter, n.d. [ca. post-1995–97]. JBV III Papers. Margaret made her home at Clover Living Center in Auburn, Maine, after Ted died in 1984 and lived there until her death in 1999. Right up to the time of her death Margaret was taking a correspondence course in writing nonfiction articles and hoped to publish articles about her travels around the world.
98. Margaret Sandliands Vickery and JBV III also took trips together. See for example JBV III to SSB III, 15 June 1959, in which JBV III talks about their trip to New York City to see the Bolshoi Ballet perform Swan Lake and to see a performance of Helen Hayes in a Eugene O'Neill play. SSB III Papers.
99. For quote and discussion of the motives for writing regional and local history see Amato, *Rethinking Home,* 4.

CHAPTER 11

1. JBV III Papers.
2. Story told to author by EGS, Jr. Quote from JBV III, "Walter G. Morrill: The Fighting Colonel of the Twentieth Maine," in Richard S. Sprague, editor, *A Handful of Spice: A Miscellany of Maine Literature and History* (Orono, Maine: University of Maine Press, University of Maine Studies, 2nd series, no. 88, 1968), 127–51.
3. Quote from Charles Franklin Phillips, *"Bates College" in Maine: Enduring Strength and Scholarship* (New York: The Newcomen Society in North America, 1952), 12. For opposition to women at Bates see Noel Davis Godfrey, "Some Phases of Collegiate and University Education in Maine—Historically Studied." Ph.D. Dissertation, School of Education of New York University, 1931, 83.
4. Godfrey, *University Education in Maine*, 97–98.
5. For teaching careers of Alice Maud Vickery, Class of 1897, and Ethel Belle Vickery [Hambleton], Class of 1901, see alumni news in *The Bates Student*, vols. 21–29, 32, 33, 35, 37, 39, 44, 48, Edmond S. Muskie Archives and Special Collections Library, Bates College.
6. See GVF to JBV III, 25 March 1933, for a good sense of the class dynamics of choosing a career in New England during the Great Depression: "I hope you [JBV III] can go to college. Our State colleges have many fine courses…. I think Farming one of the noblest things one can do and if done with a hearty desire to do it well, most satisfying. I often listen at the Radio to the 'Farm & Home Hour' and am impressed with what is accomplished by the youth of America. My son is a teacher in a boys school and we feel that a Teacher has power for great good wherever he is, to lead young people in right paths is certainly an opportunity for influence in the world. So many of our famous men have begun as teachers; if one doesn't find their vocation while in college, while teaching one finds a lead. But whatever one takes up is gone into with a hearty will to make it worth while and a willingness to take failure as a part of life's adventure, beginning again with

courage against all odds, cheerfully doing one's part in good comradeship with all our neighbors—a good & happy life will come. You do not need to decide yet." JBV III Papers.

7. See George M. Chase, *George C. Chase: A Biography* (Boston and New York: Houghton, Mifflin Company, 1924). For the history of Chase's boyhood in Unity, Maine, see George C. Chase, *Twice Told Tales* (Portland, Maine: The Mosher Press, 1923).

8. The sons and daughters of Stephen and Hannah Blethen Chase of Unity married into the Bartlett, Patee, Gilkey, Hussey, and Rackliff families; their children married into the Ayer, Bartlett, Farwell, Stevens, Files, and Myrick families who were all, of course, related to the Vickerys. See genealogical notes in JBV III Papers.

9. JBV II, "Home," to JBV III, Bates College, 27 September 1936. JBV III Papers.

10. Ibid. In a letter from CBV to JBV III, 1 January 1937, she mentions his list of subjects: English, Ancient History, German, and Biology. Carrie also laments, "I wish you (JBV III) could know some of your western cousins." JBV III Papers.

11. JBV II, "Home," to JBV III, Bates College, 25 October 1936. JBV III Papers.

12. While JBV II might have felt some skepticism about college, he respected education. When President Franklin D. Roosevelt attempted to put more justices on the Supreme Court who would aid him in passing New Deal legislation, JBV II (a staunch Republican) asked his son, "What do you hear the College people say in regard to Roosevelt Packing the Supreme Court[?]" See JBV II, "Home," to JBV III, Bates College, March 1937. JBV III Papers.

13. JBV II, "Home," to JBV III, Bates College, 25 October 1936. JBV III Papers.

14. JBV II, "Home," to JBV III, Bates College, March 1937. JBV III Papers.

15. JBV II, "Home, Sabath P.M.," to JBV III, Bates College, 10 October 1937. JBV III Papers. Because such papers are not extant at Bates College, it is impossible to know if JBV III received financial aid or a student loan. However, in 1937 Bates disbursed $24,000 in scholarship aid and about $7,000 in student loans. In 1937 669 students attended Bates, and the entering Class of 1940 numbered 231 (121 men and 110 women), which was the largest in the school's history at the time. See *Report of the President of Bates College for the Academic Year, 1937–1938*. For entering students at Bates College, the 1937–38 tuition was $250, room and board for men was $250, and books and supplies cost $40. See *The Bulletin of Bates College, 1937–1938* (Lewiston, Maine: Thirty-Fifth Series, no.5, 1937).

16. Everett Vickery to JBV II, 18 February 1937. JBV III Papers.

17. "Vickery Writing History of Unity," *The Bates Student*, Bates College [Lewiston, Maine], 6 October 1937.

18. JBV II, "Home Sabath," to JBV III, Bates College, 10 October 1937. JBV III Papers.

19. Frank M. Coffin, "Thoughts on My Relationship with James Vickery," correspondence with author, 25 June 2002.

20. See Bates College official transcripts. Copies in JBV III Papers.

21. See "Bates College 1994 Alumni Survey," Bates College Alumni Files, Edmond S. Muskie Archives and Special Collections Library, Bates College.

22. JBV III's papers are filled with the steady correspondence he kept with the lifelong friends he met at Bates College, many of whom, like the Honorable Frank M. Coffin, became prominent citizens.

23. Coffin, "Thoughts on My Relationship with James Vickery." Concerning their relationship after graduation, Coffin said: "After graduation, we kept in close touch for a year or so pending our entry into military service.... After the war when I finally returned to Maine to take up my duties as a U.S. Circuit Judge, living in South Portland, I had occasion to see Jimmy from time to time when he

came to Portland on matters relating to the Maine Historical Society in which he was a major player. However, I saw far too little of him, but we kept in touch through cards and letters at Christmas time. I watched with pride as his reputation as a local historian grew throughout the State."

24. Bates Alumni Files, Edmond S. Muskie Archives and Special Collections Library, Bates College.

25. Coffin, "Thoughts on My Relationship with James Vickery."

26. See "Enlisted Record and Report of Separation Honorable Discharge" of JBV III. JBV III Papers.

27. It was after JBV III's time in the army that he began to refer to Private David Vickery II as "Super Patriot." JBV III Papers.

28. For instance see the correspondence from William T. Silverman, Fort Benjamin Harrison, IN, to JBV III, 1955; James Maynard, United States Military Academy, to JBV III, 1960–61; Dennis E. Glidden, Fort Bragg, NC, to JBV III, 1960–62; and Michael H. Ayer, Vietnam, to JBV III, 1967.

29. SSB III to JBV III, 3 October 1942. JBV III Papers.

30. JBV III explained in 1981 why he taught English even though both his undergraduate and graduate degrees were in history: "Even though history has been of major importance to me, I didn't teach it because the history teacher is usually saddled with coaching the basketball team." See Newall, "In retirement, Vickery plans to write, travel."

31. JBV III to SSB III, 10 September 1949. SSB III Papers.

32. See JBV II to SSB III, 29 August 1949: "James right now is planning to go to Orono the best part of the year while the government is paying the G.I. College expenses." JBV III Papers. JBV III contemplated attending Stanford University for his MA degree and SSB III offered JBV III a room in his Redlands house. See SSB III to JBV III, 17 August 1949. JBV III Papers. In his 10 September 1949 response JBV III was frank about his feelings concerning the University of Maine—feelings that would completely change forty years later: "Much as I should like to I don't feel that I can come out to Redlands this fall. I certainly would like to come out and stay with you and go to school and I think that your advice is good about a California school and the change of scenery would be beneficial…. Since I have almost completed my work at the University of Maine I thought that I should finish there…. I have six hours more plus my thesis to take at Maine before I get my master's degree, which is very little. I really don't think the degree from Maine amounts to a great deal and I should take further study elsewhere. Before I had received your letter I had made arrangements for a room and made application for admission. It is really disappointing that I cannot come out this fall for there is nothing I should like better to do. At the present time I feel somewhat confused and do not know what exactly to do. I shall have plenty of time under the GI bill of education so if all goes well perhaps I may yet get to California." SSB III Papers. Later in a 15 June 1959 letter to SSB III, JBV III talked of plans to attend summer school at the University of Montana, but apparently these plans were not realized. SSB III Papers. JBV III would, however, attend summer school in American Studies at Yale University in 1965 when he was one of eleven English teachers from all over New England who was awarded a scholarship from the Coe Foundation. JBV III's Maine education, like his genealogy, became an important part of his identity: "[James Berry Vickery III] prides himself that he's 100 per cent Maine, the son of Colonial ancestors, a graduate of all-Maine Schools…. He failed to explain why, in a period of independence, he took graduate study at Yale!" Dee Fearon, "Much Has Happened In Bangor Since The Year of 1769," *Bangor Daily News*, 4–5 October 1969.

33. JBV III, his brother Eric, and his cousins Ted and Margaret Vickery were instrumental in planning and funding this Unity celebration. See JBV II to JBV III, 8 March 1954. JBV III Papers; and Dorothy E. Freeman, Ph.D. and Susan M. Simeone, *Ordinary, Yet Extraordinary: Six Decades in the Life of Unity, Maine, 1941–2001* (Unity, Maine: Unity Foundation, J. S. McCarthy/Letersystems, 2002), 134–39.

34. SSB III to JBV III, 6 September 1954. JBV III Papers.

35. Ibid. Thorndike, Maine, is one of Unity's neighboring towns.

36. Ibid.

37. John M. Cates, Jr., to JBV III, 23 January 1955. JBV III Papers.

38. See Peter Novick, *That Noble Dream: The "Objectivity Question" and the American Historical Profession* (Cambridge, England: Cambridge University Press, 1988), 332–39.

39. JBV III in the preface to *A History of the Town of Unity, Maine.*

40. Since JBV III's *A History of the Town of Unity, Maine,* a new book was published that carries on this tradition and extends the history of Unity into the twenty-first century. See Freeman and Simeone, *Ordinary, Yet Extraordinary.*

41. Elizabeth Ring, "Review of *A History of the Town of Unity, Maine.*"

42. Ibid. Elizabeth Ring was the guest speaker at Unity's 150th Anniversary Celebration. See JBV III to SSB III 12 May 1954. SSB Papers. Ring spoke about her research on the "Westward trek of Maine '49ers" from Waldo County, one of whom was her great-grandfather Henry Harvey. Letters between Elizabeth Ring and JBV III show a great appreciation for each other and their work in Maine history. See for example Elizabeth Ring to JBV III, 11 April 1954 and 11 July 1954. EGS, Jr., Papers.

43. Samuel P. Hays, "History and Genealogy: Patterns of Change and Cooperation," in Taylor and Crandall, *Generations and Change,* 29–51.

44. For the historiography of the cooperative scholarship between genealogists and academic historians see Robert M. Taylor, Jr., and Ralph J. Crandall, "Historians and Genealogists: An Emerging Community of Interest," in Taylor and Crandall, *Generations and Change,* 3–26.

45. JBV II to JBV III, 13 October 1953. JBV III Papers. In many letters between JBV II and his sons he wrote about stocks and gave investment advice. See for instance Everett Stewart Vickery to JBV II, 18 February 1937 and JBV II to JBV III, 4 January ca. 1950s, and 11 March 1955. JBV III Papers. This serious involvement in the stock market seems to support historian Richard H. Condon's statement that "the [Maine] men who farmed, fished, or cut wood, and the women who worked alongside and in addition reared the children and kept the house, had to be gamblers." Condon, "Living in Two Worlds," 81.

46. In the end JBV III charged $7.50 for his book.

47. JBV II to JBV III, 8 March 1954. JBV III Papers.

48. See SSB III to JBV III, 28 August 1947. SSB III Papers.

49. See "Quaker Hill Road Farm First Tilled By Eli Vickery In 1832," *Morning Sentinel* [Waterville, Maine], 28 April 1951. In 1961 the farm was sold to the Harriman family and they sold it in 1971 and went into the motel business, apparently feeling that the tourism industry had more potential than farming. See JBV III to SSB III, 3 July 1971: "The old Vickery farm is vacant now. The Harrimans who bought it ten years ago sold their herd of [Holstein] cows and bought a motel near Belfast." SSB III Papers.

50. See Judd, et al., *Maine: The Pine Tree State,* 532–35; and Richard Wescott and David Vail, "The Transformation of Farming in Maine, 1940–1985," *Maine Historical Quarterly* 28, no. 2 (Fall 1988), 66–84. For a poignant study of the state of

contemporary family farming see Victor Davis Hanson, *Fields Without Dreams: Defending the Agrarian Idea* (New York: The Free Press, 1996).

51. JBV II to SSB III, 31 July 1949. SSB III Papers. Cassie Hillman Hunt Vickery (1903–97) was from Hartland, Maine. Cassie and her first husband Archelous H. Hunt, who was also from Hartland, married on 6 January 1923. A family story contends that Cassie had been JBV II's "housekeeper" before they were married.

52. Actually while JBV III was away in the service his family had already begun to think about selling the farm, in part because they could not find help. See JBV III to "Dear Folks," 15 September 1945: "I really do not think that it is wise to sell the farm. Although it is a great burden now the day is coming in about 20 years when it will be a godsend to have a farm. I am going to assume the role of a prophet and predict that by that time the world will be up to its neck either in world revolution or deep depression. I think that you can get help pretty soon because if they discharge 5 million men from the army next summer, employment ought to be pretty easy." JBV III Papers.

53. Richard H. Condon, "Nearing the End: Maine's Rural Community, 1929–1945," *Maine Historical Quarterly* 32, nos. 3 and 4 (Winter-Spring 1992), 1,167.

54. SSB III to JBV III, 17 August 1949. JBV III Papers. Sometime earlier JBV II must have decided to sell the Vickery farm on Quaker Hill (probably) to Ted and Margaret Vickery. See Claribel S. Vickery to JBV III, 26 June 1939: "Even I shall feel strange to know that the old farm has changed hands as from my earliest remembrance it has been the Uncle Eli place. In a sense it will be so still, as the change would keep it in the family name but not in the direct line from father to son." JBV III Papers.

55. JBV III to SSB III, 24 July 1957. SSB III Papers.

56. JBV III to SSB III, 14 October 1959. SSB III Papers.

57. JBV III to SSB III, 17 June 1960. SSB III Papers.

58. See JBV III, "Walter G. Morrill," 127–51.

59. JBV III to SSB III, 17 June 1960. SSB III Papers.

60. JBV III to SSB III, 3 July 1961. SSB III Papers. There is evidence that Cassie received some income from the family farm during the late 1930s and early 1940s. See JBV II's "Farm Operation Charges" books. JBV III Papers. These same sources document the economic interests that Ted Vickery and Eric Vickery had in the family farm as well.

61. JBV III to SSB III, 1 November 1964. SSB III Papers. For correspondence from Cassie Hillman Hunt Vickery to SSB III see for example JBV II to SSB III, 31 July 1949: "Dear Stillman I sure can add my little say did your ears burn any this past two weeks. If so you will know the reason why. We had a raspberry pie that doesn't grow on every bush also a good blueberry pie lots of green peas & string beans. I said how I wish Stillman was here to enjoy this meal with me." SSB III Papers.

62. See Hill, et al., *Winnecook Ranch*, 46–47, 94, 114. The last years of the ranch corporation's history is an unhappy story of larceny and miscarriage of trust, notwithstanding a few dedicated shareholders and general managers.

63. See www.unity.edu/UHS/index.html SSB III talked of establishing a scholarship fund, "the beneficiary having a Unity preference," at Colby College in Maine that was to be activated after his death, and of an endowment in Unity that, among other things, would care for the graves of his parents and grandparents. See SSB III to JBV III, 1 September 1967. SSB III Papers. Apparently SSB III did establish the Evelyn Crie Berry Fund at Colby College in the name of Berry and his cousin Mildred Berry Pelletier, "primarily to provide financial support for students from Unity, Maine"; and the Ralph and Evelyn Crie Berry Memorial Fund at Stanford University, "to support the study of mollusks." See Ann Marie Przybyla,

Guide to the Papers of S. Stillman Berry (Washington, D.C.: Archives and Special Collections of the Smithsonian Institution, 1993), 67, 71.

64. Everett S. Vickery obituary, *Republican Journal*, 3 April 1986.

65. Descriptions of Eric from Eric A. Vickery obituary, *Bangor Daily News*, 23–24 March 1991. JBV III often visited his brother Everett during the years that Everett lived in Connecticut, and Everett like Eric took road trips to historical sites and museums with JBV III. See for example JBV III to SSB III, 13 August 1956, in which JBV III describes their trip to the Bedford Whaling Museum and Sturbridge Village. SSB III Papers. For other stories about "driving" JBV III see Sanford Phippen, "A dean among historians," *Maine Times*, 10 July 1997.

66. For a visit to the Bither Brook home and JBV III's library at this time see Carmelia Fogg, "Student of History: Unique Book Treasure Keeps Teacher Hunting," *Bangor Daily News*, 4 April 1962.

67. EGS, Jr., conversation with author, September 2002.

68. See Bunting, *A Day's Work*. Bunting dedicated this book to the memory of JBV III whom he called "teacher, historian, and antiquarian…. A Maine original," and Eric A. Vickery, "countryman."

69. Eric and JBV III had sold their Unity property years earlier. In 1979 JBV III wrote SSB III: "Eric and I plan to sell our Unity property. I am not ready to sell, but Eric is unhappy during the winters. It is costly to heat in winter as oil prices here are high. Most homes require at least $800 just for the four months of winter." JBV III to SSB III, 24 March 1979. SSB III Papers.

70. Christopher Smith quote in Phippen, "A dean among historians."

71. EGS, Jr., conversation with author, September 2002.

72. See Newall, *Bangor Daily News*, 21 May 1981.

73. Berlin, "James B. Vickery III," *Seven Books in a Footlocker*, 66.

74. See press release from American Association for State and Local History, 3 October 1983. JBV III Papers.

75. James B. Vickery III obituary, n.p., 14 June 1997. Bates Alumni Files, Edmond S. Muskie Archives and Special Collections Library, Bates College.

76. Mundy quote in Berlin, "James B. Vickery III," *Seven Books in a Footlocker*, 66.

77. Weber, *"Bangor's Greatest Natural Tesource."* JBV III very rarely mentioned marriage. After his induction into the army, JBV III wrote to Frank M. Coffin: "How I envy those that are getting married now. Not that I think I want to make that step, for I think it would be unwise, now that I'm in the service. It seems that you & I may be the last to take the step closer to the altar. No doubt, you will win. I have made up my mind never to marry while at least only an N.C.O. I wish a more colorful wedding such as flashing gold braid & swords crossed, a reception etc. that is the only way to get married,—also champagne in bucket fulls." JBV III to Frank M. Coffin, 11 August 1942. Copy in JBV III Papers.

78. EGS, Jr., conversation with author, September 2002.

79. SSB III to JBV III, 25 June 1942. JBV III Papers.

80. For more on JBV III's lifestyle see Tom Weber, "Mining a Historical Treasure: James Vickery Collection Chronicles Maine's Past," *Bangor Daily News*, 15 August 1997.

81. SSB III to JBV III, 25 June 1942. JBV III Papers.

82. Earlier JBV III took a trip to England with John Arthur Vickery, Jr.'s parents John Arthur Vickery, Sr., and Elizabeth Sendrowski Vickery.

83. Quote about JBV III from Weber, "Bangor's greatest natural resource."

84. EGS, Jr. conversation with author, September 2002.

85. Ibid.

86. EGS, Jr., "James B. Vickery III Eulogy," 17 June 1997. Copy in JBV III Papers.

INDEX

References are italic for images or maps.

A

A Maine Hamlet (Lura Beam), 199–201
Adams, Abigail, 60–61
African Americans: American Revolution and, 61; Civil War and, 105. *See also* slavery.
agriculture: agrarian ideal, 75, 109; American Revolution and, 53, 100; barter system, 226–27; Cape Cod and, 26; cash economy, 90–91, 100, 101–02, 104, 110; Civil War and, 105; crisis in Maine, 113; family farms, 53, 56, 61, 75, 76–79, 80, 81, 84–85, 91, 100, 104, 107, 115, 171, 198, 201, 239, 240; gambling and, 292n.45; homesteading in Wyoming, 168, 174–75; in twentieth-century Maine, 192, 198–201, 239, 289n.6, 293n.52; journals, 101–02; Maine dairy farms, 132; mixed husbandry, 71, 84–85, 90, 283n.5; Native American and, 14; potatoes, 85, 198–*99*, 226–27; Puritan settlers and, 4, 14; reform, 100–02; slash and burn, 56; slave labor and, 87; societies, 100–01; technology and, 90–91, 198–99, 100–02, 239, 287n.70; textile mills and, 80; Whigs, and, 87; western competition and eastern, 91, 100, 113, 198. *See also* cattle industry; community; depressions (economic); Farm Bureau; sheep industry.
Akron, Ohio, 57
alcohol: in West, 117, 138–39; on Maine frontier, 58. *See also* Temperance Movement.
American: first generation, 56, 61; identity, 45, 212, 214, 236; patriotism, 178, 212, 235–36; Revolution, 45–53, 61, 62; values, immigrants and, 212; values in West, 118
Anthony, Susan B., 89
Anti–slavery Movement (abolition), 83, 87, 98–99

architecture: antebellum New England farm, 84–85; Colonial Revival and, 212–13; in seventeenth-century Massachusetts Bay Colony, 7; in New Republic, Maine, 55–56, 57, 71, 79; in Unity, Maine, 57, 81, 84, *241*, 244, 283n.5; Montana ranch, 137, 163; Wyoming homestead, 167, 168, 169
Arnold, J. M. Shoe Company, 207, 285n.51
Atwood family, 45
Augusta, Maine, 55, *66,* 70, 82, 88, 91
Ayer family, 95, *96,* 97, 98, 101, 156, 290n.8

B

Bangor, Maine, *67,* 69, 77, 89, 97, 124, 200, 207, 217, 245, 247, 249, 251
Bartlett family, 55, 57–60, 64–65, 81, 95, *96,* 97, 98, 107, 124, 210, 244, 267n.2, 290n.8
Bates College, 224–29
Beecher, Catherine, 126
Bean family, 57
Belfast, Maine, *66,* 91, 129, 141, 193, 204
Berry, Ada Josephine, *frontispiece*
Berry, Alfred, 81, 104
Berry, Benjamin, 204
Berry, Evelyn "Evie" Crie Kelley, ix, xviii, 74, 94, *121*–24, 129, 135–38, 143, 147, 150–*54, 153*
Berry family, 64, 74, 76, *96,* 105, 107–09, 210, *155,* 284n.21; connection to Vickery family, 253n.17; diabetes in, 154, 274n.107; homestead in Maine, *210;* in Montana, 114, 116, 118–56, 158
Berry, Florence Ellen Bartlett, xv, 74, 149–*50,* 152, 274n.107
Berry, Hannah, 80, 81, 85
Berry, Hattie May Myrick Plummer, 74, 204
Berry, James, 81
Berry, James Edwin, 74, 105, 107–10, *108,* 152, 275n.115
Berry, John F. (Lieutenant), 105, 268n.23
Berry, Lottie, 94, 121

Berry, Mary Jane Adler, 74, 109
Berry, Olive Jackson, *77*, 81, 106, 124, 233
Berry, Olive Mussey, 74, 108, 109, 118, *133*
Berry, Ralph, ix, 74, 94, 105, 109, 118, *121*–25, 127, 129, 134–135, 138, 144, 147, 149–154, *153*, 158
Berry, Reuel Mussey, 74, 105, 120, 125, 204
Berry, Ruth Maria, 74, 124, 125, 126, 127, 148–*49*, 155, 156, *210*, 274n.105
Berry, Samuel Stillman I, 74, 81, 82–83, 88, 101, 108, 118, 120–21, 124, 129, *132*, 134–35
Berry, Samuel "Sam" Stillman II, xv, 74, 120–21, 129, 134–39, 143, 148–*50*
Berry, S[amuel] Stillman III, ix, x, xii, xviii, *51*, 94, 113, 120, 122–23, 141, *244*; birth and childhood, 150–*152*, *155*; career, 211; education, 153, 154; genealogy and, 211; health, 151–53; James Berry Vickery III and, 211, 216, 230, 232–*34*; 239–40, *244*, 249; Winnecook Ranch and, 151–52, 154–55, 187, 211, 244
Berry, Sybil Samuel (Myrick), xv, 149, *155*, 275n.107
Beston, Henry and Elizabeth Coatsworth, *213*, 287n.73
Bible, the: 8, 90, 177, 180, 182, 200; funerals and, 90; genealogy and, xiii, 71; marriage and, 59; Montana pilgrims and, 116, 141; Puritan settlement and, 13, 29; Vickery family, 71, 215, 287n.79
"Big Letter," the, 181–82, 187
Big Timber, Montana, *130*, 139, 159, 160, 163, 164, 166
Billings, Montana, *131*, 139, 182
birth control, 76, 92, 171, 279n.51
Black, Flora I., 129, 271n.19
Blue Hill, Maine, 46, 55, 58, 193
Boothbay, Maine, 57, *66*, 121
Boston, Massachusetts: crime and violence in, 17, 36; eighteenth-century metropolis, 33–34, 36; King George's War and, 35–36; Maine and, 41; sheep industry in, 140; Vickery family moves to, 33. *See also* Liberty Men; Great Proprietors; War of 1812.
Bowdoin family, 62, *63*

Brandenburg, Algia Mason, 277n.12
Brandenburg, Alverda Murray, 161–62
Brandenburg, Delilah Vesser, 161
Brandenburg, Emma (Reese), 162, 277 n.12
Brandenburg family, 160–62, 276n.10, 277n.12
Brandenburg, Jackson "Jay," 162, 277n.12
Brandenburg, Joseph, 161
Brandenburg, Matthias, 160–61
Brandenburg, Nancy Jane (Osbourne), 277n.12
Brandenburg, Samuel, 161
Brandenburg, Solomon, 160
Brewer, Maine, *67*, 157, 208, 245, 246
Bridger, Montana, *131*, 185, 187
Brooks, Maine, 193, 239
Brown, Harry M., 239
buffalo, 141, 273n.88
Budd, Kellogg, Vickery general store, Montana, 159, 160, 166, 276n.9
bundling, 84
Bunting, William H., 245–46
Burnham, Maine, 55

C

California, 107–09
Cape Cod, *20*, 22, 26, 33, 79
captivity narratives, 19
Carroll (Martinsdale), Montana, 118, *130*, 139, 140
Cates, John M. Jr., 235–36
cattle industry (Montana),114, 118, 139; relationship with sheep industry, 144–45
Charleston, Maine, 57, *66*
Chase family, 55, 81, 124, 210, 224, 267n.2, 268n.35, 290n.8
Chase, George Colby (Professor), 224
Chatham (Monomoit), Massachusetts, 16–19, *20*, 22, 25
Cheever, W. (Reverend), 207
children (childhood): 91; diphtheria, 106; clothing, 196; farm, work and, 78, 79, 85, 100, 171, 174–75; in eighteenth century, 27, 37; in twentieth century, 198, 202; in Western Vickery family, 172–78; new born, 279n.44, 283n.7; nineteenth-century middle class, 76–77, 171; photography and, 193–94; schools, New Republic and, 79–80. *See*

can, 14; religion and, 27; sheep culture and, 119–20, 127, 136–40, 147; suffrage and, 9, 28; teaching and, 80, 109, 156, 224, 289n.6; unmarried, 4, 5, 26, 166; widowerhood, 37, 47; work and, 4, 76, 78, 90–91, 101, 127, 141, 192, 200–01; work and Puritan, 14. *See also* family; patriarchy; soldiers.

mental illness, x, 22, 58, 88, 91, 99, 106, 158

Metacom (King Philip), 15

Methodists, 97

mining industry, 107–10, 114, 117–18, 165–68

Missouri River, 117, 125, *130–31*, 133, 140, 143

Mitchell family, 48, 53, 55, 57, 64, 105, 107, 210, 239, *241*, 262n.19

Monmouth, New Jersey, *34*, 51

Montana: *130–31*; Civil War and, 110, 117, 268n.35; exchange of people, culture, capital between Maine and, xviii, 110, 113–15, 118–20, 129, 132, 134–136, 140–41, 148, 158–59, 178–79, 218; description of, 128–29, 132–133; official territory of, 117; statehood, 125, 166; violence in, 142–45, 166–67

Morrill Land Grant Act, 101

Morrill, Walter G. (Colonel), 224, 242

Morse, Theoda Mears, xii, 31

Montville, Maine, *66,* 193

Moulton family, 120, 143

Mount Holyoke College, 126

Mueller, Josephine Cook (Mrs. Oscar), 113, 268n.35

Mundy, James H., 247

Murch family, 105, 107, 210

Musselshell River, *131*, 140, 143, 143, 146, 147, 158, 159

Mussey family, 85, 88, 210, 266n.27

mutuality. *See* community.

Myrick family, 275n.107, 290n.8

N

Nantucket Island, 32, 37

Native Americans: American Revolution and, 61 fish ownership and, 22; English and, 13–14, 43; French and, 18, 41, 42, 43; in Montana, 117, 141–44, 273n.88; in New England, 6, 18, 41;

land use, ownership and, 13–14, 61, 64, 142, 144, 168; work and, 14; white settlers in West and, xviii, 117–18, 124, 141–44

New England: antebellum courtship in rural, 84; embargo and, 68; first generation born in, 10; identity, pilgrims and, 116; regionalism, 213–14; settlement in southern colonies compared with, 4; slavery and economy of, 32; tourism in, 213; values, 149, 214; Virginia trade and, 32; women's rights conventions in, 89; "Yankee farmer," 198, 283n.14. *See also* immigration.

Nisco family, 285n.51

North Waldo Agricultural Society (NWAS), 101

O

O'Brien, Francis, xiv

"Ohio Fever," 57, 107

"Oregon Fever," 107

Orrington, Maine, 57, *67*

P

Paine family, 33, 261n.22

Parker family, 33

Patee family, 290n.8

patriarchy, 8, 9, 10, 197–98, 232

pernicious anemia, 182, 221

Phinney, Edmund (Colonel), 48

Phippen family, 4–5, 7, 17, 61, 255n.4

photographs (photography), xviii–xix, 193–94, 196, 245

pilgrims (Pilgrims), 114, 116, 126–27, 139, 151, 155, 212

Pittsfield, Maine, *66,* 91, 157, 196, 201; Maine Central Institute (MCI), 223–24

Plymouth Colony, 15–16, 116

Portage Lake, Maine, *67,* 230

Portland Packing Company, 192, 239

Portsmouth, (Strawbery Banke) New Hampshire, *20,* 42

primogeniture, 62

prison reform, 88, 99

privateers, 18, 35–36

property, *See* land.

Puritans, Puritanism (Congregational Church): 3–4, 9, 13–14, 16, 27–28; children and, 27; domestic violence and, 59–60; role of deacon, 26; war with Native Americans, 14–15; women and, 27

ANDREA CONSTANTINE HAWKES is a Ph.D. candidate in history at the University of Maine and a 2003 Elizabeth Perkins Fellow at the Old York Historical Society, York, Maine. Her dissertation, for which she was awarded a Gest Research Fellowship at Haverford College, is the biography of Elizabeth McClintock Phillips (1821–96), who was an antebellum Quaker abolitionist and initiator of the 1848 Seneca Falls woman's rights convention. Hawkes is a specialist in nineteenth-century United States history, as well as New England regional and women's studies. She co-edited *The Civil War Recollections of General Ellis Spear*, and edited and wrote an interpretative essay for *The Lighthouse Keeper's Wife*, the autobiography of Connie Scovill Small.